About the Author

Originally from East Lothian, Scotland, Graeme is married to Candy, his childhood sweetheart. They both work as general managers of a luxury safari lodge in Amboseli, Kenya, and when not working, live in Morbihan, France. They have two sons; the elder, Kris, lives in Shanghai with his wife Kirsty, and daughter Matilda (Tilly), and the younger, Sean, lives in South Korea with his girlfriend Gigi. Graeme loves living and working in Kenya and is heavily involved in the local Maasai community. He has helped raise thousands of dollars to build and extend the village school.

Don't Shake the Mango Tree
Tales of a Scottish Maasai

Graeme Forbes-Smith

Don't Shake the Mango Tree
Tales of a Scottish Maasai

Olympia Publishers
London

www.olympiapublishers.com
OLYMPIA PAPERBACK EDITION

A CIP catalogue record for this title is
available from the British Library.

ISBN: 978-1-80074-454-7

First Published in 2022

Olympia Publishers
Tallis House
2 Tallis Street
London
EC4Y 0AB

Printed in Great Britain

Dedication

This book is dedicated to my wife, Candy, who has shared my life through all of the trials and tribulations life has thrown at us, and helped me at every turn, to laugh, see the bright side, and continue to play the game.

The book is also dedicated to my childhood friend, Gordon King, with whom I shared many of the adventures depicted within this book, who sadly passed away three months after our arrival in Tanzania, and was the inspiration for me to begin this tale.

I also cannot fail to mention, John Simonson, and his wife, Annette, and their family, who made us feel instantly welcome on our arrival on Ushongo Beach. John appears in a number of different guises throughout the book, and as an inspiration for several characters within the book. He tragically passed away from Covid during 2021, and is very sadly missed.

The night before we departed Edinburgh for Tanzania, we enjoyed dinner with two great friends, Alan and Jeannie Raynor, who presented us with a beautiful leather-bound book. On opening the book, I remarked, "Thanks, but it is empty?" To which Jeannie replied, "That is because tomorrow is the first blank page of a story which is waiting to be told, and we know you will fill it."

Be careful what you wish for.

Acknowledgements

I would never have been able to write this book if Candy had not joined me on our life's great adventures. Nor, if I was not encouraged at every turn by my sons, Kris and Sean, and certainly not had I not been nagged and pushed every step of the way by Sandy and Peter Williams, and Jan and Tom Coffer, all the way from California! Of course, I am also deeply grateful to the people of East Africa, and the Maasai community, that I am humbled to be a very small part of.

CHAPTER 1
GORDON'S LAST SAFARI

We transplanted Scots have gathered together more by accident than by design. Gordon is working, helping to build a communal farm. My wife Candy and I are hiding out from the economic disaster that had hit the UK economy. Brian is visiting his old pals on holiday. The rest of the guys are just here because they love the fun. And we're having a lot of fun.

Valentine's Bar, in downtown Pangani on the northeast coast of Tanzania, is having its first-ever Scottish farewell party. It's just that nobody knows it yet.

Rasta Ali, Bariki, Stanley from Immigration, Hothot, Zainaboo and many other bemused locals join in at the bar as the Kilimanjaro beers and Konyagi disappear, another round arriving on cue. It isn't long before a change of venue is called for, and we all move on to the nearby Shimonie bar—on foot, by car, by *pikipiki* motorbike. Later, as dusk falls, by ferry and by car we decamp again, this time to the Jahazi in Mwera Village. Eventually, the dwindling assortment of Scotsmen and native Tanzanians, by then fairly inebriated, assembles at *Kwa Graeme and Candy*—our home on Ushongo Beach—where we all gather on the terrace, laughing still and drinking still until the sun rises over distant Zanzibar, and we each finally head to our various beds. It would be a night to remember.

In the late morning and with little sleep, Brian and I head to Mwera to service my pick-up, while Candy and Gordon are back on the terrace, sipping coffee and enjoying recollections of last night's hilarity. The morning wears on, and Gordon rises. He asks to borrow a book, which Candy promptly produces, and he heads off with a wave and a grin on the short walk along the beach to the Beachcomber bar, to visit his old friends, Tony and Faithfully.

At around noon, Brian and I return home and, together with Candy, decide to have lunch at the Beach Crab. As we pose for Brian in the garden for some holiday snaps, the ocean a stunning backdrop, the air hot and clear, the day a perfect ten, the phone rings.

"Graeme, please come quick; Gordon is sick!" Faithfully screams in my ear.

I turn to Brian and Candy and say, "Just carry on without me. I'll sort this out." Too many beers last night, I assume.

I drive the two minutes to the Beachcomber, park the pick-up, and smile as I spot Faithfully waiting in the drive. *Habari asubuhi* dies on my lips, however, as I approach close enough to see her face.

Gordon lies flat-out on the sofa, facing the sea, his favourite view. Tony is giving him mouth-to-mouth, and Rashidi pumps his heart. Gordon is grey beneath his tanned face. This is no hangover.

Clearly, he needs more help than we can give, so we drag him into the back seat of my double-cab pick-up, Tony on top of him, still doing mouth-to-mouth. Mohammed, the young barman, jumps into the bed of the pick-up, and I see the waitress, Cecilia, toss a small towel to him. She knows. The rest of us don't.

On the gravel road leading to the clinic in nearby Mwera, I pull a four-wheel skid at the corner by the mango tree, where

12

school kids spend their afternoons throwing sticks to dislodge the fruit. They stare in wonder at another crazy *mzungu*, whose wheels screech as the truck just clears the tree. My heart is pounding in my chest.

As we cross the small bridge over a little stream, Tony shouts, "He's not breathing!"

I reach over the passenger seat, and with my left hand I do my best to pump his heart while driving with my right. Tony continues mouth-to-mouth. I can hear each breath as he sucks in air, a rhythm which seems to run counterpoint to my own heartbeat.

We reach the clinic in record time, but time has run out for Gordon. One look, and the doctor shakes her head sadly.

"*Pole sana*—sorry—your friend is dead."

No oxygen. No hasty shot of adrenaline. Nothing. Just dead. Tony and I slump to the ground. Mohammed reverently places the small towel Cecilia had given him over Gordon's face. Tears streak his cheeks, and he leans his head against the car. Nothing has prepared him, or any of us, for this.

Minutes pass. It must be longer, but eventually I push Gordon's legs back into the car and close the door. We begin the drive to the hospital in Pangani in silence. In Africa, you don't call for an ambulance. In most places, there isn't one. Family or friends are responsible for the remains of their lost loved ones.

Everyone at the ferry already knows. I don't know how, but they do. In Africa, news travels fast. On the ferry, almost everyone stops to say, "*Pole sana*—we are sorry." We drive the short distance to the hospital, and already a group has gathered: Ali, Bariki, Stanley, Hothot. They are distraught. I don't know what to say to them. Slowly, the numbers rise.

Candy, Brian, Faithfully, Mike, Darko, Eyal. They all arrive.

***

The formalities don't take long. The doctor asks me how he died.

In a daze I mumble, "Heart attack, I think." The typewriter taps out the result of my first autopsy. I am astonished to discover that the hospital has no morgue.

Once again, I am carrying Gordon, his old friends helping. We bring him back out to the car park and we load his body into a *dala dala* for the trip to the morgue in Tanga, sixty kilometres away. I can't do it, so I pay the attendant to wash and clean his body. Numbed by the trivia we cling to, I empty his pockets: some cash, a cell phone, keys, a last bar bill (unpaid), cigarettes.

I return the next day to officially identify the remains. Naturally, there is no electricity, so the body has already started to decompose. Ninety degrees and no freezer facility. This is no way to store a corpse, I think, especially the corpse of a lifelong friend. I phone our embassy for help, and wish I hadn't. It appears that we're on our own.

I phone the family back home. I buy a coffin, a shroud, some perfume. We dig a grave in the red African soil. We arrange for a priest. Each friend, unasked, does his bit to help. This is Africa.

***

The night before the burial, we get a call. The villagers are holding a vigil. Gordon's son and sister have arrived from

Scotland, and together we drive to the village. We discover the street outside his favourite bar, the Jahazi, blocked off, an awning erected, and over fifty villagers sitting on the ground or on plastic chairs, singing hymns in their uniquely beautiful, rhythmic, melodic way. We stand in silent gratitude. Awe. Gordon's son finally says that this is perhaps the happiest day of his life, a comment which one day we might think odd, but which at this moment seems just right. The hymns go on and on. The deep, haunting African baritones and harmonies make the hair on my neck rise, bring goose bumps, sting my eyes. I have no words. Well after midnight, we go home. The villagers don't; they stay there all night. It is their custom.

We return early, 7 a.m. By now there are almost three hundred people gathered, still singing. They have covered the street in petals and flowers. Six cows have been slaughtered. In huge vats, rice simmers. I feel humbled. Everyone who sees me hugs me, muttering, "*Tupa pamoja*—we are together." I can barely speak.

The coffin arrives in a *dala dala* from Tanga. Accompanying it are: the ever-dependable Rashid; Rasta Ali; Stanley, the immigration official; Bariki, his massive Masai friend; Hamesi; and Nixon. They have all spent the night with Gordon in the morgue, dressed his body, and placed him in his coffin. Even Urse, a young Swiss tourist we had befriended, is there. He had come to photograph wildlife, and is now asked instead to video a funeral.

Each of them hugs me, but none can speak. The coffin is placed on a table in the middle of the street. We pray and sing a hymn. People toss flowers on the coffin. Ali Mohammed, the chief of police, helps to carry the coffin to the police pick-up that today does double-duty as a hearse: an ironic tribute.

15

Everyone follows the pick-up through the village, past the mango trees, to the graveside.

The grave is very deep. Gordon will lie forever in a stand of flame trees, surrounded by coconut palms and stately mango trees, on a hill looking down to the Indian Ocean. I have seen worse places. The stand is packed with over three hundred mourners. We all join in the beautiful, haunting Swahili hymn, How Great Thou Art.

Each close friend takes his turn to shovel the rich African soil into the grave. The red dust blows gently over us all as we stand, a moment in perfect silence. I stutter a few inadequate words, but remember to say, "*Tupa pamoja*," which is greeted with murmurs of approval by the locals.

In silence again, we walk together back through the trees to the village, where we all eat in the open air outside the Jahazi, the wind blowing the last of the petals gently down the dusty street. Tony stands and says a few words, ending with, "Gordon came to Africa to visit me, but stayed so long because of all of you." Fitting words. Probably the most fitting of the entire day.

Without a conscious plan, Gordon's closest friends start to leave, by jeep, pick-up and *pikipiki,* all heading to the Beachcomber. We gather in the beachfront bar and sit quietly sipping our drinks, very aware that this was where it ended.

Tony starts slowly strumming a guitar. After a short while, Jeff joins in with another. Rashid gathers up a *ngoma* and launches into a compelling, repetitive slow beat. Stanley joins him with another drum. Hamesi picks up the same rhythm on a wooden xylophone. More drums appear and join in. The beat gets stronger and stronger. Soda bottles are stroked with kitchen knives, adding to the rising, insistent cadence. Mike adds bass on a didgeridoo, the women begin clapping along, and still others pound the tables in time with this wondrous African rhythm. I find myself on my feet. I raise my glass and shout, "To Gordon!" The music abruptly halts as everyone leaps to their feet, echoing my toast, glasses in hand. The spell is broken; we collapse into our seats talking and laughing.

The mourning is over.

Old Mohammed, the fisherman, takes me gently by the arm, leads me outside, and in halting English and Kiswahili tells me that I am not to be sad any more. Life, he says, is like the mango tree. When each fruit becomes ripe, in its time, it falls from the tree. Just like us.

I sit alone and stare out at the red, sharp disc of the sun, setting slowly over the wild African bush, and wish somebody would stop those kids from throwing their sticks so hard at the mango tree.

CHAPTER 2
HOW HAD IT COME TO THIS?

How had it come to this?

One morning some fifteen years before, a rather cheeky email from Gordon had appeared in my inbox, informing me that he had prices for a flight to Mombasa, transport in a 4x4— to be hired courtesy of a family friend—and a random guide to help us climb Mount Kilimanjaro. What exactly, he wondered with a certain smug assurance, might be my excuse for not actually doing it? He knew, of course, that this wasn't a challenge I'd be likely to refuse, given how often we'd fantasized about it as kids growing up in Scotland, addicted to David Attenborough and his Natural History TV shows.

That email would prove to change the direction of my life. And, of course, the direction of Gordon's life, as well.

***

The Thomson holiday charter flight drops us in Mombasa direct from Manchester, and we join the queue of tourists for the bus to take us to our Diani Beach Hotel. This is not the way I had imagined our exotic adventure would start, but it was the cheapest flight available, and since Gordon is organizing the entire trip, I expect the unexpected.

We check in and swerve the Welcome Meeting and the overly eager resort representative already trying hard to sell boat trips and BBQ nights. Grabbing our kit bags, festooned with climbing boots and poles, from within the pile of bright holiday luggage on the floor of Reception, we march back through the swing doors and out up the drive. I catch a last fleeting glimpse of the hotel rep staring after us as we pass out through the gate and, to get our bearings, aim straight for the first local bar we see. A quick call to our driver, Mohamed, to confirm a five a.m. pick up, a few swift beers, and then on to another bar with the dubious name of Shakattack, where he's to meet us in the morning. We'd slept on the flight and don't trust ourselves to wake early to meet him, so, settling comfortably at a table surrounded by our kit, we decide that we should just spend our first night here.

Our rough plan is to drive from Mombasa through Tsavo, via Voi to Taveta, and there to cross into Tanzania. Then we'll journey on towards Moshi and our pre-booked hotel, the Marangu, in the foothills of Mount Kilimanjaro where we will start our climb.

We've been chatting for some time, re-evaluating our routing, enjoying the wonder of actually, finally, being in Africa, when the saloon-style doors of the bar burst open. At unreasonably high speed for an indoors transit, a very drunk local gentleman wobbles past our table on his ancient bicycle, crashing casually but noisily into the bar. This event is entirely ignored by the assembled customers, who continue their conversations as though nothing has happened. The barman, however, vaults the bar, beats the poor drunk liberally round the head and shoulders, drags him to the door and summarily tosses him back outside. Wiping his hands on the front of his pants, he returns to his place of authority behind the bar and addresses us solemnly:

"Another beer?"

We mumble, somewhat sheepishly, "Yes, please," and the locals erupt in laughter. We judge that we've passed some culturally significant test, discovering that opportunities have suddenly opened up for friendly interactions with the locals. During the ensuing hours, we somehow survive the stick-thin woman with no teeth who wants to be my special girlfriend, the guy who wants to buy my watch, the other guy with a sister who loves me, his friend whose brother also loves me, several people who are in a position to sell me Tanzanites cheap, and two Dutch girls who are more than eager to be friends with any westerner who might rescue them from the four besotted local guys at the corner table trolling for wives.

The night passes with amazing swiftness, and it's still dark outside when we jump into the minivan that miraculously appears exactly on time at the bar door. We head out at last into the inky, mysterious pre-dawn gloom—on the start of our great African adventure! A family of cheetahs at the side of the road, various buses crashed at random points along the dirt tracks, elephants monopolizing the occasional tarmac, the bewildering madness of a market in Voi, and finally Taveta, the Tanzanian border, where we bid farewell to Mohamed and our creaky minibus. Here we cross a border which resembles a veritable No Man's Land from a WWII film, complete with barbed wire and watch towers. On the other side, we expect to be welcomed by a pre-arranged guide to the ancient land of Mount Kilimanjaro and the storied Serengeti: exotic Tanzania.

The guide, however, is nowhere in evidence. I'm sensing a pattern here. We sit in the stifling heat on decades-old plastic chairs, listening to the tick of an overhead fan making an energetic but futile effort at cooling the room, while the fabric of my faith in Gordon's travel arrangements begins to fray. Minutes—perhaps hours—of silence pass. We wait. Gordon, who will not meet my gaze, chain smokes and tries to radiate a confidence I'm certain he doesn't feel. Suddenly, in the distance, we can detect through the window the rapid, erratic approach of a cloud of blue smoke from down the rutted track. Trailing the smoke, a Land Rover of at least thirty years' vintage rolls to a stop outside the Immigration Office door, and a shambling wreck of a man laboriously extricates himself from behind the wheel. He approaches us, a crumpled old chap nattily attired in a brown three-piece suit and a pork pie hat, neither of which, it's clear, has seen a laundry since at least 1955. His beaming smile is spoiled only by his graveyard teeth, and he produces with a flourish, a homemade cardboard sign bearing the words, "Karibu Golden King." I laugh out loud. Our guide has arrived.

As our guide proffers abject apologies for his "tardiness in being late", we scramble into the ancient Land Rover with our kit. He remains perfectly confident that we'll reach our destination on time, though I'm not reassured when I learn that he'd gotten lost on his way to meet us. A dazzling feat, when you realize that the tarmac road from Moshi offers but one moment of choice: a single junction leading either to Dar es Salaam or to Taveta. On the other hand, street signs are rare in Africa, though east and west remain the same as elsewhere, as do north and south. In any case, I remind myself with a snicker, this is an adventure.

We break our journey at the first bar we pass, as Engelbert, our driver (by now I find it impossible to think of him as a guide) announces that he is "proper famished" and "requires sustenance." His bar of choice proves to be a dodgy-looking hovel by the side of the main road, called "The Teenage Ice Bar." While he tucks into his goat-and-rice, a dish which looks more like it's been attacked by a maniac wielding a machete than prepared by a cook, I survey my surroundings.

Apparently, you can buy Sportsman Cigarettes here—the "cigarette of the athlete", as the advert proudly proclaims—by the packet or individually. The television has its volume stuck at full blast and is playing an odd version of video memorials to a succession of dead people, with an Irish Folk song as backing. The barmaid is deeply asleep, standing up with her head resting on a bar stool, and the only other customer is an ancient Maasai, quietly tapping his wooden club in time to the beat of that song from *The Corrs* on the TV. Gordon, The Golden King, has recovered his composure and is now proclaiming that the long wait at the border had been part of his master plan all along, a way of easing us into the African pace of life. A lesson in culture, you know. Right.

Safely back in the old Land Rover, we resume our journey. The road here is metaled and in good condition, and the scenery is stunning, with lush green vegetation broken by bursts of vivid colour from occasional bougainvillea and flame trees. Mountains loom, dusky in the distance. When the cloud cover breaks a little, we get our first glimpse of Mount Kilimanjaro. She's a shy mountain, most often clouded at the summit, only showing her face when the mood takes her. Engelbert points her out, or I'd never have noticed the mountain's sudden appearance. *Kili*, as she's locally known, is so tall and regal that her snow-covered peak could easily be mistaken for just another cloud. That we should be standing way up there in a mere four days' time is an idea a little hard to absorb, and a wary silence replaces our excited chatter.

We pass through the gates and into the drive of the Marangu Hotel, and with a last burst of black smoke, the Land Rover finally grinds to a halt only a hundred metres from its destination. We unload our gear and walk the short distance to the lodge reception, leaving Engelbert fussing under the hood in a cloud of smoke and steam. To be honest, I'm astonished the old wreck made it this far, and less than surprised when he tells me that this happens all the time.

The lodge is full. After an excellent dinner, we sit cosily in the bar behind our bottles of Serengeti beer, eavesdropping on other guests. Some are discussing the preparations for their climb tomorrow; others have just returned, and are toasting their successes and bemoaning their failures. We ponder silently how we will fare ourselves.

Morning sees us reunited with Engelbert, who has repaired the Land Rover sufficiently to carry us the short distance to Kilimanjaro National Park. After paying our fee and meeting our guides, Moses and Thomas, we set off on our climb. We've elected to do the Marangu Route, which involves two days and two nights of hill walking through jungle, then forest, then alpine terrain. This is followed by eight hours of never-ending hell as we trudge in agonized, breathless near-silence through the "saddle", a high-altitude desert landscape. From the start of our walk, we can see Kibo Hut, our destination for the day, in the distance, a kind of surreal mirage. As we progress, the hut seems ever to recede. However long we slog towards it, it remains an apparently unreachable goal.

The strong wind whipping over the plain is freezing, but the clear blue sky means we're walking under the blazing African sun. We manage to be both frozen and scorched at the same time. At over 15,000 feet, the altitude makes any exertion difficult, but in this magnificent natural theatre, with Mawenze Peak behind us, Gilman's Point before us, and a view to the left out over the plateau where we gaze *down* on the clouds, we press on. Eventually, of course, we do reach Kibo, and enjoy a well-earned six hours' rest before the upcoming midnight start to our final push to the summit. We try to prepare an evening meal, but at this altitude and with the small gas stove we have, it's impossible to bring water to a boil. We settle for yet more bananas and some energy bars.

At midnight we embark, we "Three Musketeers" (Gordon, Moses and myself) and the "dark tan Yin," as Gordon describes Thomas. We set off *pole pole*—slowly, slowly—the mantra of the mountain. Statistics prove that the longer you take to climb up, the more your body becomes acclimatized to the altitude, and the better your chances of reaching the summit. Our plan to do the climb in just three days up and one day down has not really taken these statistics into account. Our planned speed is intended primarily to keep the cost low.

This leg of the climb turns out to be a full seven hours' advance on nearly vertical slope, covered in loose, treacherous scree rocks. It seems that for every three steps forward we take, the rocks slide us back one.

Just out of Kibo Camp, we're overtaken by a group of about twenty American college kids, who jog past us in matching bright red snow suits, singing some sort of college marching song that brings to mind Marine Corps basic training films. We begin to consider that our lifestyle choices over the past fifteen years, working hard for five days and partying even harder from Friday through to Sunday night, might not have been the best preparation for an adventure like this. As we struggle past Hans Meyer Cave at about four a.m., however, we take a perverse pleasure in seeing our college contingent somewhat in disarray, several lying by the side of the rough trail, others being helped back down by their guides and porters.

Mentally, and sometimes even physically, Moses and Thomas push us forward, and we keep struggling onwards and upwards. I'm utterly exhausted and can't even take on water, as it has frozen solid in my bottle. As the first pale, rosy signs of dawn begin to appear, we can see above us the outline of the peak at Gilman's Point. Moses and Thomas appear annoyingly like two guys taking a leisurely Sunday morning stroll along the beach, while Gordon and I resemble zombies from some cheap horror movie. We struggle on and on, and finally, as full dawn breaks over the magnificent Peak of Mawenze, we summit at Gilman's Point.

It has been the longest seven hours of my life, but the joy I feel is beyond comprehension. We hug one another, we hug Thomas and Moses, and we take a few quick photographs. It's far too cold to stay still for long, though, so we continue onwards to Uhuru Point round the rim of the crater, which some bastard of a surveyor had declared was only ever so slightly higher than Gilman's. Legs burning from the climb, eyes burning from the cold, we contemplate once again the satisfaction of having accomplished what we came to Tanzania to do. Now, though, what we want most is a beer in a warm room, a shower, a decent meal and the end of pain. Our brief visit at Uhuru Point is followed by a stumbling, tumbling quick descent back down the scree as the temperature rises with the sun, until exhausted but elated we return to Kibo Hut.

Gordon collapses on a bed and I am being sick on my

hands and knees when two German girls, who are planning to summit the next night, wander by and stop to ask, "How was it?"

"You'll love it," I reply, and go back to being sick.

We recover, more or less, and set off back downhill as fast as we can manage. Our guides are amazed at our speed in the downward direction, but we're determined to reach the first camp before night fall.

On our return to Marangu Hotel, we insist that Thomas and Moses join us in the lush, cool gardens for that long-anticipated beer. With a perfect view of Mount Kilimanjaro in the background, surrounded by great blasts of colour from the glorious garden foliage, we spend the day with our two guides and some of their friends. They sing us traditional songs and perform traditional dances, and we reciprocate with Hearts Football songs from home and a Punk rock pogo.

Life is good.

By the end of the afternoon, we've given away all of our gloves, scarves, arctic weather jackets, balaclavas, climbing poles, and even my long-treasured *Trainspotting* T-shirt. Most of these guys regularly climb Kili in jeans and anoraks, with Wellington boots on their feet, and with a consummate ease, style and plain *cool* that puts us soft Western types in our modern climbing gear to shame.

Engelbert, who has had more to drink than the rest of us and cackled and guffawed his way through the entire afternoon, manages to coax the old Land Rover into life again. We rattle off down the drive, waving furiously, with great, drunken sentimentality, to our gang of new-found friends. Our lifestyles and cultures are obviously miles apart, but I have never been so readily accepted into a group, nor felt so comfortable so quickly in all my life. These are special people, and I am entranced.

It's a relatively short drive to Moshi. Or it would be, in real life, but Engelbert manages to drag it out to more than an hour as he weaves erratically along, sometimes even on the road. We have one short stop to retrieve one of our backpacks that flies off the roof rack.

"I wondered what that was," says Engelbert, when our cries of alarm alert him to the rucksack bouncing off down the road.

We eventually arrive safe and sound at The Kilimanjaro Crane Hotel and check in. A glorious hot shower, our first in nearly five days, makes me realize that I will never again take for granted the opportunity to get clean. We soon rendezvous in the Hotel Bar, where neither of us can stop grinning. We did it! We have lived our fantasy! We have climbed Kilimanjaro! What a feeling!

We are, tonight, our own heroes.

Over dinner we decide that our one night in Moshi would be best spent in a nightclub, celebrating. I ask the waitress where, if she had a night off, would she think the best place in Moshi to go? She reels off a long list of options, but warns, "Whatever you do, don't go to Club Alberto."

Like dangling catnip in front of a cat. We call a taxi, and when the car arrives, I ask him if he knows the Club Alberto. He assures us that he knows it well, and so we negotiate heavily until we arrive at an agreed-upon five-dollar fare for the trip. We climb into the taxi and are driven roughly five hundred metres round the corner, where he stops. There, a large, brightly-coloured sign welcomes us to Club Alberto. It would undoubtedly be visible from the window of my room, but a deal is a deal, and with Gordon laughing heartily in my ear, I grudgingly fork over the five dollars.

Club Alberto makes Shakattack look like a palace, but it's packed, has exciting live African music, and although we're the only *wazungu* in the place, we're invited to join the first table we pass. Everyone's interested in where we're from and why we're here, and I'm astonished to discover that even within our small company, one guy has worked in a factory in Finland and one in Germany, and they all speak English well. They have much to teach us about their country and lives. We explore politics, football, and religion. Subjects which would be fraught with danger in any bar in Scotland are here discussed good-naturedly, with tolerance of opposing opinions, and a surprising and wonderful lack of acrimony.

At nearly three a.m., we stagger off into the moonlight on our very short walk back to the hotel. Engelbert will be meeting us in three hours' time to begin the twelve-hour drive back to Mombasa. This plan seems like a good idea at the time.

At the Kenyan border at Taveta, we bid a sad farewell to Engelbert, and vow to stay in touch. I'm too tired to even be properly astonished that Mohamed is actually waiting for us, and we pile in and head off on the road to Mombasa. A slight detour through Tsavo National Park gives us our first real opportunity to witness wildlife in the bush. We spot elephants, giraffe, gazelles and a herd of imposing cape buffalos. The scenery is magnificent, and we depart the national park wanting more.

We reach Mombasa, the Likoni ferry, and finally Diani Beach and our Thomson Hotel. It's just under a week since we'd walked out our doors in Scotland to begin our great adventure. How is it possible that we've done so much in such a short time?

Peace is shattered as we reach the reception and the tour rep comes bounding over to us. It's hard to tell whether she's glad or furious that her two missing tourists have finally turned up apparently no worse for wear. She looks like she's spent the last week on a Valium diet, and with barely disguised frustration, reminds us about the dangers of leaving the hotel unescorted. I realize that I've not shaved for a week and my clothes are probably in need of a bit of laundry attention, and we both give an impression of considerable dissipation. In a minor sort of way, I find myself embarrassed. We manage to extricate ourselves by indicating that I may be interested in a visit to a Maasai Women's Jewellery Workshop for twenty dollars, including transport and soft drinks as taken. We'll get back to her on that, we promise.

My departure is set for early the next morning, and Gordon belatedly breaks the news that he is staying on for another week for some time at the beach. I learn that his wife thinks he's on the Isle of Mull, off the west coast of Scotland, inspecting building projects as part of his job for the local council. I know that Gordon and his wife are having problems, but I also know his wife. And my wife knows his wife. His mother lives three doors away from my mother. A "friend" is meeting him, he explains, for a week at the beach, and it would be a big help if I could maybe just not mention that we've been in Africa. A big help. With a sigh, I promise.

We hug, and I head to my room. I chuckle to myself— Gordon, always unpredictable, is certainly never dull. And I owe him one. A big one. He brought me to Africa.

I rise before dawn, shower, shave, and wander down to the deserted poolside bar. A waiter finds me a coffee and I sit alone at a table. The sun has just come up, shining through the palm trees. Vervet monkeys chase one another between the table legs around the pool, and a small white speed boat is oh so slowly gliding past on the glassy, flat, unnaturally brilliant blue sea.

Africa.

It's that Marmite moment. You're either going to love it or to hate it. And I realize that, for the second time in my life, I have fallen hopelessly in love.

CHAPTER 3
ON A BIT OF A WHIM

I stare for several minutes at the laptop screen. It reads: *Two open-ended, return flights, Edinburgh/Amsterdam/Kilimanjaro.*

Eventually, I smile, take a deep breath, and press "confirm." Then, with sudden, reflexive alarm, I hope like hell that Candy had really meant it when she'd texted back, "Yes, go for it!"

Through the plate glass window of the City Centre Hotel Bar, I watch the rain crashing down—rivers in the gutters, the wind pushing small waves across the car park—and hope I've made the right decision. Only time will tell, of course. The UK economy is in tatters, the construction industry even worse. My 'Retire By Fifty' plan to exit after "just this one hotel build" or "one more apartment complex" needs a radical overhaul. That much is clear. But this radical? We leave in four weeks for Tanzania. Why? For a work break? A sabbatical? A mid-life crisis? An irresistible adventure? Oh, God: a huge mistake? Time alone will tell.

By now, I've been to Tanzania many times before. To climb Mount Kilimanjaro and Mount Meru; for safaris in the Serengeti, at Lake Manyara and Tarangire National Parks, in the world-famous Ngorongoro Crater. Dar es Salaam, Arusha, Moshi: the very names make me smile. I'm daydreaming once again about driving through the bush under the hot African sun.

Back to reality, I refocus out the hotel window, on the wild grey northern sky and the wind whipping through the bare branches of the lonely tree at the end of the car park. I love Scotland, but sometimes I think the weather is sent to try us. I find myself hoping that Candy will like ugali, the staple Tanzanian dish. Perhaps she thinks, sometimes, that I am sent to try her.

Ironically, the next week I'm flown to Dubai and offered a job to complete a five-star hotel project. Given the package, it's not a bad 'Retire By Fifty' plan at all. But throughout the flight home, I find myself searching for a good reason not to accept. Shit, I might never see fifty-one. You never know what the future holds in store. The timing is right. We may never get another chance.

Yeah. Let's go for it.

Our friends think we're mad. My son offers to buy me a fez, and I nearly accept.

***

We exit the plane and descend the steps into the open air, straight down to tarmac under a starry sky. Candy thinks the hot wind is from the engine. It's not, of course. *Karibu Tanzania!*

As plans go, ours is admittedly not very detailed. But sometimes in life, the least complex route is the best. Gordon is to meet us at KIA International arrivals, and his legendary unreliability renders us ridiculously happy to see his suntanned face, standing out like a *Where's Wally?* cartoon figure among the sea of Swahili faces crowding our exit. The fact that I have his mother's paintings with me in my bag may have encouraged his promptness. He even has a Land Rover which carries us on the short drive to Arusha.

It's almost midnight, and the unremitting blackness makes it impossible to distinguish any of the landscape, though I'm aware we're driving directly past the towering bulk of Mt. Kilimanjaro. Arusha seems deserted. We glide through the darkened streets before plunging off-road for the short climb to our hotel, a facility owned by one of Gordon's friends. A few quick, cold Kilimanjaro beers in the bar to celebrate Candy's first ever night in Tanzania, and we head off to our respective rooms. Ours proves to be constructed entirely of wood with a *makuti* roof, and is perched on stilts on a hillside with a direct view onto Mt Meru. We very much hope the stilts will survive the night to allow us the opportunity to enjoy our promised view. This seems far from certain, but what in life is ever certain? Getting older? Taxes? Death?

We have leapt into the unknown.

In the morning, I wake early, and as Candy wants to relax by the pool, I go in search of Gordon and find him in the dining room. Over cups of dark, rich Tanzanian coffee, we listen in bemused silence to the lodge staff meeting being conducted at the other side of the restaurant. The manager is apparently convinced that the staff are stealing food, and proclaims that it has to stop. Her most compelling evidence is that they are all getting fat: an open-and-shut case. I have a vision of the junior chef bursting out of her uniform, presented as evidence exhibit 1 for the prosecution at some future employment hearing, but it's unclear what the eventual sentence might be. She surely can't fire them all.

I spend a rather pointless day accompanying Gordon as he

tries to sell his mother's paintings in an art gallery in downtown Arusha. The Indian owner seems unprepared to agree to Gordon's $100,000 asking price, a reluctance based, from what I can mostly gather, on the fact that he's never heard of the purportedly "famous" artist who, according to Gordon, had gifted the paintings to his Mum some forty years before.

As night falls, the three of us head out to explore the less touristic side of Arusha. *Kajengi Ju* is a sprawling local neighbourhood on the slopes of Mount Meru that has overtaken and surrounded Thomas Kicha's house. Crazy Thomas, as his name translates in English from the colloquial Kiswahili, is a Danish friend of Gordon's who makes a living as a professional hunter and tour guide. He has a beach house on the Indian Ocean in Ushongo, south of Pangani, which we hope to rent from him as our new base. We're given to understand that the Queen's Bar, Main Street, *Kijengi Ju*, is where we're most likely to find him.

From the expression on Candy's face, I get the distinct impression that only the smoking skeleton of a Blackhawk helicopter lying at the side of the road would be required to complete her vision of how closely *Kijengi Ju* resembles Mogadishu in the 1980's. The streets are unpaved, with dirt tracks rutted from cars passing when it rains. None of the buildings have windows, the roofs are a mix of rusted corrugated iron and *makuti* palm tiles, and the walls are covered in graffiti. Everyone seems to be outside, sitting on the pavements, cooking over open fires, conversing animatedly, or playing bao, a local game similar to baccarat. Smoky flames provide the only illumination, other than the occasional kerosene lamp spluttering dully in the more affluent windows.

The Queen's Bar has electricity, a fact immediately apparent from the exterior lighted sign beckoning us inside. As we park and disembark, however, the electricity supply abruptly cuts out and the welcoming façade of the bar is plunged into total darkness. We enter the packed bar and realize that this is not an unexpected event, as the clientele have all already turned their mobile phones to flashlight mode. Face-up on the tables, the phones are bathing the room's ceiling in a spotted, bluish, eerie glow. A generator splutters into life somewhere out back, the fridges return to work, and Dully Sykes—the latest Bongo Flava Dar es Salaam rapper— bursts into something like song from the towering but battered speakers in the corner.

As if any further illumination inside The queen's were required, Alfred, the owner, busy serving drinks behind the bar, is wearing a miner's helmet, sporting a directional headlamp nearly as bright as his welcoming smile. He's delighted to have *wazungu* visitors, and unceremoniously evicts three teenagers from their chairs at the nearest table to make space for us VIPs.

Crazy Thomas has taken his patronage elsewhere for the evening, Alfred informs us, but we spend a few hours chatting with him regarding the pride he takes in being the most celebrated auto rally driver, we're told, that Tanzania has ever produced. He backs up this claim by pointing out with torch light several photographs, yellowing away on the barroom walls, of rally cars in various suitably heroic situations: sliding around hairpin corners or flying over bridges in mid-air. The shots are all at a distance that renders it impossible to clearly make out whose hands are on the wheel. Really, from the photos, it could be anybody driving those cars—but it would be churlish to raise this point, I figure.

I assume that Alfred's miner's hat is merely a useful prop to assist in serving during a power outage, but it turns out to be just one sample from his many and varied hat collection. Throughout the evening, he reappears at random moments wearing a Davy Crocket hat, a top hat, a policeman's helmet, and finally, as we bid him good night and he accompanies us to the door, a quite impressive Japanese admiral's bicorn hat! Stunning!

It seems Thomas must have driven past and seen our Land Rover outside the bar, and, assuming it's us and not a new stop on a Thomas Cook tour of Tanzania, he calls with an invitation to his house. We drive only about a hundred metres along the road and stop at a white brick wall topped with broken glass, with a huge metal gate set in it. A head pops out of a hole in the door, the gate magically swings open, and we exit "Mogadishu, 1980" and enter Colonial Tanzania, 1920.

Powered by a generator, Thomas's gardens are a floodlit riot of colour from a vast array of shrubs, bushes and trees, all immaculately kept in immaculate order. A gravel drive crunching under our wheels takes us the short distance to a beautiful, white, one-story house with a massive stone chimney. Thomas is waiting on the terrace to greet us, and ushers us into his fabulous home. It's furnished with beautiful sofas and tables, all made from timber reclaimed from old Arab dhows, polished wooden floors, and walls hung with beautiful paintings of African landscapes. Gun racks, as befits his profession, are everywhere. We join his other guest of the evening, a former USA Border patrol policeman from Texas named James, who has safaried and hunted in Tanzania with Thomas for years. He's an imposing character, at well over six feet in height, with a voice like an American Sean Connery with a Louisiana accent. He's outfitted in rather stereotypical safari gear, complete with cartridge loops instead of breast pockets on his shirt, and exudes an aura of supreme self-confidence and expertise.

Candy visibly relaxes in our new surroundings. Although neither of us is comfortable with the thought of anyone hunting animals, during the ensuing conversation they explain that now, in more enlightened times, they only hunt certain buffalo that cause problems in village areas. Cape buffalo are notoriously grumpy and dangerous animals, sometimes attacking the local population. Sometimes, too, Thomas and James provide a necessary culling of old or sick beasts in areas where overpopulation endangers an entire herd, in much the same way as deer are culled throughout Europe.

Twenty years ago, when Thomas first built the house, it was in splendid isolation on the very lower slopes of Mount Meru, but the recent enlargement of Arusha Town to include actual suburbs has enveloped the house inside ever-expanding boundaries. This encroachment on his privacy has had its compensations, however. As Thomas remarks, where else can you watch the sun set behind Mount Meru from your garden terrace, and then, after a mere five minutes' stroll, enjoy an ice-cold beer served by a prominent former rally driver wearing a bearskin hat? He certainly has a point.

We discuss the rental of his beach house, and he generously agrees that we should try it for a week to see if we like it before making a more formal agreement. I ask about keys, but he's a bit vague on the subject. He says he thinks it's open, and, in any case, it's well guarded by Mingwa, a Maasai *askari* who does a good job if he's not sleeping. Failing admission by Mingwa, there's another Danish friend who has a house a hundred metres down the beach who almost certainly has a spare key! Gordon says he'll show us where the house is, as it doesn't really have an entrance, as such. Although I can see Candy from the corner of my eye, shaking her head almost imperceptibly to warn me off—I suspect she'd like a bit more detail, but I pretend not to notice—the deal is more or less concluded.

We spend a very enjoyable few hours with cold beer, chilled wine and great conversation that includes stories of some of their African adventures together. James also regales us with a few tales of his days as a border guard, patrolling the fence line between Texas and Mexico. In one particular story, we hear of repeated reports of a bandit preying on the Mexicans, who every night try to make the perilous leap from poverty in Mexico to a life of opportunity and safety in the USA. This particular bandit and his gang would pose as guides who, for a fee, could lead them across the border, but who would, in the end, shoot and kill these small groups of refugees, stealing their life savings and raping the women. James and another patrolman had one evening stumbled across this gang in mid rape-and-robbery, and in the ensuing gun battle James had managed to wound the leader in the abdomen. The bandit was evacuated by helicopter to a hospital in Texas where he underwent surgery that saved his life but left him requiring a colostomy bag. He promptly issued a law suit against James for causing his injuries, resulting in James being suspended from duty, and his department having to fight a multi-million-dollar court case.

In a demonstration of staggering stupidity, the bandit won release on parole to await the conclusion of the case, whereupon, of course, he quickly reverted to his old ways, continuing his spree of murder and robbery. The "Shit Bag Bandit", as he came to be known locally, was finally re-arrested by another officer who, doubting there were many perpetrators sporting colostomy bags operating on the border, linked him to James's case, and dragged him promptly back to jail. In these new circumstances, all legal proceedings against James were dropped, and he was free again to return to his duties, and to his travels to Tanzania.

At evening's end, we agree that Thomas should lead the way out of *Kijengi Ju*, driving ahead of our vehicle in the pitch darkness after midnight. This is not the easiest neighbourhood to navigate, even in daylight. Our efforts at following his lead— a high-speed roller coaster ride through through a maze of narrow streets—left us tense and shaken by journey's end.

We finally reach the Kibo Palace Hotel in downtown Arusha, and decamp to the lounge bar of this relatively upmarket establishment, where we have *moja kwa barabara*— one for the road. The waiter notices that there's a dead fly in Thomas's glass and offers to bring a fresh one. Thomas stops him, seizes the bottle and pours more beer straight in. As the frothy head draws level with the rim of the glass, he yells, "Bingo!" and pings the fly from where it lies on top of the foam with his cocked forefinger. It flies into the air, landing squarely on a table ten metres distant, where two solemn gentlemen in business suits are in deep conversation.

"Works every time," Thomas declares, and drains his glass.

When the fly had plunged head-first into Thomas's beer, it hadn't given the slightest thought to its immediate future. Would it sink or swim? As I look across the table and smile at

Candy, a sudden question hits me. Had I really given enough thought to what our futures would be, here in darkest Africa? Would we sink or swim? Had I propelled Candy into a new life and new adventure with the same casual nonchalance that Thomas had just dispatched that fly?

Time would tell.

As people go their own way, destiny travels with them.

CHAPTER 4
LIFE IS A BEACH

It's six a.m., and the sun rises lazily over the peak of Mount Meru, flooding the sky with a glorious fusion of orange and red. The treetops come into stark, black focus, and birds greet the morning in a volley of cheery song. Cockerels crow in the nearby village, and fires are kicked back to life to brew the morning *chai* and cook the obligatory *mandazi,* that staple, scrumptious Tanzanian breakfast donut so beloved by all.

Gordon pulls up in his old Land Rover, dragging behind him a cloud of dust. Today we've planned a drive to Ushongo Beach, just south of Pangani Town. This gorgeous stretch of coastline lies almost half-way between Dar Es Salaam and Tanga, which is near the northern border with Kenya. From Arusha, it's a journey of about five hundred kilometres, which for most of the way utilises the main road between Arusha and Dar Es Salaam. Even optimistically, this is going to be a nine-hour drive. Studying Gordon's Land Rover doubtfully, I think to myself: *very* optimistically.

Candy and I enter the car and find an unexpected additional passenger inside: a young South African girl called Mayflower. She's decked out with 1960s hippy-dippy flair in a flowing, tie-dyed dress, carrying a multi-coloured cloth bag and, completing the ensemble, a garland of wildflowers decorating her hair. A friend of Gordon's employer, Mayflower wants to start a yoga retreat at his farm near Pangani. Perhaps this is an even more optimistic plan than our hope of making Ushongo in nine hours. We all say our hellos and set off.

The drive is through spectacular scenery. We depart Arusha by way of streets lined with flowering purple jacarandas and spectacular bougainvillea hedges. Mount Meru rises majestically to the west and Mount Kilimanjaro to the east. We weave erratically through the mad morning crush of *pikpiki* motorbikes, some crammed with as many as four people in a space meant for two, and trucks blasting black clouds of oil and smoke. Buses filled to over-capacity crowd the already crowded streets, every seat filled with more than the standard two or three passengers and most with people hanging on to the roof rack outside, bracing a foot against a step for balance. The roof racks of these buses carry everything from chickens in baskets and goats secured in boxes, to water tanks and containers of fruits and vegetables. We pass one bus on top of which an actual coffin is somewhat precariously tied. It's unclear whether or not it's occupied.

In Tanzania, I learn much later from a local doctor, it's not uncommon for a family to try to transport a family member, near death but still, perhaps, clinging to life, from the hospital back home to the village for burial, a strategy intended to save on transport costs. The fare per living person would be one hundred shillings, while the fare for a coffin can set you back as much as five thousand shillings. A savings of around forty-seven hundred shillings can be had if two relatives can manage to "walk" the patient—or even his corpse—wedged between them, onto the bus, stuffing themselves into the back seat, providing physical support for the patient (or body) with their own upright frames. As long as the conductor has failed to notice that the patient is already dead when they board, by the end of the journey it can be claimed that the unfortunate relative actually passed away during the ride. *Pole sana.* An unnecessary expense defrayed by typical African ingenuity.

We snake in and out of the morning traffic, street vendors descending on every vehicle when traffic lights force a stop. We're pressed on every side to buy bottled water, fruit, cashew nuts, shirts, a chef's hat (a strangely common offering), a set of kitchen knives with its own wooden display stand, live chickens, and even a coffee table. The moment the lights change, every vehicle roars forward with as much momentum as its mechanical state will allow. Apparently, too, the simple act of blasting your horn produces additional speed and also encourages any slackers to get a move on.

The buses, though, truly dominate the roads; with Bongo Flava music blasting out of massive speakers, they tower over every other vehicle and seem capable of driving through or over anything in their path. They're painted garish and often gloriously clashing primary colours, and have inspiring messages of faith and hope emblazoned on all sides. "Jesu is our Savior," one bus proclaims. "In Allah we trust," another declares. "Alex Ferguson is the true one God!" is the peculiar message on a third. Each bus, too, has a title: "The Dar Es Salaam Dasher" or "The Tanga Warrior" or "Mombasa Madness".

Gordon invents a tactic for use in city driving in Tanzania, based on his "where does a 400-pound gorilla, sit?" theory of African traffic. The answer, of course, is "anywhere it likes," and so the solution to finding safety on these crazed roadways is to secure a position in the slipstream of a vehicular "gorilla". He can slide efficiently into the first available slot behind a bus and allow it to function as our shield while it batters its way onwards. Gordon uses this gambit to great effect, and we're soon clear of Arusha and Moshi and heading onwards towards *Sane*, a town in the middle of the Maasai Steppe.

Here it's very hot, dry, and dusty. The road is elevated, and huge, dry *korongo*, dried-out river beds, pass under the road through culverts. There are frequent signs posted warning of the dangerous, powerful winds that sweep down from the Usambara Mountains that run parallel with the road, northwards towards Kenya. Donkey trains meander alongside and across the road, carrying timber towards the Kenyan border. Everywhere, people are walking, carrying baskets of fruit: pawpaw, mango, pineapple, jackfruits, the weirdly always green Tanzanian oranges, and vegetables of every imaginable sort, from potatoes to cassavas. Large hampers containing the appallingly smelly daga fish, tiny sun-dried whitebait from the Indian Ocean, are balanced perfectly on the heads of women gliding beside the road with the stunning, regal grace of a European catwalk model. It's inevitably the women doing this work—even small girls, imitating their mothers and aunties, following single-file—walking miles to the nearest market or bringing water back to their villages, their heads protected only by a twist of cloth from the rough palm-leaf baskets and the relentless mid-day sun.

We speed onwards, past Mombo Town, and past the turn-off to the treacherous road to Lushoto, which winds upwards three thousand feet into the Usambara Mountains. We pass a bus, toppled off the road into a deep *korongo*. The coachman has perhaps misjudged a corner, or the vehicle may have been hit by the ferocious winds. Or the driver has perhaps simply chewed too much *mira* or *gatthat*: narcotics habitually taken to keep them awake and alert, but which also can have other, less advantageous effects. The landscape is strewn with the contents of the roof rack, and the injured and dead lie in the sun. Out here, there are no ambulances. The bus is on fire, and crowds of people just stand and stare. It's horrific, but there's no help we can offer, so we continue on, eastwards, our mood considerably deflated.

We pass multiple times through police checkpoints where we're obliged to stop. We fairly quickly work out that this is merely a way for individual policemen to supplement their earnings. They spring from behind various mango trees along the route, to accuse us of speeding (true), or to demand to check our safety equipment, including required warning triangles, first aid kits, and numerous safety stickers that must be displayed on the windscreen. Given that the local traffic, which is rarely stopped by the police, consists almost universally of death traps on wheels, our reasonably intact vehicle renders us an especially likely target to have ready cash with which pay a bribe. Humour and courtesy go a long way in these circumstances, however, and most often we depart from these encounters leaving officers grinning and waving us onwards.

We're asked at one checkpoint if we'd mind giving an officer a lift to Korogwe Town. He turns out to be Stanley, the local Head of Immigration for the entire Pwani/Coastal Region. Had the former *"His Excellency, President for Life, Field Marshal Al Hadji Doctor Idi Amin Dada, VC, DSO, MC, Lord of All the Beasts of the Earth and Fishes of the Seas and Conqueror of the British Empire in Africa in General and Uganda in Particular"* worked out in a gym just once in a while, Stanley could have been his double. He's carrying a

Kalashnikov in one giant paw, and a massive jackfruit in his other. We offer him a beer from our cool box and some cashew nuts we'd purchased in Arusha at the traffic lights, in lieu of that set of kitchen knives with its own wooden display stand, and he's delighted. Given his massive frame, he has to jam himself tightly into the back seat, sharing it with our many bags and cases and Mayflower's yoga mats. When I ask if he's comfortable, he replies, "I am a soldier; please proceed." When I request that he aim the Kalashnikov out the window rather than as currently positioned, pointed directly at my back, he seems mildly surprised, but happy to comply.

Our small kindness in offering a ride to this equally kind gentleman now makes us untouchable with regard to police checkpoints. Each time we're asked to stop now, Stanley, the Immigration Chief, merely sticks his head out the window and bellows, "Attention!", whereupon a miraculous transformation of attitude abruptly occurs. The hitherto intimidating policemen by the side of the road all leap to immediate attention and salute us on our way.

We reach Korogwe Town, and Stanley asks that we drop him near the police station, or to be more precise, at the bar *next to* the police station. The latter is, we notice, located adjacent to a guest house with a truly extraordinary name: the Irente Cliffs Insane Asylum Guest House. I ponder briefly the question of who might want to actually stay there. We watch for a moment through the doorway to the bar as Stanley stacks three plastic chairs, one on top of the other, to ensure they'll bear his considerable weight, then slumps down onto this pile of plastic in front of the antiquated TV set, joining the rest of the bar patrons cheering on Liverpool live from Anfield, UK. We have today made another new and important friend.

Late in the afternoon, with a three-hour drive still ahead of us, the inevitable happens: our car creaks to a halt. Gordon coasts to the side of the road and breaks to a full stop. I jump out and take the warning triangle about a hundred metres back down the road, placing it carefully as a caution to other drivers. As I begin the trek back to the car, however, the Tanga Express Bus with "Jose Mourinho Walks on Water" painted across its front blasts its horn at me, drives directly over the triangle, thunders past down the road at a speed well beyond the local limits. I gather all the pieces of triangle I can find and contemplate replacing them in a semblance of pattern back on the tarmac, consider it pointless, and return to the vehicle where some random guys have turned up to stare blankly, together with Gordon, under the bonnet. It's clear they have no more idea of how to repair the engine than Gordon does. Mayflower suggests we form a circle, hold hands, and chant a chakra to heal our poor, sick car, but we politely decline her offer. She seems both puzzled and disappointed. She takes a seated position, however, cross-legged on the road verge, and announces her intent to attempt to heal the car through meditation. We all agree that while it might not help, it can't hurt.

Meanwhile, Gordon manages to phone a friend who knows a local fundi/mechanic who might be able to help. We are sitting forlornly at the road side as dark begins to fall, when a vehicle draws up beside us. Gordon's friend's friend agrees to tow us towards Muheza, which is the next sizable town on the road to Tanga, the final stop before the dirt road we'd take for the last section of our route to Pangani Town. On the back of his truck, a sign directly in front of my face reads *Usikate Tamaaa*, which quite aptly translates to "Do Not Despair." Apt, because we're towed erratically, at alarming speed— terrifying, in fact—arriving with breathless relief in Muheza Town. Although pitch dark with no electric lights whatsoever, it is a buzzing hive of activity. Over outdoor fires, people are cooking chapati, chips, samosas, corn on the cob, and *nyama choma* (roasted beef). Tempting fragrances are wafting from a multitude of small stalls, all lit by kerosene lamps.

They tow our car under a ubiquitous mango tree, and while we make our food choices from the hundreds of people who've surrounded us, Gorgeous George, our new mechanic friend, goes to work. Somehow, after considerable suspense, he manages to rev the engine into life. From what I can see, a hammer, a set of pliers with one handle, and a screw driver constitute his entire tool kit, but the car seems entirely restored to its former uncertain health. It's possible that the ten assorted people with their heads still tucked under the bonnet jabbering *sotto voce*, nodding wisely and pointing animatedly inside the car's workings, have actually assisted somehow in the repair, but we'll never know for sure. So, we thank them all in turn, and begin a protracted negotiation which produces a mutually agreeable fee. We pay George the equivalent of ten US dollars, plus a large serving of chapatti and some hot tea, with which he's thoroughly delighted, and resume our journey, having made yet another friend promising to be at our beck and call for life, should we ever have need of his "extensive auto mechanical skills" in the future.

"I was once mechanic to the *Rais*—the President of Tanzania!" he yells as we depart. I can see the wheels turning behind Gordon's eyes. *There must be an opportunity in this somewhere*, I know he's thinking. *Rais wa Tanzania!*

The drive to Pangani from this point forward is blissfully uneventful, especially considering that we're now driving in total darkness and the road isn't a road, but rather a narrow and bumpy dirt track, meandering unpredictably through countless small villages that pop up with surprising regularity out of the dense bush. Gordon informs us that to get to Ushongo Beach and Thomas's house, we'll have to cross the Pangani River, and the only way to do this is by a roll on/roll off ferry which last crosses the river at dusk or seven p.m., whichever comes first. As it's already nine p.m., this poses an unexpected problem. In which one of Pangani's very few guest houses will we sleep tonight?

(And how will Candy react?)

Ever resourceful, Gordon has phoned ahead. Rasta Ali, Pangani's foremost tour guide, is waiting to meet us when we arrive at the town bus stand. Rasta Ali is all of five feet and two inches tall. His flowing Rasta dreadlocks are his pride and joy, and he's decked out in a flowing white *kanzu* robe. He greets Gordon with a huge whoop and a cry of, "Gordon, man, my brother from another mother, long time brother!" and explains that he's been guiding some young German girls around historic Pangani Town, informing us confidently: "The chicks really dig me in this gear, man!" He suggests we recuperate from our long drive with a cold beer at Valentine's Bar, right next door to the bus stand, the true hub of Pangani.

Rasta swiftly places an order for some *chips mayai* (a local chips omelette) with *kachumbari* (pickle) salsa and hot chili sauce, and then finalizes our accommodation requirements. Mayflower informs us that she has other plans, and we see her last weaving off into the darkness in the direction of her commune, chanting oms as she goes.

Rasta is as good as his word, and soon he leads us to a guest house on the beach called *Three Sisters*. There are only two sisters, but they both greet us warmly. They look like identical twins, dressed in a bright blast of colour: long, flowing dresses made of beautiful *kanga* cloth with matching headdresses. They're very graceful and elegant, and they bustle around the room, fussing over us, trying to force yet more food on us, eager to please.

They insist with a stern formality, however, on verifying that Candy and I have bona fide married status before showing us to our double room for the night. "We're not that kind of establishment, you know," insists Sister Number One. "If you want that sort of hanky panky, go to The One Song Bar!" chimes in Sister Number Two, glaring meaningfully at Rasta Ali, whose smile never falters.

Sister Number Two demonstrates the working of our ensuite shower, which is helpful, as I doubt we'd ever have thought to fill the bucket of water from the tap, and pour it over each other. To be fair, absent an actual shower head, it's by far the best solution.

In the morning, Rasta is waiting for us in the *makuti* thatched-roof breakfast room and offers to guide us to the ferry for fifty dollars. When we point out that we can see the ferry from where we're seated, he's entirely unfazed, offering to reduce his price to thirty dollars, since we're friends of Gordon. When we again demur, he merely smiles and re-adjusts his offer.

"Okay," he acquiesces. "Thirty dollars, then, for both of you." My expression halts any further negotiations.

"*Hamna shida*—no problem—and *PFS,*" he replies

cheerfully.

"*PFS*?" I query.

"*Pole fucking sana*, man," he grins. "So fucking sorry"—
a gentle Swahili expression, corrupted a bit by too much time
in Gordon's company in their favourite watering hole, the One
Song Bar: an admittedly disreputable establishment. It owes
its name to the fact that it only has one song on its dilapidated
juke box, played constantly and always at full volume: Tom
Jones' *The Green, Green Grass of Home*.

We depart the guest house, Gordon driving the Land Rover
with Rasta in front, and we reach the ferry in time to drive
straight onto its deck. The Pangani River is about five hundred
metres wide at this point, and almost a kilometre from the
mouth, where it enters the Indian Ocean. The ferry was
donated to the town by the Danish Government, and is fitted
with radar, sonar and two huge diesel engines mounted one on
each side, sadly maintained by absolutely no one. When it
steams off from the quay side, it quickly becomes apparent that
only one of the two engines is working. The boat begins to spin
around in a pirouette known locally as the Swahili Ballet. It
manages two full circles before miraculously landing at the
opposite side quay in perfect position for us to drive off. The
level of skill required to accomplish this manoeuvre is truly
impressive.

We're only briefly hampered in exiting the ferry by
several hundred foot passengers, mostly ladies in burkas and
head coverings, decorated Swahili-style with dazzling bright
fabrics; men in white *kanzu* robes and multi-coloured fez-type
hats known as *kufia*; perhaps twenty cows driven by a Maasai
tribesman in full *shuka*, beating each cow with a stick if it

pauses; approximately thirty *pikipiki* motor bikes; and a small boy balancing an old paint pot on his head containing a cow's head and all four hooves, ingredients for a tasty soup. The *pikipiki* bikes carry at least three people each. Rasta explains that they're known as *mishikaki*, a kebab on a skewer, and laughs uproariously. That actually is kind of funny, I allow, observing, though, that while the law states that everyone must wear a crash helmet, the police only ever seem to apply this to the driver. It seems, as well, that pretty much any form of headwear is duly regarded as an acceptable form of "crash helmet," evident from the fact that there are drivers wearing construction workers' yellow helmets, a bowler hat, and even, hilariously, a pointed black Halloween witch's hat worn with utterly unironic aplomb.

A short and glorious drive on a dirt road through a stunning avenue of brightly red flowering flame trees leads us to Ushongo Beach. We turn off the dirt road and drive quite literally through long grass and bushes, bursting out the other side to find the house of Crazy Thomas positioned with exotic perfection under a stand of palm trees, directly on a breathtakingly beautiful deserted beach only twenty meters from the Indian Ocean. The island of Zanzibar is just visible on the horizon, and we've rarely if ever been greeted by a scene of such bewitching natural beauty. The bay, completely edged by palm trees, curves for twelve kilometres in a perfect crescent shape. A fishing village lies to the north with multiple *ngalawa*—dugout canoes—fishing in the bay.

The Beachcomber Beach Bar is a kilometre away along the beach, and Rasta disappears in that direction as soon as we park. The house itself proves to have two bedrooms, a very basic kitchen, an open lounge, a shower room, and a stunning terrace overlooking the sea. It has electricity but no generator. More importantly, though, it does have Mingwa, the Maasai security guard, who speaks no English other than the name of the Manchester United football team. He greets us with his warm, hugely comforting smile and points out the essentials, communicating with surprising effectiveness the most important features of the borehole and water tower, as well as the table under which he sleeps at night—and whenever else his duties permit.

We unpack and make ourselves comfortable in our new home. Gordon suggests lunch at the Beachcomber Beach Bar. He tells us that Rasta Ali will have a table reserved for us, and we can meet his good friends, the bar's owner: Tony, a fifty-something, Tanzanian/Greek whose father had owned a sisal estate in the 1950's, and his Tanzanian wife, Faithfully.

The Beachcomber Beach Bar is a bar-cum-guest house establishment that Tony likes to describe as a "lodge," with an open-air, *makuti*/palm-thatched roofed bar area and some small rooms and bandas scattered amongst the palm trees for accommodation. It boasts, as well, a totally unexpected but fabulous sound system, booming out Bob Marley reggae music as we enter straight in off the sand.

Tony describes it as a "no news/no shoes" kind of place. His ripped and faded board shorts, t-shirt emblazoned with the misquoted lyrics, "I Fucked the Sherriff, But I Did Not Shoot the Deputy", the long grey hair pulled back and styled in a pirate's pigtail, and the fact of his very obvious glass eye rather does point to that vibe. Ali has indeed reserved a table for us, which he's sharing with Old Mohammed, a fisherman from the nearby village who is at least 80 years old. He chain-smokes Gordon's cigarettes and sips on a glass of *konyagi*, a local cane spirit. He wears a *kofia* hat and a *kanga* cloth wrap with consummate ease, with a grimy old T shirt claiming: "I shot the Deputy." His laugh is infectious, and despite not speaking a word of English, he manages to fully participate in the gathering. In everything, that is, apart from the actual purchase of drinks or cigarettes.

Faithfully appears from the kitchen with samosas, fish & chips, and rice, as Gordon makes a grab at retrieving his cigarette pack from Mohammed's grasp. Rasta, laughing, admonishes Gordon, "You smoke like a train, anyway, *kaka* Gordon."

Gordon advises Rasta to fuck off. "You've never seen a train, Rasta. How would you know?"

"Hey Graeme," Rasta yells across the room, "Did Gordon ever tell you about the time we stole a cat from the One Song Bar and sold it to the owner at Shimoni Bar for two cold Kilimanjaros?"

"Nope," I say.

"Hey, can you lend me twenty dollars?"

You never know with these guys where a conversation might be headed.

We learn that Rasta's brother had sold a cow to his neighbour the prior month, and two days later the cow walked back home. The neighbour promptly complained to the police that Rasta's brother had stolen his cow, and was a villain, cattle rustler, and all-around danger to the community. The police agreed (a set of facts apparently not in dispute), and so his brother has been in a jail cell for two weeks, awaiting trial, since no one can afford to post his bail. This tale reminds Gordon of the time Crazy Thomas was reported for shooting a buffalo near Ushongo, and when he had crossed the ferry back into Pangani the police were awaiting his arrival, promptly arresting him, along with his driver and friend, Peter, for hunting without a license. The two men were deposited in cells adjacent to the station, from which Thomas phoned a high-ranking police official in Arusha who, in turn, immediately informed the Pangani Branch to release them as the charge was absurd and without foundation. It was not mentioned that Thomas had not long before gifted the official with fifty dollars, in apparently much the same way you'd hire a lawyer on retainer. On his release from his brief captivity, Thomas thought it would be funny to play a trick on Peter so he crept round outside the police station and, whispering through the cell's barred window, informed his friend that he had escaped. He pushed a Mars Bar through the bars, advising him to "hang in there, buddy." He told his friend, sympathetically, not to give up hope, and promised: "I'll be back."

Thomas, Gordon related, then spent the rest of that afternoon in the nearby Shimoni Bar with Gordon, periodically visiting Peter at the cell window to give him updates on his promised escape plan. He finally got a naively grateful Peter released the next morning, telling him that he'd spent the entire day raising the funds for his bail. Chuckling, Gordon adds that Thomas actually had Peter paying off the bail money each month for three months before someone finally told Peter the truth.

We spend the remainder of the afternoon trying to be heard above the loud music and constant chatter of the locals in the bar. Does nobody here work? We drink, we eat, we swap tales, and at some point during the evening, we agree that a trip over to Zanzibar the next morning in Tony's wooden fishing boat would be a great idea. The agreed departure time of six a.m. seems optimistic, but we'll give it our best shot. Rasta Ali has inveigled himself into the company of three young female German NGO workers, and is extolling the virtues of his historic Pangani Bike Tour, which is available tomorrow should they wish to join him, and yes, he will accept a beer while he gives them the details, much obliged.

Tony is loudly insisting that he should play his guitar, and Faithfully is equally insistent that he shouldn't. He informs me that if I'm sticking around here, then I have to be tough on staff and set an example. Once, sometime in the past, he remarks, he'd been certain that staff were stealing the booze from behind the bar, whenever he or Faithfully left the Lodge or visited Dar Es Salaam. To solve the problem, he says, he called a staff meeting in the bar, laid out his suspicions that there was theft occurring when he was not there to see everything, and informed everyone that he'd been visited in a dream by a *ramba ramba* man, a local witch doctor, who'd told him that he needed to take action. This grabbed everyone's attention, whereupon he had leapt up onto the bar, stared at the assembled throng, pointed in an arc around them and shouted, "Even when I'm not here, I can see *all*!" With a brisk and dramatic flourish, he had plucked out his glass eye and thumped it onto the top shelf, then turned to his spellbound audience and announced again, "I see *all*."

The effect had been electric, Gordon said. Most of them screamed, and one barman had turned abruptly and sprinted off down the beach, never to return. "Back to work!" Tony had admonished the much-abashed crew, and they all had reputedly fled to their respective duties.

I turned to Tony. "So, did it work?" I naturally wanted to know.

"Of course it fucking did," Tony replied. "For the next two stock takes I was bottles OVER at every count. They were sneaking back into stock the bottles they'd stolen!"

Grand and warming laughter all around, and Tony orders another beer, resuming his search for his guitar. Candy and I say our goodnights and depart for home, strolling along the deserted beach. A full moon lights the sand and iridescent whitecaps, and we can see for miles, our only other companions thousands of ghost crabs which scurry at great speed away from us and vanish into tiny holes in the sand. The beach seems virtually alive with these cartoon characters, with their eyes on stalks and sideways scuttle. The gentle breeze sways the palm trees. We reach the house, strip off, and scamper ourselves, straight into the Indian Ocean; it's high tide and bathwater warm, and we swim and giggle, and, exhausted after an eventful day, emerge back onto the moonlit beach and return slowly to the beach house's terrace. Mingwa is fast asleep under the table there and, despite his gross dereliction of duty, it's somehow comforting to have him guarding our new home. He rolls deeper inside his Maasai *shuka*, and we open the door quietly, trying not to wake him. I can't resist, though, a few minutes later, sneaking out and hiding his shoes in the bushes. I'll wait until morning to observe him working that one out, but I am pretty certain his Maasai pride won't let him ask where they are.

Welcome to Ushongo Beach. We are indeed home now.

CHAPTER 5
NIGHT BOAT TO STONE TOWN, ZANIZBAR

We awake at the outrageous hour of five a.m., and there's neither a suggestion of a breeze nor a single cloud in the still dark, ink-blue morning sky. Just a vast, dizzying array of brilliant, shimmering stars, some seeming close enough to reach out and touch, and all surrounded by the luminous dusting of the distant Milky Way. Morning at this hour is illuminated only by that blazing yellow full moon. The only sounds are the soft, rhythmic crashing of the waves on the deserted shore, and the occasional cry of a distant bush baby, high in one of the countless palm trees fringing the beach along this stretch of lonely Tanzanian coastline. The palms stand sentinel, tall and skinny like silent Maasai *askaris* guarding their posts. The village lies in darkness. It'll be more than an hour before the first call to prayer will ring out from the Mosque tower to rouse Ushongo to another day.

We find Tony's boat bouncing in the surf directly outside the Beachcomber Bar, but with no immediate sign of him or Rasta Ali. Closer inspection reveals Tony lying fast asleep in the scuppers, cuddling his guitar. Faithfully sits on a hard plank seat behind the Captain, Kimwimyi. In this pale light, he and his mate, Mhatari, quietly slip anchor. Candy and I clamber aboard through the surging surf, and the small outboard bursts to life. Faithfully greets Candy with a hug, and they settle down together in the bow seats. Rasta Ali seems to have convinced his German lady friends that no visit to the beach is complete without a bicycle tour of Pangani in the company of the town's foremost guide, so he won't be joining us. Of Gordon there is no sign.

We're leaving the Swahili Coast bound for Nungwi, forty-five kilometres away, in northern Zanzibar, and from there we'll proceed onward to our real destination: spicy, exotic Stone Town. We're still deep in the hot and sultry African night, and when Kimwimyi silently hands round a bottle of *Konyagi*, the local fiery spirit, to toast the start of our voyage, I'm overcome with an appealing fantasy: we're a crew of pirates or smugglers, on a daring raid to a spice island where our fortune will be made! We laugh as Candy briefly chokes at the taste of the konyagi, but she gently wipes her lips and proclaims it delicious.

The small wooden boat glides effortlessly through the swell, in defiance of its ancient and worn appearance. We're heading almost exactly due east, a fact confirmed by the red disc of the sun as it slowly emerges, dead ahead on the horizon, beckoning us towards our destination. We're accompanied by small flying fish skimming the surface of the sea. A yellow fin tuna competes for our attention, dancing in the interface between the ocean and the rosy glow of sunrise. Occasionally, as we plough through the deep trough in the Indian Ocean that separates Zanzibar from mainland Tanzania, the salt spray washes our faces.

Full daylight arrives at last, cloaked in brilliant blue against which the island's coastline now stands in splendid relief. Kimwimyi suddenly shouts, "Pombo! Pombo!" and we at once observe four dolphins leaping from the sea like a team of synchronized swimmers, off the port bow of our small craft. Four more appear off starboard, and we scoot around frantically to grab our respective cameras. As they must have done a thousand times before, the dolphins reappear at random, always tantalizingly just out of frame, and we all achieve some excellent shots of nothing but sea and sky.

"*Mungu wangu*—Oh, my God," mutters Mhatari, and as we all turn to follow the direction of his pointed finger, we fall into stunned silence. As far as the eye can see, hundreds of dolphins are leaping from the sea's white-capped surface, re-submerging only to reappear seconds later. We are surrounded by this thrilling spectacle of dolphins at play. We veer to the north, and for thirty glorious minutes we can join in their joyous procession. They're spinner dolphins, migrating north in search of food. These beautiful, friendly, and inquisitive temporary companions seem to accept our presence as natural—even, perhaps, as a pleasure—and carry on in their exuberant way. Though reluctant to leave, we eventually turn again for land; we're short of fuel and have no choice, but we all gaze longingly after our friends until they disappear into the distance, with not a little envy of their life of freedom and joy.

We clear the headland and float gently over the now smooth, glassy surface of the bay, sheltered by a string of small islands. The water is so clear we can easily see the myriad multi-coloured shoals of fish teeming just below the surface, darting in and around the brilliantly-hued coral reefs that protect this exquisite coastline. We drop anchor just offshore at a seemingly endless, white powder, soft sand beach. Tony, Faithfully, Candy and I gather on the shore, grouped around our cool box. Though it's barely eight a.m., the sun is high enough in the sky to have warmed the sand, and the contrast with our home in Scotland tempts us to enjoy a cold Kilimanjaro beer. Time is uniquely elastic in Africa.

A guest from one of the many nearby luxury hotels pauses as she passes, enquiring whether we've just been on the Sunrise Boat Tour. She's clearly a bit puzzled when we all laugh, and Tony mutters, "Sort of... yeah."

Candy wonders aloud whether we shouldn't report to Immigration as, technically, Zanzibar requires entry and exit visas. Tony's reply of, "Trust me, I'm a doctor", does little to answer her concerns.

"What?" Karibu Zanzibar.

As Kimwimyi and Mhatri lay to in the bay, promising to wait for us or for further instructions, we're led to a waiting car by a driver Faithfully has organized for us. He has appeared, as if from nowhere, standing on the high-water line, and we follow him off the beach, passing through a hotel where a receptionist behind the registration counter raises an eyebrow at seeing four strangers—clearly not guests—entering and exiting her hotel so early in the morning.

The drive to Stone Town will take about an hour, but it's an hour well-spent, as we travel a tarmac road lined with hibiscus, frangipani, flame trees, bougainvillea and the lush green foliage endemic to Zanzibar. Here on the island, there's a greater sense of modernity than we've witnessed in the happy but tumbledown style of the villages on the mainland. There's glass in some windows, we notice. The illusion of western prosperity is dispelled somewhat when we pass a donkey cart loaded with fresh mangos, and have to pause in our tracks as a herd of goats, kept orderly by two small boys with long sticks, amble lazily across the road. We pass an ancient old man wobbling along on his bicycle with an equally ancient musket slung over his frail shoulders, a relic from a less peaceful but not too distant past. "He's still fighting the slaver," laughs Abdul, our Zanzibari driver.

We reach the outskirts of Stone Town and slow our speed as we wind through the narrow streets of the city. The high white Arabic style buildings seem to almost lean over to touch each other, producing an uncanny sensation of being drawn into a tunnel, the entrance, maybe, to a secret, mystical world. We grind to a halt. A lorry piled dangerously high with old fridges, bound for Dar es Salaam by dhow, has crashed, blocking the street. People mill around, shouting and offering advice, adding to the confusion, but mostly just gawping. Street boys use this as an opportunity to try to sell us their wares through the car window. They pretend astonishment that we have no need of cashew nuts or Gucci sunglasses (spelled with only one "c".)

The refrigerators have been reloaded onto the broken vehicle, and we can move forward once more—slowly—so slowly, in fact, that the cashew nut seller can keep up a final sales pitch as he jogs alongside our window. At last, we burst free. We park next to the old Moorish fort and walk the last few metres through the incredibly narrow streets to our hotel. The Coco Del Mar seems hyperbolic at best, given its crumbling exterior façade. We enter through a traditional Zanzibari door of solid coconut wood, decorated with huge brass spikes once used to ward off elephants. As we pass through to reception, I wonder if it works as well to deter cashew nut vendors. We're shown to our room, which is basic but serviceable. Candy asks the young housekeeper where to find the hair dryer, and the remote for the satellite TV?

Bewildered, the housekeeper stares back at us with an uncertain smile.

We meet Tony and Faithfully in the open-air mezzanine area. Tony has an opened, half-finished bottle of Grant's Whisky on the table. He's extolling the virtues of the design of the bottle: triangular, so as not to roll and break when stored on sailing ships, which circumnavigated the globe centuries before. "Clever bastards, you Jocks," he adds, in ironic admiration of our nation's ingenuity.

Faithfully is elegance personified, dressed in an eye-catching Zanzibari hijab of flowing cerise and black, with a magnificent headdress in the same striking colours. She produces a headdress for Candy and they both, ably abetted by the housekeeper, and with much hilarity, set about making Candy into a character from the Arabian Nights. It's not really necessary—she's already a beauty—but it's the end of the Eid festival, and it's nice to show some respect for the local culture.

In perfect contrast to our display of respect for Islam, Tony suggests we head for Livingstone's Bar to plan our evening. The tables are set directly on the beach under a huge mango tree, providing some much-needed shade. We watch the dhows sailing gracefully past, with only the silhouettes of their resting crews visible as they return from their early morning fishing. The bay is full of cargo and freight ships at anchor, adding to the pervading impressions of a bygone era. Some vessels are anchored far out in the straits which lead to the main harbour. The fast, sleek, modern ferries from Dar es Salaam provide a marked contrast. Small tourist boats heading out to the Turtle Islands crisscross the harbour, their names proudly embellishing their sun canopies: Banana, Mr Bean,

Jambo, Karibu. They're all available for hire; the price is always negotiable. One ship, which most closely resembles an enormous World War Two landing craft, is beached directly in front of the bar, its front boarding ramp lowered, offering entry into its dark, mysterious interior. We watch in fascinated horror as car after car is driven through the soft sand at breakneck speed, in an attempt to reach the ramp before getting stuck in the sand. Almost every car gets stuck in the sand, of course, providing cheerful work and apparently a lot of fun for roughly fifteen young boys who push, dig and haul the vehicles, engineering each one aboard. Faithfully informs us that the cars are bound for an auction in Dar Es Salaam.

We wander somewhat aimlessly through Stone Town's vibrant streets. The Central Market is a glorious profusion of colour and sounds; the scent of spices fills the air. Zanzibar is, after all, the Spice Island, and it's easy to imagine that you're in an old Arab casbah. Beautiful boutique hotels are carefully concealed behind the old faded façades of the traditional coral stone buildings that give the town its name. Tantalizing glimpses of shaded courtyards and cool swimming pools make the oppressive African heat of the street even harder to bear, and heighten the impression that one must peel back layer upon layer of mystery, with reverent patience, before learning how to fully appreciate all that Zanzibar has hidden in its dark and intriguing heart.

As dusk approaches, we make our way to the Africa House Hotel. Once a private gentlemen's club, it's been beautifully restored to its former glory. The walls are lined with fascinating faded black-and-white photos. Visual clues to the story of its colonial past are conspicuous in both architecture and décor, and as we head out to the sun terrace, we stop more than once to examine items which catch our eye. We order cocktails, and enjoy the last few minutes of sunshine. Tame monkeys play on the bar or wander around the terrace; there was one more, we are told, but he was sadly stolen some few nights before. His wanted poster hangs forlornly on the wall complete with a notice of reward for his return. Candy lazily wonders if they keep a mugshot ready for each of the other monkeys, just in case. Cocktails in hand, we watch the local children diving into the sea from an old oil tanker, which has crashed over the edge of the harbour quay and been adopted by them as a perfect springboard.

The sun nears the horizon, and the sky is streaked with orange. In Africa, the sun itself seems always to exit the day as a red circle, trailing orange or purple clouds to frame its crimson glow, sinking with a slowness almost suspenseful as a sultry darkness finally falls like a velvet curtain being drawn across a favourite painting. The breeze from off the water lightens the lingering heat.

We head now towards the *Forodhani* Gardens—in English, these are generally known as the Jubilee Gardens—only a short stroll through the darkened streets. Our footsteps echo from the walls. The shops have closed for the day, but the street touts never close. With some difficulty, we avoid their offers to take us to where we already know we're going. No, we don't want a tour to the home of Freddie Mercury. I picture a Zanzibari version of Rasta Ali, taking guests to a different house every day and proclaiming it as the "true" birth house. Nobody actually knows where Zanzibar's most famous son truly lived in his early years.

We soon arrive in the square. In the shadow of The Old Fort and bordered by the harbour, the gardens are illuminated by a multitude of dancing lanterns and lights. Quilts are spread on the ground, covering every available fragment of grass or pavement. Entire families, from babes in arms to frail old mamas occupy these, content to enjoy the spectacle unfolding all around. The gardens are replete with stalls serving a vast array of foods, all cooked right in the open on grills, BBQs and hot plates. Fish, chicken, meat kebab, salads, chips, Zanzibar pizza and fresh sugar cane juice, squeezed by hand through iron mangles, are all noisily offered for sale by the multitude of stall holders. Hundreds of people jostle for position, or find seats on the edge of cool fountains or the sea walls to enjoy their meals. It's an anarchy of colour, clashes of bright African patterns and demure Arab fashion producing outfits of rebellious but wonderful disharmony. Women in full black hijab drift by, bringing to bear only the flash of their eyes to convey personality. Headdresses, kangas, saris and dazzling kikois, in every imaginable colour, shade and combination, adorn young and old alike. The festival of Eid has finished and everyone's celebrating, all co-mingling joyously regardless of colour or creed. Tarib music plaintively ornaments the night breeze, drifting on the gentle trade winds, wrapping the whole scene in an invisible softness. We sit smoking shisha pipes on the terrace of the Monsoon restaurant, the rich, alluring smell merely adding to the romance. This is a typical Zanzibar night: hot, exotic, buzzing, cosmopolitan, mysterious and, by any definition, magical.

Tomorrow we must return to Ushongo, but tomorrow is another day. Tony and Faithfully are continuing on to Dar Es Salaam on the two-hour trip aboard the Kilimanjaro Ferry, and we'll be flying back direct to Ushongo. We have a meeting, the following week, with a mysterious acquaintance of Gordon called "Boss" in Tanga Town. We've been told that he wants to discuss a potential job with us. And we're looking for a job now. We've decided.

The next morning, we're at Zanzibar International Airport, bright and early for the forty-minute flight to Ushongo Airstrip. We have to pass through immigration, and while the officer questions why we have no entry stamp for Zanzibar, he blithely accepts my indignant explanation that it's not our fault one of his colleagues didn't do his job properly on our arrival. Candy's still grinning discreetly as we're escorted out over the apron to the 12-seat Cessna 208 awaiting us, the ubiquitous bush plane used throughout East Africa.

There are only two other passengers on the flight, who turn out to be the Greek Orthodox Archbishop of Tanzania and his assistant. We exchange greetings and settle down for the flight. As we taxi out, the pilot is shouting his safety briefing over his shoulder above the roar of the engine. We can't hear a word, but reckon we'll figure out what to do if the need arises. The engine reaches a crescendo of racket, and we bullet forward, only for the pilot to take a sharp turn left and pull up the plane.

"Sorry folks. Something feels wrong," he announces, and we are disembarked to a second plane.

Candy is no lover of small planes, but it appears that his Highness the Archbishop is even less of a fan, as he's visibly shaking and muttering to his companion while the pilot goes through the procedure yet again. This time, however, we sail off uneventfully into the blue yonder. The view below is fantastic.

We circle over Stone Town, easily picking out the harbour and even the ferry transporting Faithfully and Tony on their way to Dar Es Salaam, out past Prisoner Island. As we head north, the pilot issues a warning that we seem to be heading into a tropical storm. The sky darkens suddenly, and lightning slashes across the jet-black sky. By now the archbishop is actually reciting prayers. Candy's gripping my hand and I hug her close to me. We look into each other's eyes. "If I die in this plane, I'll kill you," she jokes. I mention that it might have been useful to have been able to hear the safety briefing. Suddenly, we're both laughing, and I think, "This is Africa."

The archbishop doesn't appear to appreciate our laughter, so we restrain ourselves out of respect for the genuine danger I sense we might all actually be in. Within minutes, the flight becomes nightmarish, the plane plummeting and stabilizing by turns. It's buffeted by the strong winds and pockets of hot and cold air currents caused by the storm. Zero visibility and frequent flashes of forked lightning add to the drama of a journey which seems much, much longer than it actually is. The pilot starts to circle, lower and lower, searching for a hole in the cloud. Finally, one appears, and we dart into it while the opportunity is available.

Mashado Airstrip serves the Ushongo and Pangani area all the way up the coast to Tanga. One might therefore be forgiven to expect something more substantial than a grass strip cut out of the middle of a huge sisal estate, but the sight of this scar of brown cropped scrub and soil is, when we sight it at last, one of the most beautiful scraps of land we've ever seen. And, wonder of wonders, greeting us on landing is Gordon, all grins and leaning against a tree with our hired car beside him. While the pilot coaxes the archbishop back onto the plane, and they take off to continue their journey of hops between bush airstrips all the way to Arusha, we three lean against the tree and wax philosophical about the Tanzanian aviation industry.

CHAPTER 6
TANGA, CITY OF LIGHTS

The largest city in the Pwani coastal region north of Dar Es Salam before the Kenya border at Horohoro, Tanga is only seventy kilometres from Ushongo Beach. Of that distance, there's a metaled, finished road for two kilometres inside Pangani. For the rest of the stretch, the way consists only of those typical African bush tracks, which are used by everything from enormous buses destined for the cities to sisal trucks transporting the ubiquitous timber poles used everywhere for thatched roofing structures, as well as tractors, 4x4s and private cars, *pikipikis* and *bodabodas*, motorbike taxis, bicycles, herds of cows, goats and us, when we're traveling to Tanga to buy supplies, visit a bank or undertake most any other task one would take for granted almost anywhere else in the world. When you add in the unavoidable obstruction created by the Pangani River Ferry, the fastest time one can hope to cover this drive in is two hours in each direction.

We're on our weekly supply run to stock up on food, fuel, cash, and wine, and to meet up with a friend of Gordon who wants to discuss a business opportunity with us. Candy has come to terms with the fact that I may have glossed over a few details about what Tanga actually has to offer as a shopping mecca and entertainment capital, and has even forgiven me for the fact that hardly anyone speaks English and that there's not really that vaguely promised "abundant supply" of hair "saloons," as they're locally known. (I'm interested to discover if Candy will try the "To Die For Hair Saloon," which seems to this perhaps naïve male a high price to pay for nice hair.) The only "supermarket" is in fact Ashok's Emporium of Fine Foods & Wines. Even I admit it doesn't have everything, but with a bit of patience you can usually find most of what you need there, provided your needs are few and simple. Candy, in a typical display of her talent for pathetic puns, claims she'll never forget the name of this market, inasmuch as the first time she laid eyes on it, it was "a shock to the system." Get it? "Ashok?" Sigh.

It's been raining heavily, so the road has taken a bashing, and the pick-up we're using, hired through a friend of Rasta Ali, has minimal electrics in operation. The windscreen wipers tend to work when they're in the mood and the electric windows tend to be stuck up when in searing heat or down, as now, in torrential rain. We've driven the two kilometres of "good road" through three-foot deep floods covering the actual surface of the roadway—or I should say, where the surface of the roadway *ought to be*—and have arrived at the top of a valley, where the road curves steeply downwards to where it crosses a small concrete bridge, at this moment largely concealed by a torrent of water raging over it. From this point, the road climbs steeply up the other side before continuing onwards to Tanga. The Pangani Express bus is firmly stuck up to its rear axle in deep mud just a short way down the hill, and the road grader is lying a bit further down the hill on its side, where the driver has clearly lost control and veered off the road into the bush. Several dozen bus passengers line the side of the road, their possessions balanced on their heads, picking their way through the mud and debris on foot, towards Tanga—a daunting prospect, even for those only heading part-way there.

We ourselves find the prospect daunting, too, and we have a vehicle. We set off anyway down the hill, the car slipping sideways in the slick sludge. I recover from the skid and gun it forward in low four-wheel drive mode. With the engine screaming, we crash through the water engulfing the bridge and roar onwards and upwards, sliding and fishtailing alarmingly, and as we reach the top of the incline, we're cheered on by an appreciative audience. We clear the bend and stop to inspect the road ahead, congratulating ourselves on our achievement thus far when, without warning, a brand-new Land Rover Defender speeds past us through a huge puddle of mud, throwing up a wall of filthy water, drenching me from head to toe. The driver waves a cheery hand out the window and continues at speed toward Tanga. I'm cursing like Gordon, so angry I'm idiotically jumping up and down. Candy pours a bottle of water over my head, purportedly to clean the mud from my face, but this act of dubious kindness fails entirely to improve my temper. It does mean, however, that I can see again, so, still muttering obscenities, and with Candy unsuccessfully trying to stop giggling, I get back behind the wheel, and we continue our slog forward.

Nearly two hours later, we pull into the main market square in Tanga next to the big vegetable *sokoni*—most cities have these small single-focus markets, often providing goods of far higher quality than what can be found in the supermarkets—and park opposite Ashok's Emporium. As I alight from the car, I see the bastard who had nearly drowned me waving from the terrace of The Ocean Breeze Bar and Grill. With Candy chanting a quiet mantra of "calm down, calm down, calm down", clearly intended to calm me down, we approach the asshole and are—to my chagrin—greeted by my cheerful assailant, shouting, "So, so, sorry, my friend! I could not stop; I could not even slow down, the road was so bad! I only saw it was you after we splashed through that mud hole! Please let me get you a beer; you must be soaking!"

He introduces himself as "Boss". Everybody, we're told, calls him "Boss", so now he calls himself that, too. This is the friend of Gordon: coincidentally, ironically, the very gentleman with a potential job offer, who we have come to Tanga to meet. We join him at his table and he fusses all over us, seeking to make us "comfortable", and ordering beer and chapati for all. The Ocean Breeze, a concrete-floored hovel with neither a view of the ocean nor admitting any form of a breeze, does serve wonderful chapati, and the ice-cold beer is very welcome now that the rain has stopped and the heat and humidity are kicking in, Tanga-style.

Boss gets straight down to business.

"How would you both like to become my general managers, at my safari lodge up near the Kenya border?"

He goes on to say that Gordon recommended us, having described us as honest and hard-working—traits, he tells us, that are often sadly lacking in East African management. Gordon has explained that I've had extensive experience in construction and maintenance, and that both Candy and I have worked in bars when younger. Over the years, we've each accrued considerable general management experience which, Boss feels, would make us ideal candidates for the position he's offering. I ask why he hadn't considered Gordon for the job and, once he stops laughing, he explains that he's not looking for unreliability or a scoundrel, however likeable

Gordon may be.

Boss proves to be a great salesman, describing in some detail how the lodge, while a bit run-down, is an undiscovered diamond waiting to be polished. It is located directly on the beach of a wide estuary river, within a private game conservancy that's teeming with elephants, lions, leopards, buffalo: four, in fact, of the "Big Five", with only the profoundly endangered rhino absent from the park. On a clear day, it's possible to see Mount Kilimanjaro to the west from the lodge, and it has two speed boats, an ocean-going dhow, and six Toyota safari vehicles.

"How about you spend a couple of nights there, and see what you think?" he suggests.

The lodge, he tells us, is closed for the next two months for the rainy season, and there's a lovely house for the managers. He's simply too busy in Dar Es Salaam with his other mining-related businesses, and is hardly ever around. He can easily arrange our work visas, and the salary he suggests is more than ample. Candy and I exchange glances.

She says quietly, "Well, we could go visit. Right?"

Boss takes this as written confirmation of our hiring, orders a bottle of sparkling wine to celebrate, and offers his handshake.

"You are going to love it!" he assures us. "The staff manage themselves. It's a breeze. Like being on holiday."

Though somewhat sceptical, and suspecting a smidgeon of over-promising in his sales pitch, we nevertheless agree to drive up the next day. He provides us with directions and the mobile number of Nawir, his Indian office manager in Dar who's currently holding down the fort at the lodge, and asks us to call him once we're there and checked in.

In the silence which ensues following Boss's departure back to Dar Es Salaam, we wonder what we've just done. We can always turn down the job if we think it's terrible, we agree, and then begin to laugh. I remind Candy that we've always tried to live by the motto, "Life happens while you're making plans, so JFDI: Just Fucking Do It!" I say, laughing, "This time, I think, maybe we've really done it!"

The drive north of Tanga towards the Kenyan border is gorgeous, with the sparkling, crystal clear waters of the Indian Ocean gently breaking surf onto deserted beaches to the east. To the west is thick, lush, dense rainforest, backed by the Usambara Mountains and Kilimanjaro. We turn off following the signs for Mashetani Ridge Lodge, and head east on a bumpy dirt track. The sign says 80 kilometres, and the road runs along the edge of the wide river estuary. It's stunning. The trees are full of a wide variety of birds: the majestic African fish eagle with his haunting call sign, the hilariously inquisitive red hornbill, the plumed white-bellied go-away birds, the gloriously colourful superb starlings, and a huge variety of kingfishers. The diversity seems endless.

We see recent signs of elephants: fresh dung and broken grass and tree branches. Greater kudu burst out of the bush and sprint directly across our path. We turn a corner, and, spread before us over a wide open plain, we encounter over a hundred elephants grazing. Young males face off against one another in mock battle, and proud mothers carefully conceal their tiny calves beneath ample bellies. Their mothers' massive rear legs and the hovering bodies of several concerned aunties shield the babies from any possible danger.

We pick our way carefully through the herd. They surround the track, and we stop as necessary to allow them to pass. Young, frisky males make the occasional mock charge towards us, then stop abruptly, trumpeting and flapping huge ears, making us giggle. Mostly, they're surprisingly relaxed, and simply allow us to pass unimpeded, showing little if any interest in our progress. Sometimes, we just stop and watch, speechless. This is a first for us, a revelation, and Candy holds my hand, muttering, "Oh, my God. Oh, wow. Fantastic."

We leave the herd behind us, and move through plains and riverine forest, continuing towards the lodge. Zebra, impala, giraffes, and Grant's and Thomson's gazelles abound. We can see pods of hippos on each curve of the river, and occasionally a sinister splash as a huge Nile crocodile, disturbed from basking in the sun by our passing, slithers into the deep green water. The sheer abundance of wildlife is both unexpected and utterly entrancing.

We reach the lodge before lunchtime, and Nawir is waiting for us in the car park. He greets us warmly and accompanies us to reception, a round, rustic, *makuti*-roofed structure perched on a hill looking down on the lodge. The view from here is awe-inspiring. The lodge's fifteen rooms are spread along the banks of the river on a sharp bend. Seven are facing directly east, with a view towards the Indian Ocean, easily glimpsed through the palm trees that mark the coastline. The remaining eight rooms face directly west towards Mount Kilimanjaro, which is discernible at random times from behind hazy clouds in the far distance. All of the rooms have decks or terraces overlooking the river. Central to the lodge is a bar/restaurant beside an infinity swimming pool. A second pool is located just beyond the last room looking out towards

Kilimanjaro. A raised pathway, conveniently linking the entire lodge precinct, meanders through the thick bush, allowing every room to feel secluded, providing an illusion of absolute privacy but offering easy access to the entire property.

A small bush airstrip has been cut out of the surrounding forest, and two fiberglass boats with outboards, as well as a romantic Arabic dhow, are docked at a small wooden jetty, swaying serenely in the lazy flow of the river just to the east of the last room. The view ranges over a seemingly endless expanse of open bush dotted with acacia trees, and riverine forest stretching onwards to rolling hills covered with thousands of doum palms. This is nature in its most pure, most pristine, most uncorrupted state. We're entranced.

Candy taps my arm and, as I turn towards her, she simply says, "Yes... Yes. Call Boss and tell him *yes!*"

They say the bug that bites the hardest in Africa is the safari bug, and it looks like we are both incurably infected.

The next morning, Nawir gives us the royal tour of the property, covering both front and back of house, reception, restaurant, bar, rooms, pools, kitchens, stores, laundry, garage, maintenance, and even the car park. We meet the entire staff, a bewildering seventy-plus barrage of handsome faces and exotic names. They constitute a melting pot of Tanzanian cultures, with Maasai in a traditional Tanzanian role of security due to their fearsome reputation and height, an impression of danger not in the least mitigated by their familiar bright red *shukas,* and fierce weaponry, including spear, *rungu* (tomahawk-like club) and a short, scary stabbing sword. The lodge's Head of Security, Sembuli, is Maasai, but unusually, he's barely five foot two inches tall. He easily compensates for this, however, by sporting, as well as his traditional weapons, a pump-action shotgun almost as tall as he is.

Local villagers provide most of the labour in the laundry and house-keeping departments, with some from the Usambara Mountains near Leshoto, a few from Tanga and Pangani, and a small number from even as far away as Dar Es Salaam and the islands of Zanzibar and Pemba. Each staff member greets us with a natural, welcoming warmth, but our heads are spinning by the time we sit down for lunch from our hopeless attempts to catch and remember so many interesting names: Majabu (surprise), Mtoro (burden), Mjanja (sneaky), Tano (five), Jumanne (Tuesday), Witness, Bariki (blessed), Shida (problem), Purity and dozens more. We have to suppress laughter when the ladies who run the laundry actually turn out to be named Faith, Hope, and Charity. And, as Scots, we're naturally delighted to meet our two Head Guides, Ali Mohammed Makenzi and Juma Wanyama Maclean. We point out they both have Scottish clan names; they merely smile politely, and reply, "Really?"

The restaurant/bar team all speak very good English—a very helpful advantage both to them and to us, as Candy and I are already struggling to learn Kiswahili, a project with which they will be extremely useful. Furthermore, of course, most guests will speak no Kiswahili, but will be likely to speak English. Having English-speaking staff in positions where they will be interacting with guests will make for great service.

Rose and Rosie are identical twins. Chichi, on the food-and-beverage team, informs me that they can only be told apart because Rose has a big ass—*wowowo sana*—and Rosie has not. The girls reply that Chichi is the thorn between two roses and laugh uproariously. Food-and-beverage is filled out by Jafari (we later learn "Jafari" is his Swahili-accented pronunciation of "Geoffrey"), Abedi, and the mega mixologist-cum-cocktail expert, Saidi Saidi, who says he's so good his parents named him twice, and declares himself the best Muslim barman in all of Tanzania.

Candy has returned from the kitchen somewhat dismayed, as not one of the staff speaks a single word of English, and the same proves to apply to the maintenance and garage teams, as well, though the guides all speak very good English, as befits their positions.

Naturally curious, we enquire from Nawir what happened to the previous General Managers, and he rolls his eyes. "Long story," he sighs. "He took to the *pombe* (palm wine) and she took to the cream cakes, and before too long, she could not get through the door and he could not get through the day." While we don't find this particularly helpful, or, to be honest, even remotely believable, we choose to look forward and not backwards, though I do warn Candy off the cream cakes, getting me a well-deserved punch on the bicep.

After lunch, we wander around the rooms, inspect the pools, and stroll down to the boats riding high at the jetty. There is a tidal surge in the river that jumps four metres from low tide to high tide. Mohammed, the boat Captain, explains that we have to time our excursions very well or risk having guests stuck on a sandbar in a crocodile-infested river. I make a mental note of the issue.

Boss phones us later that day. We reassure him that, yes, we'll take the job, and he whoops with delight. He tells us he'll get started on work permits, and can we start tomorrow? Laughing, we tell him, "Hey! We've already started!" Another quick call to make arrangements for our gear to be collected from Ushongo at Crazy Thomas's house, and we move the small overnight bag we've brought with us from the guest room where we had spent the previous night into our new home: the General Manager's House. This feels so right.

Boss has told us to make the house our own: to change whatever we want, add whatever we want, make ourselves comfortable. It's important, he insists, that we have a nice place to relax. The two-story house needs decoration and re-organizing, but it's very, very nice, with a downstairs lounge and W.C., an outside terrace, and an upstairs viewing deck adjoining a large bedroom and shower room with a second W.C. From the viewing deck the view is insanely, ridiculously beautiful. We can see the Indian Ocean to the east, Mount Kilimanjaro to the west, and the river directly in front of us, snaking through the trees. A large waterhole just to the north is currently being visited by a large, enthusiastic family of elephants, drinking and socializing. We take this as a magical welcome from the bush, and are beside ourselves with joy at having found what seems to be just the right place and just the right position for us, at just the right time in our lives. We hug from a sense of genuine relief. This gamble, Africa, was a risk that will pay off in ways we cannot possibly as yet anticipate, but it's plainly going to be life-changing, and we can already sense that it's going to be wonderful.

We unpack and get settled for our first night as General Managers of Mashetani Ridge Lodge. After an early, truly scrumptious private dinner in the restaurant, we head back to our house and, from our roof terrace, enjoy our gin-and-tonic sundowners while watching the sun—a giant orange disc, throwing dazzling light onto the snows topping Mount Kilimanjaro—slip sensually towards the horizon. We sit silently, in awe, as dusk turns to full night, the sky begins to sparkle, and the Milky Way slowly comes into focus. Jupiter and Mars can be seen with crystal clarity; even Saturn and the Southern Cross share the sky with a crescent moon. We're bewitched by Africa, and retire to bed thoroughly enthralled with our new surroundings.

We wake with a violent crash against the wooden bedroom wall—a snarling, raging roar that jerks us instantly from sleep to terrified wakefulness!

"What the hell is that? screams Candy.

I leap from bed and, pretty much terrified, peer out of the mosquito-netted window. On our terrace, directly beneath the window, a female leopard has a bushbuck gripped by the throat in her massive, powerful jaws. As it fights for its life, the bushbuck's hooves are beating a desperate, dying tattoo against our flimsy timber wall. Candy joins me, and we watch in horrified fascination as the leopard drags her victim over the terrace, up the stairs to our roof top deck and then vanishes with a leap, still carrying that heavy burden, into the adjacent trees. A leopard will usually deposit her vanquished prey in the treetops to prevent its being stolen by other predators. Our first close-up encounter with nature's sometimes harsh dynamic becomes, appropriately, as authentic a welcome to this unique opportunity we've seized, and to life in the bush, as the idyllic herds of elephants and the brilliant African stars.

Welcome to Mashetani Ridge Lodge. And to paradise, with a few sharp edges.

CHAPTER 7
LIFE IN THE BUSH

We quickly settle into our new lives and jobs. This may be paradise, but the lodge does *not* run itself, and the staff are terribly disorganized. They've always tried hard, but have only been allowed to do what they thought best and not what was best, so we have a big challenge ahead.

Candy discovers, especially when dealing with the kitchen staff, that she doesn't like the words *hamna*—none—or *shida*—problem—but she does love *hamna shida,* which means "no problem". This is very confusing at first for both of us, as our Kiswahili, gleaned mostly from watching *The Lion King* with the kids, had led us to believe that "no problem" was *hakuna matata*. But *hakuna matata* is Kenyan Swahili, and therefore wrong here in coastal Tanzania. Tanzanians, and especially the coastal or island Tanzanians, are very proud of their beautiful and poetic mother tongue. We learn that Swahili is actually an Arabic word for "coastal," and that it developed first as a trading language. It's a rich mélange of Bantu, Arabic, Indian, and English, with a smattering of other European languages. As it was never a written language until colonial times, its modern written version is fundamentally phonetic, which helps—sometimes. We make progress, and the staff all try hard to assist, but we still make howling errors. Candy tells one of the Roses in her best Swahili to please pick up her bottles and place them on the bar, and the entire food-and-beverage team dissolve in laughter. In this learning-through-humiliation process, we discover that *chupa* means "bottle," while *chupi* means "underpants". Luckily it was Rose and not one of the guys who was directed to put her underpants on the bar. The guys all consider themselves comedians, and no doubt would have been tempted to call Candy's bluff.

Candy is working with the kitchen and food-and-beverage teams on a new seven-day menu for the guests, and I have the mechanics servicing all the vehicles and boat engines. Moreover, I've introduced the novel idea of keeping service records, which all and sundry regard as a brilliant innovation, and so we have the stores all cleaned out and parts and spares all recorded. The maintenance team have been tasked with completely redecorating all of the rooms and public areas, so we've just begun with Room Number One and will move on from there. After the first day, the fundi/tradesman tasked with painting Room One is surprised that I'm displeased at finding more paint on the floor than on the walls. After a long discussion, I tell him he might die in that room, but he is not leaving before he has cleaned and painted it properly. In my best Swahili, I tell him I want the lamps painted completely, as well, and when I return, I discover he'd taken this to include the bulbs. I make a mental note concerning the dangers of instructions being interpreted literally. Progress, however, is being made.

The food here is becoming amazing with the improvements Candy has introduced. We purchase direct from the local fishermen for all our jumbo prawns, mangrove crab, lobster, calamari, red snapper, yellow-fin tuna, kingfish and even barracuda, as well as an amazing local fish called *kole kole*. The seafood is delivered hanging over the back of a bicycle that a local fisherman rides over the bush tracks from the village, to bring direct to the kitchen. At one lunchtime, I spot a mangrove crab gallantly making a run for it, racing from the kitchen in a futile bid to escape back to the river, pursued by an irate chef. You simply cannot get any fresher than that!

We have some contractors on site assisting, and one evening, when we're relaxing back at the house, I hear Sembuli, our Head of Security, hailing me from outside.

"*Hodi hodi* (knock, knock!), Bwana Graeme!"

He tells me that the contractors are intent on driving to the village in the lodge cars, and although he has told them not to, they won't listen to him. We have a strict no-driving-after-dark rule in the conservancy. It's dangerous, as there may be elephant or buffalo on the road, absolutely invisible in the pitch dark. Further, we're in the border area, so it's possible to get lost and wander inadvertently into Kenya, or to simply have a major breakdown or damage a car.

I tell him to remind them that I have said that this is not possible, and he disappears into the night. I consider a moment, and then tell Candy that I'd better go and ensure that all is okay. I grab two Maglite torches and head off towards the garage, and as I arrive, I see one of the Land Cruisers reversing out of the parking bay. A perfect opportunity to employ Tony's advice about establishing the hierarchy early on, I decide, and so I smash my torch against the driver's window. He jams on the brakes. I demand that he return the vehicle to the parking bay, get out of the car, and go back to staff quarters. The contractor responds with verbal aggression, maintaining that he intends to go to the village, that he has the right to do what he wants, and that I should get out of his way. His expression is arrogant, rigid, combative. I call Sembuli over, and then turn back to the contractor.

"If you want to go to the village, you can walk there, if you dare," I tell him. "But you're not using any company vehicles. You know the rules. No driving after dark."

He glares at me, dangerously. The staff are now gathered in the shadows, enjoying the entertainment, so I really feel the need to establish my authority.

"Sembuli," I say, not taking my eyes off the angry face of the contractor. "No cars are authorized to leave the garage at night, under any circumstances. If you see someone attempting to take a car out, then you should consider it theft, and should shoot the thief at once."

In the surrounding silence, the sound of Sembuli locking a round into the pump-action shotgun's chamber is shockingly loud.

Addressing the assembled staff, I smile. "Thank you all for your time. Sleep well." I turn and head back to the house. Candy asks if everything's okay, and I assure her all is under control. Two minutes later Sembuli reappears at the door and hands me the keys to all the cars, and even those to all the boats. I wish him a good evening and he runs off to resume his patrols.

The next day I'm sitting in the office, and as each staff member arrives to sign in, I'm greeted very formally, by each, with, *"Shikamoo, Mzee."* I reply with equal formality, *"Marahaba."* *Shikamoo* is an important address of respect in Swahili culture, reserved for elders and very important people, and I'm feeling pretty good about myself. This renewed self-confidence is immediately shattered, however, when Candy stalks into the office from where she's been working in the kitchen.

"For God's sake, Graeme, please tell me you didn't threaten to shoot people last night!"

"Well, not technically," I tell her. "I just instructed Sembuli to shoot…"

She's having none of it. "You cannot do that! That is inappropriate!"

The Roses have given Candy a play-by-play of the former evening's entertainment, apparently in graphic detail. While nobody ever again tried to take a car out at night, we did establish that Candy and I have very differing management styles. There's always more than one way to skin a cat, in my view, but Candy will always prefer methods which don't involve pump-action shotguns.

The lodge is slowly coming together. As each room is completed, the housekeeping staff descend upon it and, under Candy's excellent supervision, begin to transform it into a mini holiday utopia. Straw sun hats, kikoi wraps, soft slippers for the guests to use, pictures on the walls, curtains… all those details so important to creating a warm and inviting room. A women's group in Tanga makes an amazing, fragrant bath soap that Candy introduces, which both softens the skin and benefits the community. The lodge is beginning to live up to its potential. It is becoming a luxurious and beautiful retreat, at once rustic and elegant. The staff is coming together, as well, a genuine team of individuals working together, who have become fond of one another, and of us. We have become a little "family" in the middle of nowhere, relying on one another, appreciating one another, enjoying one another's company, conversation, presence. Even paradise can become a *better* paradise with the right people.

One evening we decide to do a test run on our proposed

sunset river safari, so together with Saidi Saidi the mega mixologist, witty Jafari, and our captain, Mohammed, we slip our anchor and head slowly down river two hours before sunset. At the river's "meander" point, it winds its way slowly towards the distant Indian Ocean, and on nearly every corner we encounter pods of hippopotamus. They grunt as we approach, then silently submerge to just below the surface where, like portly astronauts, they enjoy their underwater moonwalk, keeping a watchful eye on us. Crocodiles bask lazily in the evening sunlight, on the sand bars and on the banks above us. Due to the tidal surge, the river banks in some places appear as sheer sand cliffs of deep, rich red African soil, towering some four metres above us. It's slightly unnerving to have a crocodile looking down on you from above, with his permanent, sinister smile seeming to take the measure of you as you slowly drift past.

Kingfishers—malachites and brown-hooded and pied—adorn nearly every horizontal option. African darters and black-headed, grey, and striated herons perch atop the trees lining the banks. An enormous Nile monitor lizard watches us with suspicion, as he pauses in his hunt for eggs amongst the intricate mix of mangrove tree roots which grow directly from the shallows. As we turn a slow bend, we're delighted to witness a procession of elephants crossing the river in majestic single file. We laugh as one elephant slightly loses his dignity, sliding down the steep bank on his folded front legs and crashing quite indecorously into the water. We ease off the outboard and give way; the lion may think he is the king of the jungle, but that's only because the elephant doesn't blow his own trumpet.

We've come near enough to the delta to see the ocean,

and, finding a very wide, quiet bend, we ask Mohammed to anchor here in the middle of the river. The boat turns on the anchor rope, and we're facing directly towards the west. The sun is slowly sinking past the tops of the mangroves into the jungle below. Saidi Saidi and Jafari jump into action. They have a cool box packed with crushed ice, so produce the coldest Kilimanjaro beer I think possible, even in paradise. I love the Kilimanjaro beer slogan: "If you can't climb it, drink it!" Candy has a chilled glass of her favourite rose wine, and from another box they produce vegetable samosas, cold chicken kebabs and mini prawn skewers with a hot *pili pili* sauce. Twenty metres from the boat, the eyes of a dozen hippo appear with all the timing of synchronized swimmers, warily observing us warily observing them. Outside the water, the hippo is Africa's most dangerous animal, and their mood can change in a heartbeat. But this moment seems as idyllic for them as for us.

A fish eagle scoops his catch from right by the side of the boat, and perches high in the tree line to enjoy a crunchy sundowner of his own. The river has turned crimson, and there's a purple band between it and the sinking sun. We tell the staff that the guests will absolutely love this excursion, and that we plan to offer an identical early morning version, except with a sunrise at the mouth of the river.

Jafari shakes his head and laughs. "Crazy *wazungu*. Why do they love this thing? This happens every night."

"Yes," I reply, "but sunsets and sunrises are absolutely free, and our guests should not miss so many of them. They pay to see what you and I are lucky enough to see every day." Jafari smiles agreement.

We raise anchor and begin our return to the lodge; it's

going to be a busy day tomorrow. Our first guests are arriving by a scheduled Coastal Air flight, and we have to be prepared.

Our private air strip is actually just a grass "runway", some twelve hundred meters long and fifty meters wide, cut directly out of the bush. Our windsock was badly in need of repair and our tailor's first attempt at a replacement looked like some large, exotic ladies' underwear. Today I am amazed to see a very professional replacement fluttering in the slight morning breeze. Closer examination reveals that he has cut up and resewn together twenty-seven high-visibility construction safety jackets to complete his creation, and I'm once again astounded by Tanzanian ingenuity and knack for innovation.

Under a towering tortilis acacia tree, we've set a small table, complete with ice-cold eucalyptus-scented hand towels. We also have ice-cold Buck's Fizz and champagne flutes to hand. After lengthy discussions with the staff, we're debuting a number of agreed-upon strategies to make our guests' arrival super-unique. To this end, Jafari, Chichi and Saidi Saidi are dressed in their white, flowing, coastal Muslim Kanzu robes, and the Rose twins present an exciting splash of colour in their traditional coastal *darisha* dresses. Jafari has a *ngoma*—an East African drum—and they are all crazy excited. We hear the hum of an engine, and then pick out a speck in the distant blue sky that turns within moments into a plane. It's a Cessna 208 with twelve passenger seats, and it describes a slow circle above us as the pilot prepares for landing. Once satisfied that we've cleared the airstrip of stray giraffe and zebra, the pilot thunders in, engines howling, in a cloud of dust and sand, before easing gently to a stop directly in front of our acacia. Welcome, ladies and gentlemen, to Arrival Gate One-and-only at Mashetani International Airport, Tanzania!

With the propeller blade still turning lazily in the sun, the pilot opens the rear door and the guests shakily descend onto the dirt air strip. Our two guides, Ali and Juma, are already collecting the guests' luggage and stowing it in the safari vehicles. Our merry band are waiting at the bottom of the steps already singing:

> "*Jambo, Jambo, Bwana,*
> *Habari gani?*
> *Mzuri sana,*
> *Wageni, wakaribishwa,*
> *Tanzania yetu,*
> *Hakuna matata*!"

Yes, the lyrics include *hakuna matata*, but this is, despite its ubiquitous familiarity throughout Tanzania, a Kenyan tune:

> "Hello, hello, sir!
> How's it going?
> I'm very well!
> Strangers are welcomed,
> Our Tanzania,
> No worries!"

Jafari beats a tribal tattoo on his *ngoma* while the rest of the team dance in a circle around the guests, and the two Roses offer them cool, fragrant hand towels. I greet the clearly impressed group of guests and then lead them to the shade of the tree. Chichi offers them the ice-cold Buck's fizz while the singing continues. The pilot is laughing out loud in the background, despite the fact that his other passengers—those not staying with us—have all disembarked as well, and are busy taking photographs; our efforts at hospitality have entirely ruined his quick turnaround schedule. One of the guests turns his wide-eyed gaze to me and exclaims, "Holy fuck, is this for real? First, we land in the middle of a god-damned jungle, and then we get champagne!"

"Welcome to Mashetani Ridge Lodge," I welcome them, beaming, very damned pleased with myself!

The guests join Ali for a lengthy game drive back to the lodge, while the rest of the team and I pack up, wave off the Coastal pilot, and hasten directly back to the lodge to ensure that we, together with Candy and the rest of the staff, will be fully prepared for their arrival.

I've no sooner arrived at our office overlooking the car park when I see Mumbi, our massive Maasai *askari*—perhaps the most physically imposing of our entire security staff— dragging something behind him through the bush. Mumbi's primary responsibility is for the security at our diesel storage tank and dispensing area, situated way back-of-house at the edge of the bush. As he draws nearer, I can see that what he's dragging is a person. Moreover, it's a person bound with rope and bleeding from several cuts about the head and body. I leap to my feet and run down to the car park. Mumbi explains that he has discovered this unfortunate chap poking about in the bush near the diesel tank, assumed he was up to no good, and thought it best to beat him, tie him up, and bring him to the office for further instruction.

With some encouragement, the shaken victim cautiously reveals that he's an itinerant and was walking from his home in the bush towards Tanga. He claims that he hadn't even known there was a lodge here, and he'd had no intention of stealing anything. Mumbi is not convinced, but we decide to send him by *bodaboda* (local motorcycle taxi) to the village and let him explain himself to the village chief and— mwenyeketi wa kijiji (chairman of the village), and they can decide if he should be taken to the police. Nothing in tribal Tanzania is decided without the approval of the *manikiti*. The last I see of him, he's jammed between the *bodaboda* driver and Mumbi, though, as they depart, he does manage to wave to me and smile through his broken teeth. We subsequently learn that the village declares him harmless, in the end, and one family takes him into their home, feeds him for several weeks, provides him with clothes, and gives him money for his bus fare to Tanga so he can continue on his journey.

You will meet no more generous people in the world than the peoples of East Africa.

The guests duly arrive: a group of six, all from various states across the USA. Candy completes a safety briefing, and they adjourn to their rooms to unpack and prepare for a lunch which we'll serve under a canvas shade on the pool deck overlooking the river. An important part of the briefing for our guests is safety, especially concerning life within the lodge precincts. Since we're in the middle of the bush and adjacent to a river, the wildlife does have the inconvenient habit of treating the lodge as their own. It's not uncommon to find a crocodile sunning himself close to the restaurant or a group of elephants having an early lunch under the marula trees on either side of the walkway. At night, we often have lions either actually on the grounds or nearby roaring contentedly, and our friendly female leopard is often spotted doing her rounds. Sometimes, guests think the show is over when they return to the lodge and need occasionally to be reminded to be on their guard. All rooms have radio hand sets and an air horn alarm, and at night they must book a time in advance to be escorted to and from the dining area by an *askari*. One evening an elderly German guest, mistaking the air horn for mosquito spray, almost had a heart attack when the deafening blast of air erupted as he innocently sprayed a mossie!

Sembuli keeps his pump-action shotgun in a canvas carrying case over his shoulder at all times. When I asked if he thought a lion would wait while he undid the Velcro to retrieve the gun and protect the guests, he knitted his brows soberly.

"That is a good thought, Boss."

I'm dismayed but not surprised, therefore, that after lunch when the guests request an escort back to their rooms, Sembuli appears instantly, priming the pump action with a Rambo-style flourish before their astonished faces. Clearly, we must work out a compromise.

The next morning, we set off before dawn on the supply run to Tanga. Candy and I are joined by Saber, the driver, and Moki, the mechanic, who needs to visit a clinic to see about a stomach ailment. We're in the Toyota double-cab and have a trailer attached, as well. We have to bring in virtually everything needed at the lodge, most things expected, and others often not. Fresh fruit & vegetables, beers, wines and sodas, meat, dry goods, rice, maintenance items, housekeeping supplies—pretty much everything, except, of course, for our seafood—needs to be transported into the bush for us, and for all safari camps and lodges throughout the country. This is one reason for the high prices of safari accommodations in Africa. Running a western-style establishment in the middle of nowhere in a third world country is expensive.

Just outside the lodge, we pass a pride of six lions sleeping in various poses on either side, with one young, handsome male flopped obscenely on his back in the middle of the track. Hearing our approach, he reluctantly but quite generously rises to allow us to pass. As daylight breaks through the riverine forest, we spot a troop of around thirty baboons, all occupying the topmost branches of a sprawling acacia tree, all facing the rising sun. This is where they sleep at night, safe from predators. Only coffee cups in their hands could make them look more content.

We reach the main road and turn towards Tanga. A little further on, we encounter the Mombasa/Tanga Express bus blocking the way. The passengers are all milling around outside of the bus, and a rather large black-and-white Frisian cow is lying in the middle of the road mooing in distress. Clearly, the bus has collided with the cow. I joke to Saber that this is lucky, as it will save us a visit to the butcher's, but soon find myself having to drag him back to the car. He has leapt into action, fetching a huge cool box and a *panga* (bush knife) from the vehicle. In any case, somebody has beaten him to it, and the cow has been quickly dispatched onwards to cow heaven with a swift cut to the throat. Moki and Saber explain the cow is now *halal*, as it was killed in the correct manner, and is now acceptable for the mainly Muslim population to eat. We edge past the throng who are in the process of butchering the unfortunate beast, and continue onwards towards Tanga.

Arriving in Tanga is always a joy. It's by far the largest city on the coast north of Dar Es Salaam, and the number of bicyclists on the busy streets must, in this respect, rival Amsterdam. Some are attached to wooden carts, and we pass one which seems to be carrying the contents of an entire house, including a sofa and armchairs, piled high on the cart with a guy fast asleep on the sofa. The streets are lined with small *duka*s, shops selling everything you could need or even imagine. Displayed outside *duka* doorways are beautiful, carved wooden beds and tables for sale at the Mashariki carpenters' shop. Oddly, as well, coffins are on offer, alongside the beds. I try to imagine a circumstance when I might be tasked with purchasing a bed for my home and think, "Ah, perhaps I should pick up a coffin while I'm here."

A full catch, it seems, of those appallingly smelly *daga* fish are drying in the sun, laid out on a roundabout. Plumbers and hardware stores are conveniently adjacent to one another. Outside hair salons, young girls—hair stylists—attach braided hair extensions to customers' heads, using wax directly from a lit candle as the customers chat idly with their friends. Countless shops sell clothes, *kangas*, *kikois,* and fabrics of every conceivable colour.

Saber and Moki drop us off at the Neema Crafts Coffee House and head off to start collecting the various orders we've placed in advance with the assorted merchants we use. Candy and I are both quite excited, as friends have assured us that Neema's has great coffees, even cappuccinos, and fantastic internet, so we're anticipating a rare treat. We enter through their craft shop, a marvellous wonderland which offers a large array of items made on the premises by disadvantaged people from the local area. On display are exquisite, colourful lightshades, hand-made table runners, mugs and crockery, woven fabrics, and recycled glassware.

We mount the stairs and enter the coffee shop, selecting a table by the window overlooking Tanga bay, with the Tanga Yacht Club in the distance. No one comes to take our order, so I approach the counter and ask for two cappuccinos, please.

The server just stares at me blankly, so I slowly repeat my order. We continue staring at one other during an awkward silence, and I finally notice a note pad on the counter. I take out my pen and write "2 cappuccinos, please," and hand it to the server. His expression immediately lights up. Beaming, he points to my table. Slightly mystified, I return to Candy at the table to wait for our coffee. Candy, has meanwhile been reading, that workers in the café are disabled members of the local community, and the servers are all in fact deaf and dumb. The disabled provide not only the products on offer, but the majority of services available at Neema. I feel abashed, but relieved at the same time. This is not a mistake I'm likely to ever make again.

The coffees arrive in due time and are absolutely delicious. As I sip contentedly on my cappuccino, our son calls us on Skype from Shanghai, where he works as a teacher. It's great to hear from him, and we chat away happily until he asks, "Dad, what is that noise in the background?"

I turn to confirm my suspicions, and reply, "Would you believe, it's a dwarf with a cleft palate singing *Amazing Grace*?" Very little in Africa surprises us now.

Following the coffees, we adjourn downstairs to do some shopping for the lodge. Candy excitedly chooses lamp shades made from local kikoi material, table runners woven here in the factory, and an assortment of recycled glasses, decanters and candle holders. All will look wonderful in the lodge. We choose a large candelabra made entirely from re-cycled wine bottles that seems perfect as a centrepiece for the bar area, and I ask the lady behind the counter to please assist us with retrieving it from the hook where it hangs from the ceiling. She merely points towards it, and I'm vaguely puzzled, but try my best to reach up to unhook it. I'm not quite tall enough, so, first I stand on a coffee table, with no luck. Then I try a large box which seems sufficiently sturdy, but have no success with this solution, either. Exasperated, I look around the shop for something to use, all the while silently watched by the lady at the counter. On the point of giving up, I look behind the counter to discover that she, too, is a dwarf, seated atop a set of step ladders. Problem solved, as she graciously allows me to use them to retrieve our purchase before popping back up on her perch with surprising grace to take our payment.

We stroll back through the town together, and nearly every child we pass shouts, *"Wazungu!"* at us, the perfectly polite term for a European or Caucasian. We wave each time, and call back, *"Jambo!"* There aren't many Europeans walking the streets of Tanga Town. We're an event.

We reach the Ocean Breeze and enter, pulling up a chair to await Saber and Moki. The doorway darkens and the strong sunlight is momentarily obscured as the giant frame of Stanley, our old Immigration Officer friend, squeezes inside. His voice booms out: "Graeme! Candy! *Habari siku ningi, kaka na dada.* (It's a long time, brother and sister)."

We greet him warmly, and he joins us at our table, first carefully stacking three plastic chairs on top of each other to accommodate the vastness and weight of what he describes as his "prosperous posterior". He props his Kalashnikov machine gun against the wall and orders two beers twice. When I ask why not four together, he winks and explains that these fellows in here are so slow he could die of thirst in between orders if he did not carefully plan ahead. We laugh, and chat, and catch up on all that's been going on since we last met, and then I suddenly remember Stanley's uncanny knack at showing up whenever there's free beer on offer. I have a good idea that we'll be footing the bill here.

A group of young backpackers is stationed comfortably at the table just beside us, and they're bemoaning the difficulties of crossing the border to Kenya, and how hard it is to renew a Tourist Visa so far from Dar Es Salaam, if it runs out. One guy quietly admits that his expired the previous week, and he can't afford the time or money to travel to Dar to renew it. Stanley kicks me under the table and winks. He then stands, draws himself up to his full formidable height, straightens his peaked cap and grabs the youth's hand. He slaps a handcuff round the young boy's wrist before attaching the other to his own wrist and announcing himself to his stunned audience.

"I'm Chief of Immigration for Tanga & Pwani Region, and I believe you are residing in my country with incorrect paperwork. Come, I must interrogate you."

He forthwith drags the near-hysterical youth to our table and plops back down.

"You see, Mr Graeme, the contempt the youth of the day have for proper institutions? A disgraceful disregard for my Office and His Highness, the Reis, our glorious President."

The backpackers are frozen in silent terror, and when their friend attempts to speak, he can only muster a strangled croak. Stanley's far from subtle second kick on my leg prompts me into action.

"Perhaps, I could suggest a solution, Officer Stanley," I offer. "Maybe if our young friend could purchase for you, two beers twice, or perhaps even thrice, it would show the proper respect for the Tanzanian government, and you could resolve his current dilemma."

Stanley pretends to grudgingly ponder this suggestion,

then announces, "This could be possible."

As the two beers thrice begin arriving, he magnanimously uncuffs the young man and demands to see his passport. With a dramatic flourish, he produces his official rubber stamp, rifles through to the correct page, and stamps loudly several times, admires his handiwork, cocks his head, and announces, "That will be fifty dollars, please." You'd think the beers would be enough, but an opportunity is an opportunity.

Upon payment of the fifty bucks, Stanley peremptorily dismisses the group, who depart as quickly, and as sheepishly, as their remaining dignity will allow.

"I always like to help our country's visitors whenever I can," Stanley pronounces between slurps of his beer. "I thank you for your wise suggestion."

Suddenly, a commotion unfolding outside the Ocean Breeze draws our attention. Customers and staff crowd the terrace and windows, and we hear the women shouting, "*Mwezi! Mwezi! Mwezi!*" (Thief!) A youth riding a bicycle he has stolen is weaving through the crowd between the *Sokini* Market and Ashok's Emporium, keeping just yards in front of the chasing mob. As he looks back over his shoulder, the Rasta who sells daily newspapers from under the big, shady mango tree jumps to his feet and abruptly drop kicks the youth in his face, sending him crashing to the ground. The mob descend on him, kicking and beating him as he lies helpless on the dirt road.

We look to Stanley, but he gravely shakes his head and quietly says, "Do not try to interfere."

Luckily for the youth, there are four policemen exiting Ashock's Emporium, and they approach the scene. The mob parts like the Red Sea around them. They use their sticks to beat the youth a few more times, then pick him up and throw him into the open back of the police pickup and drive off. For a few moments, silence falls on the market place, then the spell breaks and everyone returns to their daily routines. Stanley explains that had the police not intervened, the youth would have been beaten to death and the body burned. Stealing someone's bike is stealing someone's essential transport—that bike allows someone to travel every day to work, to be able to feed his family and send his children to school. They would all suffer because of one youth who is too lazy to work, and so dishonest he would steal a good person's belongings, denying him the chance to work.

"In Tanzania we do not tolerate *mwezi*," Stanley says with a sigh. He avows that even the youth's family would not have collected the body, so great is the disgrace. "He was a very lucky young man," is Stanley's final observation.

Saber and Moki arrive, and we depart with promises to let him know next time we visit town, or if there's anything he can do to help us, although we are now both convinced that Stanley knows even before we do when we enter Tanga Town. This is hardly surprising, however, as often when we visit Tanga, we're scarcely past the first roundabout before Rasta Ali phones to greet us—and coincidentally also visiting town that day. The Tanga Telegraph works very well indeed, we agree.

Saber takes the road north and zigzags his way through the throng of cyclists, donkeys, and street vendors. We've left it late, and as the sun begins to set, mosques begin the call to prayer. There is something haunting and beautiful in the sound, as each mosque competes with the next to remind the faithful that God is, indeed, Great, and that we should all be grateful to have been spared for another day.

The sun gradually transforms all the minarets into silhouettes, backlit in sunset colours, and we are once again reminded of Hemingway's observation about Africa, words that inspire us to embrace each day with a special joy: "I never knew of a morning in Africa when I woke up and was not happy."

Nor have I. Nor have I.

CHAPTER 8
FOUR FUNERALS AND A WEDDING

Early in the morning, Ali Makenzi shows up in our office to inform us that Moki is still not well. The staff have conducted a meeting, and have decided to ask if we could please assist in paying for a local witch doctor to come to the lodge and treat him.

My head is instantly full of questions. Is there a particular witch doctor you have in mind? (In my contacts book, will he be listed under "w" for "witch" or "d" for "doctor"? Does the petty cash spreadsheet have a category for "Witch Doctor"?) I do know that Mwera Village near Ushongo Beach is considered the local centre for all things related to witch doctors, or *ramba ramba*, as they are known in the vernacular. How does one actually hire a witch doctor?

When, many months after his death, Gordon's son and daughter visited us to see his grave, we arrived at the spot and I instantly noticed a stone jar covered with Arabic script which had been carefully placed at the centre of his grave. While his son and daughter were comforting one other, I surreptitiously took a look at the jar and discovered it was full of human hair and animal bones, and covered in neat Arabic script. I managed to convince his kids that it was merely a present one of his friends from the village had left as a mark of respect, but I suspected that there was more to the story.

Subsequently, I asked old Mohammed about it. With his

customary grin, he explained that this was all completely normal. An aggrieved husband, as it happened, had employed the witch doctor to put a spell on one of his neighbours who he suspected was sleeping with his young wife. Who better to disturb the neighbour's sleep than the ghost of a giant, crazy *mzungu*? The entire village were all in agreement that this would be the ideal solution. The fellow would be unable to sleep at night, and therefore would have no strength for anything, let alone chasing other men's wives. Problem efficiently solved! The jar of human and animal parts would serve to identify exactly which deceased *mzungu* was being called upon to haunt the neighbour. As this incident, I decide, had taught me something of the ways and uses of your average witch doctor, I might well be considered qualified as more or less a *ramba ramba* expert. And so, I promise Ali that I'll try to organize a visit to the witch doctor for Moki.

Two days later, Mohammed, Candy and I are sitting around a charcoal fire inside the witch doctor's tiny thatched hut in Mwera Village. His three wives are fussing around a three-legged iron pot balanced on stones above the fire, its contents bubbling away. I really hope it's soup for lunch, but fear I'll be disappointed, so I don't ask. Candy mutters, "First scene from Macbeth," as we squat down and Mohammed explains our problem to the witch doctor. After much back and forth negotiating, he agrees to help and the fee is settled. In addition to the actual fee, however, I will have to purchase two chickens which he'll need for the ceremony. He wants the equivalent of $10 each for the chickens. I protest that I can buy two chickens in Ashok's Emporium, plucked and ready for cooking, for three dollars each, but Candy is hissing at me under her breath that bargaining with a witch doctor is perhaps insensitive. Discretion being the better part of valour, as they say, I agree to his terms, comforting myself with the thought that live chickens will perhaps be better suited to the event than the frozen version.

The staff are all delighted that the arrangements have been completed, and there's an air of anticipation throughout the lodge. Moki continues to look quite unwell, and I try very hard to convince him that a bus to Dar Es Salaam and a visit to a clinic there would be much the better approach. All to no avail. He refuses.

Friday night arrives, and we have a full lodge with almost forty guests. A mini, United Nations gathers in the bar, with guests from the USA, Europe, the United Kingdom, South America, and Southeast Asia. Candy and I are busy organizing river safaris, early morning game drives and snorkelling trips to the sand bar in the Indian Ocean. The lounge bar is buzzing. We're sharing Manhattan cocktails, expertly prepared by Saidi Saidi, with a nice couple from New York. Early diners are enjoying seafood platters with fresh calamari, mangrove crab, jumbo prawns and succulent lobster thermidor, all caught earlier that morning. Kissy, our resident large-spotted genet cat, is entertaining a group of guests from Germany, warily weaving her way through the shadows, occasionally darting in at lightning speed to steel a chicken drumstick. Sometimes, in perfect imitation of a meercat, she sits up on her back legs, checking for further opportunities. She is a real star with the guests, with her ringed tail, black-and-white-and-grey body spotted like a leopard, and her sweet, mouse-like face. She is beyond cute.

There's a small commotion as the food-and-beverage team break into a dance while singing "Happy Birthday" to the wife of a delightful young couple from Santiago, Chile. Jafari goes the extra mile; he's down on one knee, serenading the guest with the classic Swahili hit song "*Malaika*" ("My Angel, I Love You . . . If Only I Had the Money, I Would Marry You, My Angel"). I see Ali Makenzi on the edge of the throng mouthing in my direction: "*Ramba ramba, tayari!*" The witch doctor, it seems, is ready, so I make my excuses and Ali and I walk together over to the staff quarters where all not on duty have gathered. Already, the witch doctor is dancing in a tight circle, emitting moaning noises as his three assistants beat out a crazy rhythm on their drums. The drums are made of cow dung, sun-dried to a very hard consistency, with a goatskin over the top end and bells fitted at the bottom end, in the Zanzibar Tarib style. It is very evocative—and quite eerie.

The witch doctor is stripped to the waist, and his body is covered with what looks like blood, but which I actually surmise is a mixture of mud and blood. As we arrive, he slits the throat of the second chicken, which explains the origin of the blood. He lets it flow freely from the slaughtered chicken, entirely drenching his head. It's only then that I notice Moki, also drenched in blood from the dead chickens, lying on the ground in the centre of the circle of assembled staff. Candy arrives at my side and grips my hand. The witch doctor throws some scraps of cloth around the prostrate Moki. They burst into flames, drawing gasps of fear and astonishment from all of us. Some of the house girls are sufficiently frightened that they run away and hide in their rooms.

The drumming reaches a crescendo, and the witch doctor is screaming verses in a strange tongue and stamping his feet. Suddenly, he collapses on top of Moki, who shrieks in alarm, then goes silent. The drums have stopped. It seems as though everyone present has stopped breathing. I search the faces of the assembled staff members. They seem frozen in place; the mood is trance-like. I look back to where Moki lies immobile and silent, and the witch doctor has disappeared. I look around again, and find that the drummers have also vanished. Ali and Saber help Moki, who is shaking uncontrollably, to his feet, and lead him to his room. The remaining staff silently disperse.

In the morning, Moki is dead. He has died in his sleep.

I authorize a car, and Saber drives Moki's body back to his village, Sakura, on the coast south of Pangani, where the preparations for the funeral will begin. I call Boss to let him know what has happened. Moki has been employed by Boss for many years, and he's genuinely upset to hear the news. He immediately offers to contact the family and pay for all the costs, a generous gesture that will be extremely well-appreciated within the community. In Tanzania, when anyone dies, the village *mwenyekiti* (chairman), or perhaps a close family friend, will pass a paper around the community for donations. Each person will contribute what they can. Some only pennies; others, a great deal more. The family, it is felt, should not have the added burden of any financial strain to contend with in this time of mourning. Boss says it's important that both he and I attend to represent the company, and so we arrange to meet at Sakura the following day.

We organize four cars for all the staff who are able to attend the funeral. In Swahili coastal tradition, the body is usually buried the same day as, or the day after death, so timing is important. When we depart early the next morning, I am driving the pickup, while Candy and the remaining staff remain behind to look after our lodge full of guests. The show, as they say, must go on. We meet Boss on the rough road south from Pangani towards Saadani National Park and drive together towards Sakura. The village is packed with friends, relatives and neighbours from all the surrounding villages. There must be over five hundred people in attendance; Moki was a very popular and respected member of the community. Boss and I are ushered into the *mwenyekiti*'s house, where we sit cross-legged on the floor with the elders of the village and the senior male members of Moki's family. All the women are absent. They're gathered separately at his house, attempting to console his wife and children. We're offered food: *maharagwe* (local bean stew), *kuku* (chicken), and *kachambari* salsa with rice. Boss whispers to me, that he is too upset to speak, and that I must represent the company and give a speech at Moki's house before the body is taken to be buried. It will be a great honour for him that his employer shows him this mark of respect.

"What? Are you serious?" I hiss.

"Please," pleads Boss. "You will be great, and I just can't do it."

I am suddenly eating more slowly. What should I say?

We finish our meal, and Boss, the village elders and I move silently through the assembled crowd to Moki's house. The surrounding crowd ripples apart to let us through and closes behind us as we pass. Moki is lying in an open coffin, as tradition dictates, his expression serene, peaceful. This helps little in dispelling my apprehension. The *mwenyekiti* calls for silence and indicates the table upon which I should climb so that everyone can see and hear me. I ask Ali to translate for me, as I am suddenly concerned that I'll make a mistake with my Swahili that could unintentionally upset someone. I take a breath, try not to take any notice of Moki's sightless eyes staring up at me and begin in a loud, and I hope clear, voice.

"It's a great honour for me to be invited here today to represent Boss and the company that Moki worked for, for so many years." Ali is translating almost simultaneously. "He was an extremely valued worker, a popular member of the staff but, above all, a great person. He will be sadly missed for his humour and charm, and his skills with music which entertained us all on so many occasions. I feel very humble to be here. People like Moki have made me, a visitor in your land, feel very safe and welcome. I've been lucky in my life to travel all over the world, but I feel more at home here amongst you all than in most of the places I've known. This is a special place, with special people. It has been people like Moki who have made us want to stay here, and he is a very big part of why I have chosen to stay here, and live and work amongst you."

I take a breath and continue, more relaxed now. "Moki was a shining example of everything we should all aspire to be: gracious, gentle, forgiving, and generous. A friend to everyone he met. A wonderful father and husband. A provider. A vital member of a unique community. He will be missed. We can never replace him, but we can follow his example. As we say farewell to Moki, we will understand that he may be gone from us but he will never be forgotten. *Tupa pamoja.*"

This phrase seems to have become a recurring theme in my life—a comfort in the face of death. *Tupa pamoja.* We are together.

The crowd begins to cheer, calling back as one, "*Tupa pamoja!*" Someone helps me down from the table and leads me to Moki's coffin. It seems I've earned the honour of being a pallbearer. I am to carry one side at the front of the coffin. I'm by far the tallest of the coffin bearers, and when the other three suddenly begin moving toward the graveyard, weaving from side to side in a kind of progressive dance, it's all I can do to keep my corner balanced precariously on my shoulder. Three corners of joyous African natural rhythm, one corner of stumbling Scotsman. I'm concentrating with a sweaty desperation, terrified that I might drop him. The other coffin bearers rotate out frequently, so that each member of his family and his closest friends can share the honour of bearing Moki to his final resting place.

I can barely see; sweat is dripping into my eyes by the time we reach the grave. We lower him into the ground and the coffin lid is fitted in place. For a moment I hallucinate that Moki winks at me as the lid slides home. Final words are read aloud; a hymn is sung.

Boss whispers in my ear, "Well done. Keep this up, and you'll be voted chairman by next month."

The red, red soil is shovelled on top of the coffin and many people come to me to shake my hand or pat my back. From all directions, I hear the ringing refrain of "*asante sana*" (thank you very much) as we return to our cars for the long drive home.

During the journey, I'm alone with my thoughts. This is my fourth African funeral. First, Gordon. Next, I attended the state funeral of the local Member of Parliament in Bagamoyo, again representing Boss. I was the only *mzungu* there, mistaken, as a result, for being important and ushered, much to my horror, to sit in the very front row. The President, also in attendance at this important occasion, glanced along the row of seated dignitaries. Our eyes met and he nodded in apparent, but mistaken, recognition and smiled at me. The surreal feeling was further heightened as we were all filing out behind the President and a group of Maasai arrived late. They were pushing through the crowd when, in sudden recognition, they surrounded me, greeting me warmly with much high-fiving and hugging. This drew a decidedly puzzled look from the President. Mingwa, our sleepy *askari* from the House of Crazy Thomas, introduced me to his clan members before I finally managed to melt into anonymity at the periphery of the proceedings.

My third Tanzanian funeral was for the sister of Kimwimyi, Tony's boat captain at the Beachcomber. Eight months pregnant, she had caught malaria. She couldn't take the treatment without risk of losing her baby and had tragically died as a consequence. Tragic, but not uncommon, especially when medical help is all too often not within easy reach. This had been his second sister to die in the same way.

I think suddenly of Candy, last Christmas season, who thought she had recovered from a bout of malaria and didn't bother to go for a final test. We were hosting guests, pre-dinner, when she told me she just had to leave, as she was feeling really awful. She left the party in a rush, heading towards our house. I raced after her and managed to catch her before she collapsed. Carrying her to our bed, I proceeded to call the local doctor, Dr Upendo—Dr Love, as his name translates—who arrived almost instantly on a *pikipiki* motorbike, with a paper bag under his arm containing his medical kit and supplies.

Dr Upendo quickly set about taking Candy's temperature, which was very high. He at once administered an injection—of what I'm still unsure. He told me that the parasite that carries the disease had not been fully killed by the previous treatment, and that immediate action was required. After four attempts, he found a vein, leaving the sheets splattered with blood. Inserting an IV drip of saline and then another of glucose, one in each arm, he searched for a way to hang the bags high enough to allow the drip to work. He solved the problem by using the cord from Candy's dressing gown attached to the wooden frame of the mosquito net.

We watched apprehensively as the bag of saline slowly emptied. By the time the drip had finished, Candy began to look a bit better, but we knew that she was far from safe. Upendo replaced the saline with a litre of quinine solution: both a preventative and a treatment for malaria, dating back to colonial times, when it was widely used by the British, its bitter taste concealed as a component of gin.

Faithfully appeared in the doorway, having come immediately upon hearing that Candy was unwell—alerted by the jungle drums, or perhaps Upendo. She sat beside the patient, holding one hand while I held the other.

"Worry not, Greem," she said. (She has never been able to pronounce "Graeme.") "She will be fine. This is normal."

Normal or not, I was hardly reassured. Few people who live in East Africa—or, for that matter, anywhere across the massive malarial zone which encompasses the majority of sub-Saharan Africa—escape infection with the mosquito-borne malaria parasite. Two forms exist, with *cerebral* malaria being the more severe—and the more deadly. But even the milder form, if left untreated, can kill. After an initial infection event, even following seemingly successful treatment, the parasite can survive in the blood and cause recurrent episodes. This is extremely common in Africa, and in many third-world countries around the world.

Upendo took another call and informed me that he had to leave, as a pregnant lady in the village was in labour and needed his help. "The quinine will work its magic," he reassured me as he departed.

"Would you like a glass of Robert?" Faithfully asked.

She meant wine, but always called it "Robert." I have no idea why.

As Faithfully and I shared a glass each of "Robert", Candy's eyes opened. Very quietly, from behind the white, billowing mosquito net, she said, "Hello, Faithfully."

We were thrilled and relieved that she was finally responding to the treatment. My optimism was somewhat dashed, though, when she then said, "What a lovely wedding dress you're wearing, Faithfully. You look so beautiful. Tony is so lucky to have you."

As Candy drifted back off to sleep, Faithfully and I regarded each other nervously across the bed. Gingerly, I touched Candy's forehead with the back of my hand. She was still very hot. I looked at the IV, and saw that the drip seemed to have stopped working. I tapped it a few times, but without result. I adjusted it slightly, and opened the dispenser trap a fraction, and it started to flow once more. Faithfully was cooling Candy's forehead, with cloths soaked in the ice bucket to try to reduce her temperature. Suddenly, Candy began to convulse. She shivered uncontrollably, and was violently sick. I cradled her in my arms, trying to soothe her. Faithfully was already trying to call Upendo, but he arrived as if by magic. He adjusted the quinine drip and looked at me accusingly.

"Too much quinine too fast is not good," he admonished me.

Candy's shaking subsided, and she drifted off to sleep. Upendo reassured me that the fever had passed, and I vowed to myself never to take any further part in medical treatments in the future; one autopsy on my record is enough.

In the morning Candy woke at about eleven a.m., and her smile filled me with hope and strength. She was clearly going to make it. Faithfully smiled, ruffled my hair, said, "I told you she would be fine, Greem," and left for home to get some sleep.

Who decides who lives and who dies? Is it God? Gods? Fate or mere luck? Privilege? Or is it those damned kids, shaking the mango tree?

***

With Candy fully recovered, albeit following several weeks of depleted energy, we have a wedding to look forward to! We're truly excited. It will take place in Tarangire National Park, where two of our friends are to be married in the safari lodge owned by the bride's parents. It's a beautiful lodge which is spectacularly positioned on a bluff overlooking the Tarangire River. Tarangire National Park itself is most often the first park encountered by safari-goers on the popular overland northern circuit safari. The usual itinerary, which frequently concludes in the vaunted Serengeti National Park, draws tourists from all over the world for an adventure which usually also includes some portion of the amazing Great Migration. Tarangire, a first stop on the route, is most famous for its large elephant herds and beautiful, varied landscapes. In the dry season, it has virtually the only water sources for miles around, creating its own mini-migration of not only elephants, but a stunning diversity of other wildlife coming into the park to drink and bathe in the year-round waters of its river and swamps. The upcoming wedding promises a welcome reunion with friends we don't see nearly often enough, a chance to socialize on a grand scale, and, not least as an inducement, the chance to revisit the beauty of Tarangire National Park itself, one of our favourite places anywhere.

We have a long drive ahead of us, however: at least nine hours, if everything goes smoothly, which is never guaranteed. We'll travel via Tanga, Segera, Korogwe, Mombo, Sane, Moshi and Arusha, and then on to the park. We plan to leave early, at first light, and to skirt Tanga to avoid traffic. We rise at four thirty, have a quick breakfast, and depart around six a.m. We plan to overnight in Arusha for much-needed haircuts, provisions, and to freshen up before our arrival at the lodge. As we approach the outskirts of Tanga, there's already a road block with many police and immigration officials milling around. About twenty young guys are sitting cross-legged on the road verge with their hands clasped on their heads, under cover of police with guns. As we coast to a stop, the familiar hulking figure of Stanley appears at my window.

"*Habari, Kaka*!" he roars. "Can you give me a lift to Arusha?"

The jungle drums are pretty loud in these remote parts of Africa, I ruefully surmise.

Stanley settles his considerable bulk into the back seat, and explains he'd been tipped off that a bunch of Somalis were trying to pass through the area on their way to seek work in Dar Es Salaam.

"But they have to be up early in the morning to outsmart me!" He spies the cool box. "Oh. Is there beer?"

And so, we begin our journey. Once again, we are thankfully "police proof" as at each approaching police check point, and every time a police officer leaps from his hiding place behind a mango tree, the cannonball head of Stanley appears from the rear window to bark a command, and we are once again saluted onwards towards Arusha. Even the incredible amount of beer he appropriates from the cool box fails to detract from the fact that he's a valuable asset to have onboard for any journey by car.

We speed ever onwards, through the high-altitude desert of the Maasai Steppe, with enormous dust devils whipping up miniature storms from the ultra-dry, fine, red dust, dancing across the horizon and conjuring images in my mind of Wile E. Coyote and the Road Runner. The wind whirling in through the wide-open windows of the car is so hot, it's like a hairdryer blasting full-force in your face. As we approach Moshi Town, we move into Mount Kilimanjaro's own unique micro-climate. Towering, dark blue and black clouds gather overhead. With a deafening crack of thunder, the heavens open, and torrential rain begins lashing the car. The temperature immediately drops what seems like ten degrees. The windscreen wipers struggle to cope with the sheer amount of water that the mountain has unleashed, and I have to slow down quickly to be able to see through the rain.

As suddenly as it started, however, the downpour ends, and within minutes we're once again driving on bone-dry roads, surrounded by a dusty landscape seemingly untouched by water. As we hit the outskirts of Moshi Town, Stanley directs me to stop at the first police check. The officers there greet him as an old friend, and we all go through the polite ritual of introductions and swapping phone numbers that's such a fundamental aid to survival in Tanzania. Here, we part company with Stanley, and continue on towards Arusha with assurances that nobody will stop us on our way. These reliable jungle drums can be damned useful sometimes.

We manoeuvre our way through the omni-present city traffic into the centre of Moshi Town, and park up near the bus stand. We're looking for a certain bar, the Spotted Zebra, and, sure enough, we find it on the second street back from where we're parked. As we enter, Candy seems doubtful. We are, as expected, the only *wazungu* customers in the room. My name rings out almost at once, though, and as I look around, I catch sight of a lone man standing at a table, far away in darkness at the back of the bar. I recognize Bahati Mbaya, who limps forward to embrace us. I have met him before, in Arusha with Gordon, some years ago, when we made a deal to buy some uncut tanzanite gems from him. His father has a small mine somewhere way out in the bush, and after many, many, many nights of negotiation involving many, many, many bottles of *Konyagi*—that fiery local cane spirit some idealists liken to gin—a figure of five hundred dollars for one kilogram of stones was agreed upon.

As we wait for our late lunch of chips *mayai* (potato omelette) to arrive, Bahati Mbaya once again extolls the virtues of his tanzanite, even pouring an assortment out onto the table. In the dim light, they make a singularly unimpressive mound of dirty-looking stones in a variety of very dull colours. Candy is extremely unimpressed, but I feel I have an obligation to honour the agreement we made many years before.

Bahati Mbaya's name translates to Bad Luck, a nickname with a wild backstory. He has moved into the family mining business only recently, since giving up his previous job as a tour guide, taking mostly Eastern European guests fly-camping in very remote parts of various national parks. He figured that, since his English language skills are terrible, it's just as well he specialized in people from countries where English isn't spoken all that much or all that well. This had certainly made for some interesting and chaotic trips, he tells us.

One awkward incident had occurred when he pitched the tents for his six Serbian guests close by a river in Ruaha National Park. After a successful day of bush safari followed by an excellent dinner served around the camp fire, everyone had retired for the night. Nature called, as it does, and Bahati Mbaya walked out into the bush to relieve himself under a nearby tree. Midway through this activity, a female lion pounced on him and, gripping his left buttock firmly in her jaws, started to drag him deep into the bush. His anguished cries for help had finally roused his Maasai *askari* from deep sleep, who managed somehow to salvage Bahati Mbaya's mangled ass from the lioness. Luckily, one of his Serbian guests was an accomplished emergency physician with actual war-time experience gained during the Kosovo conflict, and he was able to stop the bleeding. They immediately rushed Bahati Mbaya to hospital, arriving in time to prevent the inevitable infection a predator's bite will cause from setting in too deeply to be treated. For months afterwards, he had limped around Moshi, constantly muttering to all and sundry, "It was only *bahati mbaya!*" This led to a nickname that has stuck firmly; I doubt that even he remembers his real name.

I pay him the agreed sum, wish him *bahati njema* (good luck), and we set off again towards Arusha. My grimy tanzanite stones are stored safely under the driver's seat in an old rice sack. Five kilograms of mixed stones and dust is Candy's wry assessment.

We're treating ourselves to a night at The Kibo Palace Hotel, situated near the famous Clock Tower roundabout in central Arusha. This is famed for being the mid-point in Africa between Cairo and Cape Town. The hotel is a favourite of ours, perfectly situated in Arusha for getting around town, and given the traffic in Arusha, this is a big plus. We head to a shopping mall to indulge ourselves in the luxury of looking at shops stocked with everything we could possibly need, even if the reality is that we don't need it. Still, fun. We experience the odd familiar feeling of near-panic when faced with a supermarket aisle that offers almost one hundred varieties of shampoo. This is virtually overwhelming, as what's available in Tanga is painfully limited. Once, while on a visit back to Europe, we visited a French hypermarket and actually hyperventilated at the staggering choices we were faced with, and, leaving the trolley in the middle of an aisle, hastily exited the store without buying anything at all!

We retreat to the courtyard and the Wild Dog and Whistle Irish Bar to reorganize our thoughts, and while enjoying a cool glass of sauvignon blanc, Candy spots a "hair saloon" on the upper floor of the mall. With a sad lack of tact, she suggests that unless I want to arrive at the wedding looking like a "nutty Professor," I might think about paying it a visit. As it happens, they can fit me in, and the receptionist says they even have a stylist from Ghana in West Africa who is an "expert" in *wazungu* men's hair styles. What a relief!

Jean Paul introduces himself and seats me in front of the mirror. I explain to him quite clearly how I would like my hair cut. He stares blankly. A passing stylist says, "Oh, *pole sana, he does not speak English.*" No problem, *hamna shida*, and I offer my very basic instructions once again in Swahili, yet still he does not understand. Once more in French? He shakes his head so I mime what I would like and receive a wide grin and vigorous nodding of his head. He then takes a toilet roll and starts to wrap it carefully around my neck. Round and round. And round and round—using most of the roll. I signal to stop, as by now I'm having difficulty breathing and resemble at least a priest, if not an actual cardinal with my massive "dog collar." On goes a standard hairdresser's cape. Then, he promptly produces from nowhere a menacingly large pair of electric clippers which I veto immediately with vigorous sign language and mime scissors as a better option. At this point, he disappears and goes rummaging intently around the salon. In time, he returns triumphantly with a pair of scissors. These he places in a microwave oven I hadn't before noticed and presses the "on" button. Even the microwave's whirring and dinging, which apparently indicate that the scissors are done, cannot fully drown out the chortles of suppressed hysterics emanating from Candy, whom I can see, via the mirror, convulsed in her chair. Jean Paul adopts a series of thoughtful changes of pose, studying my cranium, and at last grabs a hunk of my hair from the top, pulls it straight upwards such that it resembles a samurai topknot, and then hacks through it at the roots!

"Fuck this! Have you ever even cut hair before?" I shout, grabbing the scissors from his startled grasp and flinging them randomly at the microwave. I throw off the cape and storm indignantly towards reception. What little dignity I do possess by now, however, is further shredded, as, attempting to unravel the infuriating toilet roll from around my neck I begin to pirouette like a spinning top. Candy and the female stylists are laughing hysterically, and the last thing I hear is the microwave dinging again as I stomp off down the stairs and back to the sanctuary of calm that is the blessed Wild Dog and Whistle.

Candy reappears a couple of hours later with her hair beautifully blow-dried and styled, a perfect, pretty picture of well-coifed femininity, all ready for the wedding. Beauty and the Beast. Lady and The Tramp. Bonnie and fucking Clyde.

The next morning, full of excitement, we depart early for the three-hour drive to Tarangire National Park. Stanley is as good as his word, as every police check waves us through without delay. We climb high up onto a wide plain dotted with Maasai manyattas, the small, circular villages of mud-and-dung thatched *bomas* so emblematic of Tanzania. The sheer escarpment of the Rift Valley looms in the far distance on the horizon. We turn off the road that will ultimately lead to Lake Manyara and the Ngorongoro Crater, before crossing down onto the endless plain that is the magical Serengeti.

Tarangire Ridge Lodge is one of our favourite lodges anywhere, perched high on a bluff looking down onto the Tarangire River and a vast savanna adorned with baobab and acacia trees and teeming with wildlife. The central, open-air bar/restaurant area features a lounge furnished with coffee tables carved from the wood of old Arab dhows and sofas cushioned with deep, plush pillows. From this point, tents spread out in single file in each direction along the top of the hill. An extensive, spectacular terrace overlooks the river and the plain below, the perfect vantage point for an armchair safari. Elephants drift past through the trees in enormous family groups, and impala, Grant's and Thomson's gazelles graze among the foliage. Multiple troops of olive baboons congregate in the treetops and vie for branch space with white-backed vultures. Buffalo and waterbuck and Maasai giraffes make use of the cool water afforded by the shallow river. The scene is idyllic; it's Africa from the picture books. It's Africa from the movies. It's Africa, for real.

The lodge is closed for the weekend, and over a hundred family members and friends have gathered to celebrate the wedding of Silvie and Marc. They have come from all corners of the globe—everywhere from the USA and Europe, to Mauritius and Australia. James and Annie are the most gracious of hosts, and Brian, the brother of the bride, is truly a boy born to the bush. He has spent his entire life here in Tarangire, and is training as a safari guide. James and I are enjoying a beer on the terrace, when Brian advises his Dad that there are seven female lions walking in the car park. James sighs, finishes his beer, and asks us both to try to keep the other guests away from the car park. We form a tiny, but effective human wall, as a mass of curious spectators try to take photos over our shoulders. James jumps in his jeep and confidently herds the lions out onto the plain. The lions appear to be extremely affronted at this disruption, but apart from a bad-tempered snarl or two, they do rather meekly comply.

The wedding is absolutely splendid. The staff have cut a large circle of grass down on the plain, directly adjacent to the Tarangire River, under the shade of an enormous, ancient baobab tree. There's a makeshift altar constructed from bush breakfast tables covered with brilliant white linen cloth. Arranged in semi-circular rows are over one hundred safari chairs, all facing the altar. Every seat is occupied by family members and friends anticipating the arrival of the bride. The priest is resplendent in his full formal white robes, and Brian, as Head Groomsman, is on guard, dressed in his safari khakis with a Henry lever-action .45-70 hunting rifle slung casually but meaningfully over his shoulder. The lions have not been invited, but it seems everyone loves a wedding in the bush, and they've been spotted flitting in and out of the surrounding scrub. The congregation are bravely giving a rendition of *Abide with Me* while peeking surreptitiously over their shoulders from time to time to check anxiously for invisible predators.

The hymn changes to *How Great Thou Art*, but which transports me instantly back in time to Gordon's funeral—the last occasion at which I'd heard this sung. Candy takes my hand and whispers, "It was exactly five years ago today that we buried Gordon." I'm astonished that I hadn't remembered the date, and the coincidence brings goosebumps to my arms and raises the hair on the back of my neck.

I turn and gaze out over the bush, recalling that the first time we ever visited here was with Gordon. I look around nervously. I'd rather the lions appeared than that the spectre of Gordon should rise up out of the bush. It's an irrational, superstitious moment, a kind of impulse which comes from being surrounded in the African culture of belief in the inexplicable, in shadows and ghosts and the immediacy of the past imposing upon the present.

The spell is mercifully broken, as a camouflage-green safari vehicle winds its way down the slope towards us. The bridegroom, best man and the remaining groomsmen disembark. Marc, together with his elder brother, Jan, and three close family friends, all from Mauritius, who have spent their formative years living in Moshi, climb out of the vehicle. A second car appears in which the bride is clearly visible.

She's utterly resplendent in her traditional white bridal gown, somewhat incongruous in this natural bush setting. She's radiant, beautiful, incandescent in her obvious happiness. Her brother, Brian, carries the two rings inside a baobab seed pod that he has cut in two, hinged, and varnished to create a perfectly unique and lovely ring box.

The ceremony itself is quickly concluded, and the congregation rise as one, cheering and applauding, as the Irish clergyman announces, "You may now kiss the bride." No one cheers louder than the combined lodge staff, all of whom have known Silvie from the day she was born, and all of whom adore her. We all begin the lazy meander back to the lodge terrace, high above us, some quickly—but not too quickly, as we've all been reminded that lions like nothing better than fleeing prey.

Everyone attending the wedding has helped to transform the terrace into an enchanting, otherworldly, one-off reception venue. Ribbons and bows hang from the trees; kerosene lamps adorn shrubs, and walls, and pathways. The Honeymoon Suite bath has been temporarily requisitioned, and is centre stage, filled to the brim with ice, and packed full of champagne, wines, beers, and spirits. Tables are laden with fabulous buffet fare. Many guests who have travelled from overseas countries, with slightly more food options than are available in Tanzania, have brought with them cooked meats, fancy cheeses, pate, and Foie Gras. There are salads fresh from Lushoto, and prawns and fish flown in direct from the coast—an abundance, in short, rarely seen in Africa.

The staff are dancing and singing. Incongruously, a jazz band has struck up, and disco music is being readied for later. The typical, enormous, eight-foot-tall speakers, much-loved by every self-respecting Tanzanian DJ, are being wrestled into place. They were delivered earlier on a cart pulled by a *pikipiki* motorbike through a national park. This doesn't happen every day.

"Banana Zorro and the E Street Band" follow the jazz section. He might not be "big in Japan," as they say, but he's certainly big in Dar Es Salaam! The staff go wild when he's joined on stage by Dully Sykes, the original Bongo Flava artist and *the* man of the moment. The bride and groom lead the dancing to Azonto by Fuze, a hugely popular number from Ghana that has the floor full and the speakers at their absolute limit. I'm wondering what the lions are thinking. I consider asking if he has ever met a hairdresser from Ghane by the name of Jean Paul.

Candy and I are out on the terrace, enjoying the breeze and the full moon washing the plain below us in such a soft and golden glow. The Irish priest approaches us, now in street clothes, and enquires where he might know us from, as we look so very familiar. "Have we met before?" he wonders.

We tell him that we're General Managers of Mashetani Ridge Lodge, and he freezes in what can only be described as horror. He then quite obviously pretends to spot someone across the terrace, and dashes off without another word.

We dissolve into laughter, remembering what he at last has recalled: last Christmas, when the lodge was full to capacity and we had no room for walk-in guests, or even seats for dinner, he had arrived, asking for a room. He had first been turned away by security, and then by the gate staff, where, much aggrieved, he'd demanded to see the managers. Security brought him to the lounge, and we politely explained that we simply didn't have room for guests without a booking. He was beside himself with fury. What followed was a spectacularly foul-mouthed tirade which ended with me being named, "a hard-hearted, miserable, Jock bastard who could stick his lodge up his arse." At the time we had no idea we had just made the acquaintance of the Archbishop of Arusha.

We sit in the moonlight, hand-in-hand, and reflect on what a privilege it has been to be a very small part of such a wonderful occasion. The love of the bride and groom shine through as strongly as the full moon above us. I smile as I remind Candy of the time Chichi told me that he'd been very excited to attend the funeral of Moki. Not just to pay his last respects to a good friend and work colleague, he clarified, but as a fabulous opportunity to find a potential bride.

Finding this strange, I asked him to expand on this statement.

"Well," he began with utmost gravity, "any girl can look beautiful and smile at a wedding, but at a funeral it takes a special girl for her true inner beauty to shine through her tears and grief. So, a funeral is most assuredly the best hunting ground for the discerning bachelor."

When a mango tree is shaken, more than grief, it seems, may be on offer—if you know what to look for.

CHAPTER 9
T.I.T.

It's Candy's birthday, and I've arranged a boat trip. We've provisioned the fiberglass speed boats with cool boxes packed with ice and a selection of rosé, sauvignon blanc, champagne, beers and sodas, as well as fresh food for the BBQ. Captain Mohammed has packed the fishing kit. We're all ready to go! Our plan is to set off down the river, head south once we reach the Indian Ocean, pick up Tony and Faithfully at Ushongo, and then Jan and Stephie, who manage a beach lodge further down the coast. We've heard of a small river with a sandbar just offshore, and it sounds ideal for our day out. Our own desert island!

We pull into the bay, and the guys are already under a palm tree waiting for us. Boarding through the surf is a challenge, and there's much hilarity when Tony topples backwards into the sea and disappears below the surface. As he resurfaces, thoroughly drenched, he is devastated to discover he's lost his false teeth. He dives overboard in a fruitless attempt to retrieve them, while Jan pulls me aside and produces the missing dentures that he'd found lying on the deck. He hides the wayward choppers deep in his board shorts, as Tony, disgruntled, reappears and climbs back aboard.

The engines gun to life, and we bounce out through the surf, clearing the coral reef and heading straight for the island. Under the ever-watchful eye of Captain Mohammed, I put the two 85 HP outboards to full throttle, and we speed across the waves under a clear azure sky. Spray lashes our faces and the feeling of perfect freedom is intoxicating. I reduce our speed as we reach another reef, and with the fishing rods trailing lines, we trawl back and forward along the reef between the shallow coastal waters and the Zanzibar channel. The reef is teeming with fish, and we soon have a rich haul of *kole kole* and red snapper.

Jan winks at me and says he'll prepare the fish for the BBQ lunch, and sets about gutting the catch. Mohammed is trawling the boat, while Tony pulls in even more fish, and I keep the ladies' glasses charged. A sudden roar from Jan startles us.

"Oh, my God!" he yells. "Come look at this!"

We all gather round, and like Jonah ejected from the belly of the whale, Jan produces Tony's false teeth from the guts of a red snapper. Tony grabs them with glee, pouring some whisky over them. Triumphantly, he rams them back into their rightful place in his mouth.

Grabbing the fish, he yells into its very dead eyes, "You ate my teeth, you mother fucker? Now I am going to eat you! With my teeth!"

Candy, Faithfully, and Stephie are completely bewildered, unable to understand what's happened. Jan and I are literally doubled over, laughing, but have vowed to each other never to reveal the sleight-of-hand behind the "miracle of the teeth."

As the tide is receding, we spot a tiny sand bar that is just appearing out of the ocean, and we anchor just off it. Mohammed and Saidi Saidi set up a shade net they've brought with them on the branches of a mangrove tree. While we snorkel and swim in the bathtub-warm shallows, they set a table complete with white linen tablecloths, and have the fish on the BBQ enticing us to gather for lunch.

Saidi Saidi produces his widely acclaimed margaritas, and before we begin to eat, the bottle of champagne is opened with a loud flourish. We all belt out a somewhat discordant but enthusiastic "Happy Birthday to You!" in Candy's direction. Tony demands that Saidi Saidi identify which specific fish is his thieving red snapper so he can complete its karma. We all kick back, relish a luscious meal, and soak in the sense of peace and utter contentment established by the blue sky, the warm breeze, and the inviting sounds of the Indian Ocean lapping gently around us.

As we're packing up, getting ready to depart, Mohammed says he's picking up a mayday call on the boat's radio. It's very hard to hear, but I can make out the voice of Greta, who operates a dive centre on the beach with her boyfriend, Dieter. She gives us GPS coordinates, and we set off to see what's amiss. We find her on a very small island where they often take groups for diving, as it has amazing coral walls, positively brimming with fish.

As we approach, we can see Greta frantically waving her arms over her head to attract our attention, and we slowly slip in and beach a short distance from her. Jan and I jump overboard and wade ashore. Greta is on her own, with just her captain, Saleem, with her. She points to the high-water mark, and Jan and I approach the site. The dead body of a young guy is lying in the sand, dressed in jeans and a Manchester United shirt. His right arm has been eaten by crabs, so that only the bones remain. Otherwise, he looks at peace.

"There are three more further leeward," Greta whispers

behind us.

We manage to raise the Coast Guard by cell phone, and they inform us that the Spice Islander ferry travelling from Stone Town in Zanzibar to Pemba Island had capsized the night before in the Pemba Channel. It was licensed to carry 450 passengers and deck cargo, but the first reports estimate that perhaps 1500 people were on board. No life boats, and very few life belts. The Coast Guard can't help us, as they have no fuel for their boat.

Captain Mohammed is beside me and has been listening.

"Tell them the body has a pocket full of cash, and they'll find fuel," he snarls, and angrily storms down the beach towards the boat.

Jan, Tony, Mohammed, Saleem, and I wrap the corpses in our white linen table cloth and picnic shade net. We load the bodies onto the dive boat and Saleem says he'll speed them ashore. We follow in our boat, trying to comfort Greta, who has been badly shaken. As we arrive at the beach, we find that the villagers have already buried the four bodies under the palm trees, above the high-water line. They had no identification, so their graves are marked only by their football shirts, each tied to a stick, fluttering in the onshore breeze. Perhaps, it is hoped, a relative will pass this way one day searching for news of them. Probably not.

Over the next few days, with the morning high tide, the ocean offers up more bodies from the deep: a tragic daily harvest. Over twenty are discovered on this section of coast alone. Each is treated with all possible dignity, and is buried near where they're found.

We stayed overnight on the beach in a small nearby lodge—six very sad people trying to celebrate a special birthday which suddenly no longer seems so special. We try to lighten the mood. We toast Candy, we toast Tony's dentures, we toast his fish, and we try our best not to allow this tragedy to entirely overwhelm our moods.

At around midnight, Jan insists on going by *pikipiki* to collect some special rum he knows is kept in stock at another lodge a few miles away. Despite our reservations, off he speeds, down the bush road into the moonlight. Around one a.m. he limps back into the bar, T-shirt in tatters, twigs in his hair, with a badly swollen knee, and sporting a sizeable burn on his thigh. Grinning delightedly, the bottle held aloft, and despite his injuries, he's like the winning captain in a football match: triumphant! He'd lost control of the bike somewhere near the entrance, he mentions in an aside, but he's confident that we can find it in the morning, once it's light. Most importantly, he does have the rum!

As dawn breaks, my phone rings. Jan, at the other end, whispers excitedly that his knee is locked and he can't get out of bed, but there's an intruder in his bathroom who seems to be smashing up the place. Can I help?

I leap from bed and run to his room, and am relieved at what I find. To this day, Jan remains the only person I know who has been terrorized by a bush baby. These adorable little primates, with their huge eyes and teeny noses, thrive in the coastal palm regions and are heart-stoppingly cute, though very inquisitive. One of these delightful little guys is busy in the shower eating Jan's hair gel, and most of his and Stephie's other various creams and potions are scattered all over the floor. He looks at me, startled, gives a shriek, and with a few hops and a leap he's out the window and away. I tell Stephie she can come out from hiding under the covers.

"I hope it doesn't take Tony's teeth!" she laughs.

As we cast off from the beach to return home, we wave fond farewells. Jan begins the hunt for his motorbike in the bushes just as we round the headland on our journey back to the creek. At the very mouth of the creek, where the river meets the Indian Ocean, we pass a very large crocodile swimming inwards from the sea! Old Mohammed the fisherman had once told me:

"In running water, expect crocodiles; in still water, expect hippo. Don't swim in either."

Wise words, given the fact that hippos kill more people by far in Africa than any other animal except the mosquito. As if we need any further demonstration of this, as we glide slowly upstream, we observe two large male hippos in a vicious fight. We can hear the roars of the dominant male from very far away, and the submissive "honk, honk, honk" of his unfortunate victim, who has strayed into the much larger animal's patch of the river. We round a slow bend just as the dominant male chases his opponent down the bank where they both disappear below the surface. Suddenly our boat erupts upwards, rising out of the water like we've hit a mine or some sort of powerful explosive charge. One of the hippos has surfaced without warning directly beneath the bow of the boat, throwing us all to the deck. Captain Mohammed, with remarkable calm and considerable skill, immediately engages full reverse throttle and we careen crazily backwards. Luckily the hippos, engrossed in their own disagreement, completely ignore us and continue their battle for supremacy towards the far shore. As we regain our composure, Captain Mohammed checks that we're all okay. I tell him he owes me a beer, as I've spilt most of the one I was drinking, and we all burst into the nervous laughter following a near-death experience. Candy announces ruefully that this has been a birthday she'll certainly never forget, but that she feels a full five years older than yesterday!

The lodge appears through the riverine forest and we catch sight of the two Roses' big and little bottoms, along with Chichi, waiting for us on the jetty with cool, scented towels and a glass of ice-cold champagne for each of us on a tray. Jafari is leading the rest of the staff in yet another rendition of "Happy Birthday." It's good to be home.

The lodge is busy as usual. Our unique blend of remote bush game drives with the opportunities for close-up encounters with elephants and other wildlife, together with our offerings of river safaris and Indian Ocean fishing and snorkelling trips makes for a tempting holiday combination, and is probably unique in East Africa. Owning our own airstrip offers easy transport. We're often fully booked, and Boss is delighted with our success. We have guests from every stratum of society and culture. For some people, a safari is a once in a lifetime, bucket-list vacation that they've saved for their entire life—an experience never to be repeated. Others have been bitten by the safari bug and will return time and again to assuage the painful withdrawal symptoms; it's universally known in the industry that the safari bug bites the hardest of any "predator" in Africa. Some simply can't stay away. Others see it as just a novel venue, allowing them to tick a box, and some others choose this most exotic of locales to celebrate a special occasion.

Tim and Sharon are from the East End of London. Tim has sworn us to secrecy, because he wants to take Sharon on an exclusive snorkelling trip to a private island in the middle of the Indian Ocean where he plans to propose to her. He has made a waterproof sign saying, "Sharon, I love you! Please marry me!" which he plans to produce six feet underwater, and he has the ring already on a thong around his neck. The only flaw to this exciting and unique plan is that Sharon has become violently seasick—so much so that they didn't sail fifty meters from the jetty on the river before Mohammed had to turn back. Undeterred, Tim has reserved the pool, and plans to pop the question submarine-fashion. A further complication, however, is that Sharon has been making very full use of the lodge's all-inclusive drinks policy which has contributed to her unfounded suspicion that Tim has fallen under the charms of one if not both of the Roses.

All of these issues taken into consideration, however, the proposal goes better than we could reasonably expect. Neither party drowns, even when Sharon tries to say, "Yes" underwater. A new problem arises, however: the ring. Sharon suspects that Tim has bought a fake diamond, as he foolishly let slip the fact that he had bought it from a fellow market trader in Mile End. Fortunately, though, a stunning coincidence allows me to save the day. One of our guests, Brigitte, hails from Belgium, where she happens to work as an expert in the precious gems industry and a director in the diamond and rare stones importing business in Antwerp. At my request, Brigitte produces a jeweller's loupe and examines the ring carefully. Luckily, she's able to declare the stone top quality, and all of two full carats, as well.

A celebration naturally ensues, with Tim buying drinks for the entire bar, casually forgetting that all drinks are included and thereby reducing lodge profits by an appreciable amount. This incident, though, gives me an idea: I seek out Brigitte to thank her and ask her if she knows anything about tanzanite stones. Indeed, as it happens, she does and implies they are the next big thing. Over a cocktail, I tell her that I have one, and ask if she'd mind looking it over, but I omit to tell her that I have a shoebox full of them under my bed that I bought from a limping, ex-safari guide called Bad Luck. In the end, I give her a stone that's the size of the top joint of my thumb. We exchange email addresses, and she promises to check it out and drop me an email with her thoughts once she returns to Belgium. First, though, she still has to complete her safari, which is set to include the Maasai Mara in Kenya, a gorilla trek in Bwindi Impenetrable Forest in Uganda, and the awesome Victoria Falls in Zimbabwe/Zambia.

***

At breakfast the next morning, several people point out that I have a rather large and obvious bite on my cheek. Either Faith, Hope or Charity—I can never tell which one is which—points at my face and informs me, "*Kubwa kuliko chuchu yangu.*" Chichi clarifies for me that she has said that the spot on my face is bigger than her nipples, a simile resulting in much hilarity among the rest of the food and beverage team. She has a point—though, of course, I cannot literally verify the comparison. My face is throbbing, and by lunch time, my cheek feels stretched to the breaking point. I am reminded of an old John Wayne movie, and retire to our house with the intention of lancing the bite to get some relief. Dousing what seems the most appropriate tool in my trusty Swiss Army knife with whisky which I then set alight in hopes of killing any bacteria surviving the whisky bath, I gingerly slice over the top of the bite. A disgusting, horrible river of pus runs down my cheek, and the relief is instant. A few dabs with an alcohol swipe, a couple of sterile strips and I feel as good as new. Even if I say so myself, I think it adds a certain dashing air of danger and resourcefulness to my appearance.

The next morning I'm not sure what is worse—the unrelenting pain in my now even more swollen face, or the chagrin from Candy's pointed reminder that my last medical interventions consisted of a cursory autopsy on Gordon and the administering of too much quinine in an attempt to cure her malaria. She's right, as usual. I'm an idiot. The redness has now spread from my cheek down to my neck and I do, if I'm honest, feel a little light-headed. This is clearly a serious infection.

Boss is not in Dar, but away on business, but when we contact him, he instantly agrees to fly me to Dar Es Salaam. None of the scheduled airlines have space, however, as it's high season when domestic travel is at its heaviest. Eventually, he calls back and tells us that he has located an Indian one-man operation out of Zanzibar and arranged for a four-seater Cessna 206 which will be arriving at our airstrip within the hour. Captain Rohan will deliver me direct to Dar, he assures us. "Worry not."

Candy has called a clinic on the peninsula and the "doctor on call" is briefed and awaits my arrival. While we are seated in the car at the airstrip, I'm smugly regaling Candy with the many benefits of having access to one's own private charter flight when Captain Rohan arrives. I kiss Candy *au revoir* and jump on board. Captain Rohan is a sixty-plus, overweight, Tanzanian-born Indian whose considerable girth instantly makes the 4-seater 206 a 2-seater.

He greets me warmly, gives me a high five, and then exclaims, "Holy fuck, bro! You been fighting with a buffalo, or something? What did you do? Try to kiss the son of a bitch?"

Pleasantries over, we speed down the airstrip. A piece of clear tape covering a large crack in my window comes free and starts repeatedly slapping my face until, in frustration, I rip it off. Captain Rohan performs a low-level fly-over in a tight circle around the lodge, yells, "Just getting my bearings!" and we're soon out and over the Indian Ocean. He's flying parallel to the coast, and I can see, first, Pemba Island and then Zanzibar. We head out to the east briefly as we cruise towards Dar. The control panel of his plane has several red lights blinking, and I enquire casually what they are, as generally, even in a car, red lights are not good news. "It's just my fucking disco, bro," he explains, as an Indi Pop, Bollywood track blasts suddenly from the speakers, proving at least that they're fully operational.

Dar Es Salaam appears through the heat haze, and Rohan sticks his head out of the window, much like a dog enjoying the view from a car. Apparently, he doesn't trust fancy GPS electronics, but prefers the traditional visual approach. Blessedly, we land without incident and he taxis to the domestic arrival terminal. As we disembark, Rohan follows me into the terminal, beseeching.

"Bro, bro, can you pay me now? I don't have any fuel to get back to Zanzibar!"

I explain that I have no cash with me; I've been in the bush for three months, and, in any case, Boss is supposed to pay him. It's now four thirty and night flying isn't allowed. His eyes are pleading. He's a fucking obese puppy. I tell him I can get one million Tanzanian shillings—approximately five hundred dollars—from the cash machine, but that's the maximum I'm permitted to withdraw in a twenty-four-hour period.

"Perfect bro! Perfect! I would kiss you, but have you seen your face?"

All three ATMs in the concourse are out of order, so we continue into town in my taxi. On the sixth stop, we find an ATM that works, and I give him the cash. With a whoop, he high fives me one last time, then regards my taxi dejectedly.

With a hang-dog expression, he asks, "How am I to get back to the airport?"

My cheek beating like a bass drum, I sigh, then, predictably, relent: "Take the fucking taxi."

Rohan screeches off towards the airport as the sun dips speedily in the west. I hail a passing *bajaji*, one of those three-wheeled motorcycle taxis found in most African cities.

"The International Clinic on the peninsula, and fast as you can. *Haraka haraka, bwana*," I instruct the driver, as it's now a quarter to six. This was an act of desperation, but admittedly also an error of judgment, as these drivers are certifiably crazy enough without any added encouragement. We hurtle down side streets towards the peninsula, across pavements, through goods yards and shanty areas, and between buses and lorries coughing smoke and fumes, arriving at long last at the clinic. I ask the driver to wait, as I'll need to go on to a hotel at the Waterfront to spend the night.

I rush into the clinic and breathlessly inform Reception, "I'm here to see the doctor on call. He's expecting me!"

"Ah! *Pole*. He has been called out," she tells me, adding "Oh, my God, have you seen your face? You should get that seen to!"

I swallow my frustration, resigning myself to a long wait. Eventually, a staff nurse gives me some antibiotics and pain killers. I'm also given a new appointment for the next morning at 07:30. I jump back in the *bajaji,* and the driver deposits me at the Waterfront Hotel, where Reception informs me that they have no rooms left. Seeing my face and taking pity, however, they suggest I come back in an hour when they will have a room prepared for me.

I cross the darkening courtyard towards the waterfront open-air restaurant, find a table in the corner and order a bottle of an oldish Cabernet Sauvignon in the belief that if you're taking pain killers and antibiotics, they deserve to be washed down with a decent vintage. The sun has sunk well below the horizon, and the Friday night Dar crowd are gathering to kick off the weekend in style. I'm exhausted. My canape of pain killers and main course of antibiotic has dulled the pain and seems to be working against the infection. I pick up my bag and head for the exit door when I suddenly remember that I've kicked off my flip flops and am barefoot. It's somewhat embarrassing to have to return to the table, now occupied by a group of businessmen, and crawl underneath to retrieve my foot wear. I emerge from under the table, mutter *pole sana* and, with as much dignity as I can muster, saunter towards the door. This is the result of working in a "no shoes, no news" kind of establishment, where being barefoot is the norm!

I take the short walk back across the courtyard towards the hotel. A local prostitute, trawling for early clients, approaches me. Her tried-and-tested opening line of "*Habari, bwana*! Do you want me to take you to heaven and back?" barely registers on my distracted brain before she follows up with, "Oh my god! Have you seen your face?" She offers to carry my bag and assist me to my hotel, but I have a vision of

137

trying to chase a fleet-footed prostitute down the road to retrieve my bag, and refuse with thanks. After a short but strenuous game of tug-o-war, she gives up on my bag and I retreat backwards into the hotel reception. My room is ready. I collapse on the bed.

I wake with the alarm at six a.m. I feel like shit, but manage a shower, skip breakfast, and head by taxi for the clinic. The female German (I suspect East German) doctor is waiting for me in reception.

She greets me with a cheerful, "Ah ha, you must be the asshole lodge manager who thinks he is a surgeon!" Then, the now obligatory, "Oh, my God! Have you seen your face?"

She ushers me into an examination room and I lie down on the bed.

She mutters, "This is going to hurt—a lot." With that reassuring sentiment, she produces a scalpel, and proceeds to cut open my cheek. She explains she needs to expel the poison, and I'm pretty sure she's smiling as she begins to dig both thumbs into the wound. It seems to explode. I smother a groan.

"You're a few tiny steps away from septicaemia," she admonishes me.

At last, she slathers my cheek with ointment, dresses my wound, gives me a range of tablets to take, and cheerfully presents the heartening, wonderful news that I'll need to return each morning for at least the next three days for the process to be repeated.

When I reflect on all of the agonizing adventures that I've endured in only one day, I wonder what the next three days have in store for me. After all, T.I.A.—This is Africa. I've begun to feel, however, that today deserves an even more specific very special honorific, amplified all the way to full-fledged T.I.T. status—This is Tanzania.

CHAPTER 10
MEET THE NEIGHBOURS

Ernest Hemingway's famous paean to Africa, "I never knew of a morning in Africa when I woke up and was not happy," reverberates in my brain as I awake a few days later in my room at the Waterfront. It's a notion that has recently been severely tested, as I must once again visit the clinic on the peninsula. Dr Gretchin, with what appears from my perspective to be a perverse and grim pleasure, is set to operate on my face one more time. This morning she's scheduled to lance my cheek and drain, hopefully for the last time, the remaining poison from my wound. I've convinced myself that she must be the granddaughter of Dr Joseph Mengele, hiding out in East Africa. Yet I do have to concede that she certainly knows what she's doing. In fact, should I ever again have need of non-anaesthetized facial surgery services in Dar Es Salaam, I know where to go.

Following my appointment, still slightly shaken but not too stirred, I make my way from the clinic by taxi to the domestic airport. Boss has arranged a commercial flight back to the lodge which thankfully does not involve Captain Rohan. The journey to the airport is suitably chaotic, of course, as pretty much all transport inside Africa tends to be. It traverses the city from the leafy, gracious peace of the peninsula area through the central business district, and onto the main—that is to say, only—road to the airport. White uniformed police abound at every junction and intersection, whistles blowing shrilly and aggressively, but to no apparent purpose. At one point, five lanes of traffic converge onto the statutory two lanes, with traffic signals pointing in every direction yet utterly ignored by one and all.

At last, we arrive and I check in for the flight. As is usual in Tanzania, it will be a far from direct flight. We'll be landing first at Zanzibar, then proceeding via Saadani and Mashado to Pemba. After this, we'll progress onwards via Tanga City to Mashetani bush strip, where I'll disembark. The plane, without me, will continue on to Arusha via Moshi. The plane itself is yet another Cessna, and bodies already fill the twelve passenger seats. Since all seats are booked for the first leg of the journey, I have the honour and privilege of sitting up front in the right-hand seat beside the pilot. This is Benji, a Belgian pilot with many, many years of bush experience, and I know him well from his frequent visits to our airstrip, dropping off and collecting our guests.

During the flight, we get to chatting about how he'd moved from flying for Médicins Sans Frontières in Sudan to commercial flights in Tanzania. He tells me that his former company here in Tanzania wouldn't release him from his work visa when he had an opportunity to really jump forward in his career. In Tanzania, when switching employers within the same industry, you must first gain a "Letter of No Objection" from your current employer before you can accept new employment. This situation had dragged on for several months before Benji decided that drastic action was required.

He was to collect a plane full of travel agents on a familiarity trip from Ruaha in southern Tanzania, and take them north to Arusha to continue visiting lodges in the

Serengeti. Once all the agents were seated on board, Benji had climbed into the passenger section of the plane through the rear door. On this particular day, he wasn't wearing his crisp white uniform, but rather board shorts and a Hawaiian shirt, plus flip flop sandals. In his hand he held an open vodka bottle in which he had substituted water for the vodka. Slugging direct from the bottle, he made his way between the seats, climbing over passengers as he introduced himself as the pilot and gave that day's version of the safety briefing before vaulting the last few seats to take up his position in the captain's seat. Tossing the empty vodka bottle onto the floor, he yelled, "Let's get this baby rocking!" and lurched off at full throttle down the grass runway. With a roar of "Whooah!" he took off and soared northwards.

Over his shoulder, Benji had shouted, "Surely, of all the wonders of the world, the horizon is the greatest!" These were the very last words spoken by anyone on the flight. Uneventfully, the flight continued in complete and utter silence, and one hour after landing he had his Letter of "No Objection," along with a warning never to darken the doorstep of his now former employer ever again.

After Benji's recitation of how he had managed to re-arrange his employment situation, I observed that it had been a somewhat drastic solution. Benji only roared with laughter and began his descent towards Mashetani airstrip. "Africa teaches resourcefulness," he reminds me. Quite true, I thought.

On this leg of the journey there are only the two of us left onboard. He'll be collecting eight of our guests from the lodge, outbound for Arusha. Taking advantage of this, he therefore flies directly along the twisting creek at what seems to me like a mere two feet above tree height, and we roar past the lodge;

the entire staff, laughing, wave furiously as we buzz the restaurant roof before landing on the nearby airstrip.

I disembark, and am met by Candy and our departing guests. The two small plaster strips and small piece of gauze on my cheek obviously do not provide a suitably heroic impression, as when Candy introduces me and informs the guests that I'd cut myself shaving, but like a typical male, had run off to hospital for treatment. It's great to be back. I've missed Candy's understated sarcasm.

In the evening, Candy and I are enjoying pre-dinner cocktails with guests in the lounge bar, when the evening's silence is abruptly shattered by the loud yelping and fiendish laughter of a clan of hyenas somewhere in the darkness nearby. We all stare out in the direction of the sounds, which continue to reach new crescendos. I radio security and soon Sembuli arrives with news. A hippo, injured in a fight for territory with another dominant, has been cornered by upwards of forty hyenas who are in the process of devouring the unfortunate beast only about seventy meters or so away on the other side of the creek, nearly directly in front of the restaurant.

The security team lights the area with torches as much as possible, and the guests are treated to a gruesome spectacle as the soup is being served. Forty hyenas fighting over a live buffet is not a quiet affair. It is the way of hyenas—they begin to tear meat away from the still-living prey without bothering with the tedious job of actually killing it, and the poor animal succumbs eventually from shock and blood loss. There are many who will claim that this method is actually less cruel than the method used by the big cats—suffocation—as the shock works as an anaesthetic, and the hyenas' prey feels less pain than terror. The initial roars of the hippo have faded now, and only the creepy vocalizations of the hyenas fill the night air.

Suddenly, overshadowing even the racket of the hyenas' meal, the mighty roar of a pride of lions approaching reverberates through the dining room. They're so close you can almost feel the bass of their growls inside your chest as they arrive, intent on stealing the hyenas' supper. Being unable to see these magnificent predators actually rather intensifies the experience. The guests huddle together in the restaurant, eyes glued to whatever movement the torches of the *askari*s are able to pick out. The lions chase off the hyenas, but the retreat is only to a small distance away. From there, the hyenas dart in and out, attempting sneak attacks to steal what morsels they can. By now, of course, the poor hippo has died—within days, there will be no evidence at all that it had ever existed. Vultures and jackals will remove any leftovers—nature's clean-up crew.

Nobody is going to sleep much tonight. Candy tells the guests that this is a good lesson that the safari is never over just because you return to the lodge. We live in their kingdom, and are lucky enough to be allowed to share their space. We wander into the wild, often, perhaps, losing our way, but inevitably finding our soul.

***

Dieter, one of our elderly German guests, asks to be escorted to his room. He's partially disabled and needs two walking sticks to get around, so we've given him the room nearest to the restaurant. Mumbi, the *askari*, takes Dieter's arm and I accompany them the thirty meters to his room. About halfway there, Mumbi stops and very quietly says, "*Hatari. Simba nakuja.*" I put my hand on Dieter's shoulder and whisper, "please stay very still." At this moment three large—at this proximity, VERY large—female lions pause while crossing the path not more than ten feet in front of us. All three lock eyes with me; I can almost taste the rangy smell from them, they're so close. Mumbi edges Dieter behind him, and says, "Trust me," then brings himself up to his full height and spreads his arms while holding the hems of his Maasai *shuka*. The effect is to make him look much bigger than he is. One lioness grunts. Then, with a seemingly pretended nonchalance, the three lions resume walking and disappear into the riverine bushes to join the rest of their pride feasting on the hippo.

I break the silence: "Well, Dieter, shall we continue to your room?"

Dieter doesn't know whether to laugh or cry, and is shaking his head muttering, "Trust me? Trust me? Oh, my God, it's not like I can run away!" Which, actually, would have been the worst possible reaction, as any cat will instinctively chase a moving subject! Yet remaining still is a lot easier to recommend than to achieve, with those pitiless eyes boring into you.

The next morning at breakfast, Dieter has the entire table of his fellow guests enthralled as he describes in graphic detail the previous night's encounter with the lionesses when he had confronted and stared down not one but three lions. I confirm to his friends his courage in the moment, and how he never flinched. The restaurant team insist on calling Dieter *Bwana Mwakubwa Simba* (Big Lion Boss) for the rest of his stay. I think he loves it. I know I would.

As a consequence of this exciting story, for the next week

we have quite a hard time enticing guests out on early morning game drives. First, the lions feast on the hippo, and then the hyenas and jackals return, only to be followed by vultures. This "bush cleaning crew" manage to turn a huge, adult, male hippo into gleaming white bones in less than a week—all in full view of and not seventy meters from our restaurant. Who needs to leave the lodge? We all have ring-side seats for an armchair safari. Nature in the raw.

The incident with the lions has brought into renewed focus, however, our need for a retraining session on the use of the hand-held radios we rely on within the lodge for communication. I gather all security personnel, plus one staff member from each department in the restaurant after all the guests have departed for the day's game drive, to begin the training. We go through care for the handsets, charging, battery care and such. I emphasize the need for constant, clear, and accurate communication, citing the lions in camp as an excellent example. I remind them that we must always communicate in English, and that we have to use standard phrases so we minimize the chance of misunderstanding in what could be an emergency situation. "Roger that, roger that." "Affirmative." "Negative." "Come in." "Break, break." "Go ahead." "Over." "Over and out." "Wilco." "Read you loud and clear." "Tango Base."

As we simulate situations and separate into teams to go through practice drills, I'm really pleased with how well it's going. It's a very productive training session, and we finish up with an open forum. I encourage all staff to ask for clarification or raise any points about which they may be unclear. Again, it has been a very constructive morning.

"Any last questions?" I ask, as we prepare to pack up

before the guests arrive for lunch. Abedi, one of our brightest waiters, whose English is excellent, immediately raises his hand.

"Yes, Abedi, please share with us your question."

"Can I please be Roger?" he asks.

Before I can even respond, Saidi Saidi interrupts, "If Abedi gets to be Roger, then can I be Wilco?"

Just then, Candy's voice comes over the radio: "*Wageni wanakuja sasa.* The guests are arriving now." Every radio set erupts to life when a chorus of ten people all answer, "Roger" and "Wilco" at the same time. I slump over the table with my head in my hands. Training over. On to lunch.

***

Ben Silet, one of our local Maasai walking guides, is to be married this afternoon, and Candy and I have the very great honour of an invitation to join the ceremony and celebrations. The entire ceremony will unfold over three full days, but we've arranged to visit on the first afternoon only.

We regularly go for walks in the bush with Ben guiding us. There's something magical about being on the ground, surrounded by nature. You see so much more than you ordinarily see from a vehicle, and Ben's knowledge of all things great and small is amazing. It's always amusing, as well, to hear the childhood fables passed on to him from his father as a child and how believable they become with his telling. We have learned why, for example, the baboons do not trust the hyenas after an incident which occurred while a crocodile was giving them both a lift across a deep river, and the hyena stole the baboon's favourite hat! This story is intended to explain how, whenever hyenas are around, baboons will always climb to the tops of the nearest trees and shout warnings to each other: "Beware! Hide your hats! Hyenas are around!"

Some of the challenges of life in the wild have been met by the Maasai with solutions which may seem cruel or horrifying to us, but which have served them well in maintaining the survival of their people. For instance, Ben, like all Maasai, has ring marks burned into his cheeks. This is undertaken as a baby, he explains, since when a baby is too young to swipe flies away from its own eyes, it may risk blindness from flies laying eggs in them. An open raw wound from a burn will attract the flies away from the eyes and reduce the risk of blindness. Likewise, the ritual of removing the two bottom front teeth, usually with the large Maasai knife, leaves a very distinctive look, but also allows for a person suffering from tetanus, or "lock jaw," as it's conventionally known, to be fed milk and cow's blood through a straw until he can recover.

Ben is imposing, at well over six feet in height, dressed always in his traditional Maasai robes, complete with his *rungu* (a tomahawk-like instrument), *upanga* (a long, stabbing knife) and spear. The Maasai keep their heads shaved clean, and sometimes daubed with bright red ochre.

Walking with Ben early one morning, we came across the corpse of a wildebeest enveloped by vultures. On our approach, the vultures all scattered, settling atop a nearby tree, watching us intently. With his *rungu*, Ben plucked the tail from the dead wildebeest, happily informing us that this would make an ideal fly whisk. He pointed out the numerous lion footprints all around the carcass, and was giving us the timeline surrounding the events of the wildebeest's demise.

First, the lions had killed the beast the previous night, gorging on the fresh meat and then moving on, leaving the remainder of the animal for the rest of the food chain, he explained. As we started to continue onwards, Candy enquired as to the whereabouts of the lions. "Oh, they will not be far," comes Ben's less-than-heartening reply. I pressed for more detail.

"If we do just happen to stumble upon these lions, Ben, do you have a plan?"

"Oh yes. I will just walk up to them and tell them, "Mr and Mrs Lion, I am sorry, but I do not want to disturb you today, please let us pass.""

Candy wryly remarked, "Well, I'm glad you have a plan. Very reassuring, indeed. I feel much better knowing that."

During our return hike to the lodge, we passed a small herd of giraffes galloping gracefully not more than twenty meters in front of us, as well as many zebras and Grant's gazelles, who observe us warily, but simply retreat a little distance away before resuming their grazing. We love these walks, immersed in nature from a different perspective, surrounded by the sights and smells you often miss from a vehicle. We love having the time to examine the footprints and tracks, the animal highways, and the stories their droppings can tell—especially in the company of such a gifted guide and storyteller as Ben.

***

It's the day of Ben's wedding, and we drive the short distance to the Maasai village for the ceremony. The circular *manyatta* is ringed by fences made of thorn tree branches, intertwined with walls made of dried cow dung. This same construction is used for the outer walls of the many village houses or *kraals*. The houses have no windows, only slits from which the Maasai can observe or shoot arrows. In the centre of the village is a huge dung pile—itself sometimes fenced—and this is where, every evening, the cattle and goats return to spend the night, safe from attack by lions and hyenas. To enter a *kraal,* you have to bend over, as the doors are very, very low. The ladies who build the houses tell us that this ensures that each time their husband enters the home, he must dip his head towards her—a gesture which, in Maasai, is a display of great respect. We would love to think this is true.

There are many dogs about, kept, in part, to bark and growl at the first scent of a predator. They are so effective that even gazelles and impalas often gather near the manyatta at night for their added protection and warning system. Predators of every sort fear the Maasai in general and their dogs in particular. Once we watched a yappy little Maasai dog chase a massive hippo along the riverbank for several hundred meters. When it finally stopped its pursuit, the hippo kept running, and the scrappy little guy let out one last yelp in its direction in a seemingly final admonishment: "AND DON'T COME BACK!"

As we disembark from the car, Ben is waiting for us with a group of elders from the village, and a large group of ladies. The ladies are magnificent. Their usually colourful shuka robes are further adorned with a multitude of small silver discs that reflect and jingle with every movement. They wear, as well, intricate, multi-coloured beaded wedding necklaces, and wrist and ankle bands. Ben is resplendent in a bright red robe, and his head is adorned with an ostrich feather headdress that makes him seem even taller. His face is adorned with red ochre highlighting the ring marks on his cheeks. We are surrounded by everyone and led inside the *manyatta*. Even before we enter, Ben asks me if I like the girl in the yellow dress. I agree that she's very beautiful, and he nods and informs me proudly, "She is going to be my second wife."

I check to see if he's smiling, but he seems perfectly serious.

"My first wife is ugly," he adds, "but she comes from a family who produce many sons. I am very lucky."

"You sure are," I agree.

We enter the *manyatta*. His bride-to-be is now nowhere to be seen; she's with the elder women inside her own hut, and takes no part in the proceedings. The centre of the village holds a crowd of Maasai men, all magnificently decked out in full tribal attire. The monotonous, hypnotic, repetitive humming sound they make as they chant is broken only by high pitched screams and commands as they subtly change from one chant to another. They continuously bounce in a trance-like rhythm. With a scream a young warrior will randomly dash forward from the group and begin the high jumping that is much admired in Maasai culture. These dances can last for hours.

After a time, Ben leads us just outside the village and we sit under a huge towering mango tree where a goat is being roasted over a fire of acacia branches. More specifically, *parts* of a goat are being roasted. I can still see the fur covered leg. I am sure I can make out the heart and kidneys speared on sticks in the middle of the small fire. An elder is in charge of the cuisine. It's a great honour for Candy to be allowed to join us under the tree, as in Maasai culture, the women are never allowed to eat with the men.

I don't think Candy has ever been so grateful to be

vegetarian—a fact which Ben already knows—as it means she's absolved of the need to eat the wedding meal. The elder/chef hands me a goat leg and helpfully peels back the fur to expose the meat. All eyes watch me as I start to nibble away. Amazingly, though it has come straight from the fire, it's only warm, and the flesh is barely cooked. I manfully nibble at the raw grub. Ben has signalled to a *morani*—young warrior—and he hastens over to where we sit, producing from somewhere near his armpit under his *shuka*, with a flourish akin to that of a magician pulling a rabbit from a hat, a bottle of Guinness! I assume that in the view of the Maasai, the Scots and the Irish are interchangeable, and I am beyond honoured by the gesture. The effort Ben must have made to find and deliver a Guinness especially for me in the middle of the bush must have been considerable. It's the first time I've consumed a Guinness warmer than the meat course, but the honour is profoundly felt.

With the wedding meal complete, Candy and I leave for the lodge. It's been an amazing experience and we're very humbled at having been included. We're barely one hundred meters from the *manyatta* when a herd of more than a hundred elephants amble into our path. We're soon surrounded by these calm and beautiful beasts. They're returning, as they do every evening, from their day in the swamps to spend the night in the foothills close by the Tanzania/Kenya border. In the distance, we can see Kilimanjaro with the setting sun lending its snow-covered summit a rosy, pink glow. We spot a Maasai child no older than seven dart out from a group of his peers towards the last passing elephant. He has dipped his hands in the ash from the cooking fires. He sprints forward, slaps the nearest elephant on the rump, leaving a distinct hand print, then sprints, screeching in triumph, back to his friends who are already running for the Manyatta gate. It's a game Ben had told us about that Maasai children often play. We hadn't totally believed it until now. The old matriarch elephant turns and follows the children with her gaze, and I swear I see her smile, then shake her head and continue onwards towards the setting sun.

CHAPTER 11
J.F.D.I.

The excitement is intense. Throughout the lodge, there's an energy, an almost tangible feeling of something building. The staff soccer team, The Mashetani Devils, have made it to a Cup Final. Not just any Cup Final, but the Goat Cup Final!

This is a highly prestigious affair. Already, multiple guests have approached us, requesting to substitute their scheduled evening game drive with being driven to the game. It's all the staff are talking about. Lions, hippo and leopards can pass by without anyone losing focus on "The Match." It's to be held in a large village twenty kilometres from the lodge, and a record crowd is expected, as the opponents are the all-conquering Tanga All Stars, direct from the bright lights of Tanga City.

Candy and I are parrying questions in the evening. It's sundowner time, and we're on the covered deck overlooking the waterhole where a large elephant family have graced us with their presence. They're noisily chasing away some impertinent hyena who have been taking too much of an interest in the elephant babies who are adorably mixed and muddled up directly, safely beneath their moms' legs. The sun is starting to set in the west, bathing distant Mount Kilimanjaro in muted gold just before it falls into blackness.

"So are The Devils going to serve up a stellar performance tomorrow?" an aging solicitor from Los Angeles demands of me.

"Ve are not missing ze football tomorrow now?" enquires a lovely Swiss couple.

John, a retired CEO of Con-Ed in New York, has joined us for cocktails and announces he wouldn't miss the game for love nor money. Saidi Saidi is mixing Manhattans and Margaritas, and we overhear him telling a Dutch guest that he's known as *"Paka."* This is "cat" in Swahili, I explain, appropriate in that he's our goal keeper.

"For his agility and reflexes," I add, "but, having seen him play, it's much more likely apt because he shits in his neighbour's garden."

My smart-ass remark is at first greeted with a quizzical look, and then a howl of laughter as the guest's wife translates into colloquial Dutch.

John is very young to have been a CEO—far less as a now retired CEO. We've had many, deep and interesting conversations with him on life and love and death and everything in between, and generally agree that the three of us have together solved the problems of the world. He's travelling alone, and tells us he had a health scare and a divorce before retiring, selling everything, and now devoting his time to travelling to all the places he'd dreamed of visiting while being too busy earning the money to do it. While working at Con-Ed, he'd leave the office on a Thursday night, catch a red-eye flight from JFK, and return on Tuesday morning. He'd always loved the reaction he used to get at the office coffee station.

"Do anything at the weekend, John?"

"Yes, actually. I visited the terracotta warriors of Xian," or "Yup. I visited the Gorkhi Terelj National Park near Ulaanbaatar."

Apparently, this was his way of exorcising past ghosts,

and spending on himself some of the monthly alimony he'd been forced to pay to his grasping ex-wife on something he wanted to do!

It's Swahili night tonight, so we're serving Tanzanian specialties. Swahili coastal cooking has been heavily influenced over the years by the trading with Indian and Arabic merchants, so curry and spices feature heavily on the menu, along with "*nyama choma*" (grilled meat.) There's no dish more likely to excite a Tanzanian than *nyama,* and almost every restaurant along the coast and in Dar Es Salaam and Tanga specializes in this dish. Whether it's beef, chicken, pork, or goat, huge quantities can be consumed at each sitting. Even the mostly Muslim coastal population cannot resist the roasted pork, so much so that it is commonly known as "*kiti moto*" which translates as "hot seat"—the perfect description of a Muslim gentleman eating pork, but constantly shifting guiltily in his seat and looking over his shoulder in case he's seen eating this forbidden delight.

As the guests are enjoying their meal, the staff bursts into a song and dance routine they practice religiously. We actually had to open this up to all staff members, rather than just the restaurant team, as they love this performance so much. This evening, we have waiters and bar staff, the head chef, the accountant, the storekeeper and most of housekeeping, with Salum, our heavily overweight, 6'2" monthly supply truck driver from Dar es Salaam, leading them all in the centre of the front line, stamping his way vigorously through the routine. We had to alter the weekly menu to coincide with his delivery schedule, as we discovered he was inventing breakdowns and punctures to ensure his presence for the dancing. The guests love it, and when Salum drags a "reluctant" elderly French lady into the midst of the throng, it only adds to the warm feeling of acceptance and togetherness. You can show guests lions, but you cannot beat the amazing, welcoming ambiance that only happy and content staff can create. *Karibuni wote* (welcome all) to Tanzania.

The next morning, we have a staff meeting in the canteen. As always, it starts with a prayer, and it warms our hearts that no matter which religion or sect is represented in the room, everyone joins in and shows full respect. We're meeting to discuss the travel arrangements for the big match tonight, and to decide who'll have to remain as the skeleton staff. Also, Candy has written and posted a memo to all staff stating that if a staff member doesn't understand either Swahili or English, then he or she should request translation from their Head of Department or a Committee member, as there have been complaints that some staff members aren't finding out news or changes. This all seems straightforward until Nanga, one of the Maasai laundry assistants, raises his hand. I invite him to speak, and ask Moses, the head of the staff committee, to translate, as Nanga only speaks Maa. He launches into a very long-winded tale, and those staff members who understand the Maa language are first smiling, and then laughing out loud. Nanga is gesticulating and becoming quite animated. Even Moses, our very serious Committee chairman, is smiling broadly.

He turns to us and explains that Nanga suggests that two heads of department be present during any translation to ensure accuracy. Nanga feels strongly about this as he has recently suffered in precisely this respect. He had a transistor radio that kept breaking down, he explains, and he took it several times to a radio fundi in Tanga, who made a repair and charged him each time. However, each time he returned home, it would stop working again the same day. He finally returned to the fundi and demanded that, after one final repair, the fundi must write him a guarantee for his work. The fundi, well aware Nanga speaks no Swahili and is illiterate, had written out a long and impressive document, and Nanga, naively satisfied, returned home. That evening when the radio failed to work once more, he was furious. When his neighbour translated his "guarantee," it read as follows:

"Dear Nanga, my esteemed customer,

Never bring this piece of shit back to my shop ever again. It is a worthless, ancient relic and should be thrown very far into a very deep river.

Signed, George W Bush."

By now, the meeting has dissolved into chaos. Everyone is laughing, and Nanga is seated at the back, arms crossed, a picture of pained dignity. Point proven, and duly and solemnly recorded in the minutes.

***

At three thirty, our caravan of cars departs for the match. We have twelve guests from Belgium, the USA, Holland, and Switzerland on board, along with the team and twenty staff members. The girls are all dressed as finely as if they were going to a wedding: a riotous assemblage of colours and patterns and joy. The guys are sporting football shirts from all

157

over Europe. For the guests, we have cool boxes packed with ice cold beers, sodas and snacks.

Our soccer safari reaches the village, and we park up under the shade of a stand of mango trees. There's already a large crowd gathered and an air of excited anticipation. Every side of the pitch is two-deep in spectators who happily make space for us near the centre line. The Tanga supporters are packed behind one goal and many have climbed high into the jacaranda trees for a better view. Supporters of both sides have cut tree branches and are waving them above their heads as they sing and dance in impatient anticipation of the game. Many fans have inflated condoms that they are banging together above their heads, making a deafening racket. I think: Well, the Anti-AIDS program should be proud of this unusual but inventive ad hoc advertising campaign.

It has crossed my mind that The Goat Cup is an unusual name for a competition, but all becomes clear, as a group of *kijana* (youths) appears. They're leading a goat on a rope leash around the pitch. One youth is stripped to the waist, his face decorated with white ash, and he's dancing in front of the procession as they march along. Moses explains to Candy, the assembled guests and me that the winning team will be awarded the goat, which they'll later enjoy as the main course for dinner. He explains, as well, that the face paint of the *kijana* signifies that the goat is soon to be roasted. The guests need our confirmation to believe this, and there ensue long explanations and discussion in a variety of European tongues. A mental image leaps into my head of Diego Maradona holding aloft a wriggling goat rather than the World Cup, and I struggle to dismiss it.

The teams are out warming up, and Candy is asked to

make the kick off. To huge cheers, she starts the game with a rather prim and lady-like kick of the ball. It's not every day that a blonde *mzungu mama* starts the Goat Cup! Most of the players are barefoot (it's only a lucky few who can afford the luxury of soccer boots), but the standard is high and skills quite incredible. The Devils take the lead, followed by a pitch invasion, led by the ladies performing cartwheels, and ululating shrilly. The referee regains a semblance of control. By the second half, The Devils are still leading by one. Mumbi, our Maasai security guard, is leaning on his stick next to me.

"Will we be doing this again?" he asks me.

"I hope so," I reply.

"In that case, next time I will bring more footballs," he offers.

I ask why, and he clarifies, "Well, they are all chasing the one ball, and if I bring more, everyone will get a chance!"

I peruse his face for clues. He's perfectly serious.

Chichi, AKA "The Train," has come on as a substitute, and his first contribution is to run directly into an opponent and concede a penalty. Moses discloses that Chichi is known as "The Train" because he can only run in a straight line. This explains the penalty, of course. The crowd, however, is incensed, and disputes the decision. The referee, blasting his whistle like a traffic policeman during rush hour in Dar Es Salaam, brings relative order, and the Tanga All Stars equalize from the penalty. As the referee places the ball on the centre circle, a group of *kijana* armed with their tree branches charge the referee who turns, and with the ball tucked securely under his arm, begins running as fast as he can towards the open door of the police station, hotly pursued by the youths. Three police officers emerge and stop the mob in its tracks. From the safety of the police station, the referee holds a red card above his head and waves it at each youth in turn—a "sending them off" effort to regain his dignity. The police escort the referee back to the pitch, and the game resumes with a roar.

With five minutes remaining, Abedi, with the name "Roger" proudly emblazoned on his back, scores with a spectacular overhead kick. The pitch is once again invaded by cartwheeling and cheering supporters, and I catch a glimpse of the Swiss couple dancing arm in arm around the centre circle with some of the jubilant crowd. Order is once again resumed, and with the light fading, the final whistle is blown.

The Mashetani Devils are the champions!

The players are mobbed by the ecstatic crowd and carried shoulder-high from the field. The Tanga All Stars fans make a futile and unsuccessful attempt to steal the goat, but, thwarted, return to their tree top vantage points and continue to boo. I persuade one of our American guests to present the prize, and he leads the goat into the middle of the pitch and presents it to Jafari, our Captain. Jafari leads the team and all our staff on a triumphant, impromptu circuit of the pitch, and even the poor, doomed goat seems to be enjoying the occasion.

In the growing darkness we all return to the cars parked under the mango trees. The guests are in high spirits. When they'd spent long evenings in their cold North American and European homes, planning their African adventure, they'd certainly never anticipated being part of such a spectacle as The Goat Cup—nor being so unconditionally accepted and embraced by the local community.

The drive back to the lodge is like a carnival, with car horns blaring and boisterous song ringing out from the safari vehicles. The guests have cleaned out the cool boxes, and everyone is enjoying the triumph. When in Africa, it pays to expect the unexpected. This evening, the excited chatter around the dining room is not about cheetah cubs spotted or lions on a kill, but rather Abedi's goal, Chichi's absurd tackle, and Saidi Saidi's fingertip save, all of which get better and better with every telling! Tonight, we're dining together as a group of all twenty guests in the lodge, rather than in the individual dining format we normally favour.

Good naturedly, Candy and I juggle the inevitable questions of how we—two Scots—have ended up in a very remote part of the African bush.

"He lied to me," Candy says, laughing. "We took a wrong turning on the motorway to Paris."

We turn the conversation back to what our guests hope to see during the rest of their safaris. John is in great form, and holds the table in thrall with tales of his many and varied travel adventures. People from a wide variety of different countries and cultures, ages and dispositions are joined tonight by a common love of nature, people, and travel. A great dinner ends a fantastic day, and slowly, at last, all the guests are escorted to their rooms.

It is said that travel is the only thing you can buy that will truly make you richer. We certainly cannot disagree!

The next morning is a typical busy lodge day: guests heading out on early morning game drives, river safaris, bush breakfasts, sea trips for fishing, and some departing on scheduled and charter flights. We are, of course, preparing for the arrival of new guests, having a very short window between departures and arrivals to ensure that the process is seamless. Tents are cleaned, laundry washed, lunches prepared, cars serviced. And then, suddenly, we notice that John has departed without our having had the chance to bid him a fond farewell.

Later that morning Mtoro, the housekeeper who had been looking after John, hands an envelope into the office. She says that John gave it to her to deliver once he had departed. We open and read the hand-written note he has left us. He must have written it the night before—a letter we still treasure to this day:

Graeme and Candy's Guide for a Happy Life, by John:

1. Remember what is important (and what is not).

2. Don't sweat the small stuff (and it's mostly small stuff).

3. Patience is a virtue. (Like all talents, this requires practice to become a virtuoso.)

4. Be kind, and respect others.

5. First, seek to understand, not judge.

6. It's not what you have, it's who you have in your life that matters.

7. Take care of your obligations, and follow your heart.

8. There will always be things to complain about, and there will always be things to be grateful for. Choose the latter.

9. Laugh.

10. Don't let the facts get in the way of a good story.

11. If you're unhappy with your life, change it.

12. Enjoy the journey.

13. Live for today; we're not promised tomorrow.

14. Love one another; learn from one another.

15. J.F.D.I.—Just Fucking Do It!

CHAPTER 12
THE SCOTTISH MAASAI

Village One, as the local Maasai refer to it, is situated only forty minutes' drive from the lodge, out on a wide, flat plain dotted with tortilis acacia trees. Dry and incredibly dusty, it offers sparse grazing for the multitude of cows and goats that are the Maasai's walking bank accounts and larders. The entirety of their wealth is expressed solely in the number and health of their livestock. It takes an exceptional circumstance for them to consider selling even one of these animals; perhaps the serious illness or imminent death of a wife or a child requiring hospitalization could initiate such drastic action—after having, of course, first tried all herbal remedies. But virtually nothing else could prompt a Maasai to part with any of his livestock.

It's only a short walk to the Kenyan border, and the Maasai pay not the slightest attention to this, to them, it is an arbitrary border. They believe that God gifted them every cow on the planet, and that they have an absolute right to roam wherever they wish, so a line on some *wazungu* map is utterly insignificant to them. Each and every member of the Maasai tribe aspires to having as many cows, goats and wives as possible—and in that specific order of importance. This has led, historically, to many conflicts, as tribes raided other tribes and stole cows and wives whenever the opportunity arose. Tribes and individuals are all interlinked through clans and families not dissimilar to the Scottish clan system, including the propensity for rustling livestock and attacking neighbouring tribes. The plaid, predominantly red *shuka,* or robe, is similar, as well, to the Scottish kilt, and when I don my own kilt for special occasions, our Maasai friends are all suitably impressed. We don't know if it's true, but one of the Maasai ladies assures us that their men also wear nothing under their garments, "ever ready for action," they giggle. Just like a true Scotsman!

In years gone by, Maasai *shuka*s were made of dried goat skins dyed with ochre to a deep blood-red. It isn't only lions, but many rival tribes, as well, who have come to recognize the red colour of a Maasai warrior striding through the bush as a sign of clear and imminent danger. They have their own very distinct language, Maa, which bears no resemblance whatever to Swahili, except for those words with no traditional Maa equivalent, for which the Swahili word is adopted.

Within the tribe, males are divided into age sets of a roughly five to seven years' spread; the women, regardless of age, are assigned the same age set as their husbands. Members of this group pass as a unit through all their rituals of life together, and stay in their set for an entire generation. These lifelong groupings begin with the circumcision set, at fourteen to eighteen years of age, when boys are sliced with a sharp knife and initiated into "manhood." During this ritual, for the boy to even grimace or show the slightest discomfort is enough to find himself ostracized by even his own family. My recent experience with my cheek and a certain German doctor in Dar makes me question how I would have coped with that experience.

The next stage for this age set's progress is to become a

"young warrior"—a *morani*. Traditionally, this is the fighting group of the clan, armed with stabbing spear, *rungu* (tomahawk) and short stabbing knives. Proudly displaying an intricate braided hairstyle, their heads and bodies are adorned with blood and ochre. Their distinctive cheek scars and missing centre bottom teeth remind me how inconsequential is my lightly scarred cheek. *Morani* progress after fifteen to twenty-five years to become junior elders, and they in turn eventually become true elders who administer, by consensus, the entire clan. This is a system both fair and honest, in the main.

When any of our Maasai staff return to work from days off or a longer leave, and report to the office, we go through a ritual of elaborate greetings suitable to such an occasion. We must always enquire as to how the wives and children, if applicable, are faring, since we always first hear in considerable detail how the cattle and goats are thriving, or—God forbid—not.

One of the greatest of the many joys and passions we experience as general managers at the lodge is the opportunity to interact with and assist this unique community, and in particular, we love being able to help the local Maasai village school. Over the years, Boss—with the help of generous donations from guests—has assisted in building classrooms to provide the Maasai with their first school in the entire area. Before the new campus was built, teachers taught the children under the shade of a massive, very old mango tree. A blackboard was nailed to its trunk. Benches and "desks" were fashioned from branches or dead trees. This rudimentary arrangement serviced twenty children, who were always on

165

time and always prepared. They wore freshly-laundered uniforms and carried with them a genuine passion for learning.

The campus now consists of a quadrangle of class rooms around a central courtyard, with a flag pole from which the Tanzanian flag flutters each day. The children arrive at school each morning while it's still dark, having been guarded along the way by two *morani*, as their route runs through an elephant corridor, often with watchful lions as road crossing guards.

We sponsor a young girl whom we met on our very first visit to the school. Perhaps a *ramba ramba* brought us to the school that day, because when we were introduced, we learned that her name is Kosenga. The coincidence was striking, as Candy's mother, who died tragically when Candy was only seven, was named Senga. In life, such things are meant to teach, or to inspire—in some way to prompt you to action, we believe—and we both immediately felt the touch of a greater hand directing us.

We learned that the headmistress had rescued Kosenga from being married off at twelve years of age, by an uncle who had taken her in when her parents had both died in an accident. On hearing her story, we immediately volunteered to pay for all her current and future school fees, uniform and books. At a cost of a mere two hundred US dollars per year, it would be but a small financial burden for us, and life-changing for Kosenga. She's painfully shy with us, still, but is flourishing in her education. Each time we return from leave in Europe, we bring her story books, magazines, and books on famous women in important roles in society, in order to expand her world view beyond her Maasai upbringing.

We've long since discovered that there's a vast difference between lack of intelligence and lack of education. Many of these kids are extremely intelligent, lacking only opportunity. David, one of our stores staff who employs daily a very sophisticated computerized inventory system, was one of the very first pupils to graduate from under the tree. At every opportunity when guests ask us about the Maasai, we encourage them to visit the village and school, and, where possible, become involved. It is for many of them a revelation.

Often, I'll be enjoying an evening cocktail with a guest from some sophisticated Western country who tells me that the visit to the Maasai village was fascinating. The dancing, costumes, hospitality, laughter—all an extraordinary experience.

"But how do they live like that?" they frequently ask.

I tell them truthfully that the Maasai are equally astonished that our guests want to commute in a car they rarely own outright, to work ten hours a day in order to buy a home they almost always never own outright, and rarely spend much time in because they have to work ten hours a day. The Maasai can spend their days with their family and friends, eat goat, drink milk, make love with the women of their age set, walk in the bush, sing and dance, and maybe buy more cows. Their houses, they will tell you, are only to sleep in, and if you cannot carry all you own in your two hands, then you surely need less than what you have. Some guests laugh out loud, and some think a little deeper. But many—many—give very generous donations, prompting us to have set up a GoFundMe page to raise money for the building of a school library.

***

The plan for the fundraiser is to march from the lodge for ten kilometres through the bush—lions notwithstanding—dressed in my kilt and accompanied by the village chairman, our walking guide Ben, Ali Makenzi (keeping the Scottish contingent front and centre), Candy, a collection of guests, and any staff wishing to join us. We're delighted that our oldest son and his wife, on vacation from Shanghai, will be here to walk with us. Kris has assured me that he'll also be bringing his kilt for the occasion. Our younger son and his girlfriend are both teachers living in South Korea, and they've set up the GoFundMe page and are marketing like mad! We hope to raise five thousand US dollars.

The guests are very generous, but we're most deeply touched when the two Roses appear in the office to donate twenty dollars each—for them, a genuine sacrifice. This display of typical African generosity is followed by a fifty-dollar contribution from Ali, the guide, and additional donations from many more of the staff. Village elders donate two goats, a contribution more difficult to reflect on the GoFundMe page, but quite a lavish bestowal nonetheless!

Kilayo, one of the Maasai elders, appears one morning at our office and presents us with yet another goat for the cause. He has also brought me a beautiful belt, intricately beaded in Maasai fashion, and a stunning wedding collar of bright Maasai beads for Candy. These are gifts, he tells us, for our kindness, and the goat a donation for the walk. A few months prior, we had received a call in the very early hours of the night. Kilayo's young wife was in labour, and something was terribly wrong. I radioed Ali, whom we dispatched with a car to transport her to a hospital four hours' drive away. Sadly, she lost the baby. As if that tragedy weren't enough, his wife, too, died one month later from an infection the hospital had missed.

Kilayo's gifts reflected his gratitude for the small, and sadly futile, attempt we'd made to help his wife and child. Once again, we are humbled, and deeply touched.

The lodge staff committee purchases the goats from us, providing cash to go towards our target, and we have an impromptu staff party: any excuse to eat goat! This is bush cooperation at its most efficient. The fund is rapidly increasing in value. We hope that over the fast-approaching Christmas season we can add even more.

***

The lodge is completely booked for the holiday period, with every room taken. For New Year's Eve, we've planned to bring in a troupe of performers from the Arts and Cultural Institute in Bagamoyo. They've promised a fabulous show, full of tribal dancing from the length and breadth of Tanzania and, in addition, a fire eater act! I worry that underneath our thatched, *makuti* roofs is perhaps not the best setting for such a show, but they manage to convince me that they do this all the time, and have never burned down a venue.

Candy and the head chef, Soudi, are concocting a spectacular Christmas Day menu, and our guests will get an impressive New Year's surprise at midnight. The maintenance team have made a colossal sign constructed from reinforcing bar, welded to form "*2018*" in numbers eight feet high. They plan to wrap the numerals in mattress material soaked in kerosene, and at the stroke of midnight on New Year's Eve, set them alight on the beach beside the river. With the ink black forest behind, it will be a spectacular sight from the restaurant.

Saidi Saidi appears in the office to protest that it's not fair that he has to work over Christmas. When we point out that he is Muslim and doesn't celebrate the birth of Christ, he's unabashed, but does concede the point and returns to work on his festive cocktail list.

Nearly everything is in readiness for the much-anticipated holiday season—a favourite time of year in the bush for everyone.

***

We've been waiting for the two Roses, Rose *Mkubwa* and Rose *Mdogo* (Big Rose and Little Rose), to join us for a service meeting. It was arranged for eight a.m., and it's now nine a.m. Even allowing for the fact that the world *kamili* (exactly) is the most pointless word in the Swahili vocabulary, this is still late. It suddenly dawns on us, however, that once again we've forgotten to specify which clock to use. We're using the Western clock and the Roses are using the Swahili clock.

In a country without watches, the Swahili day starts when the sun rises. This close to the equator, regardless of what time of the year it is, the sun more or less rises at six a.m. This is regarded as the start of the day. The sun invariably sets at around six a.m. Therefore, the Western seven a.m. becomes *saa moja asubuhi*—one o'clock in the morning. This system proceeds throughout the morning, with eight a.m. as *saa mbili asubuhi*—two o'clock in the morning—until midday or *saa sita asubuhi*—six o'clock in the morning. One minute after, it's no longer "morning," so all times following that become the hours of the *mchana,* or afternoon. This seems straightforward and manageable until you arrive at four p.m. (Western) when the time then turns to *alasiri*, or late afternoon

170

prayer time, until 18:00 (Western) is reached and the system progresses to the hours of *jioni,* or evening, which are, of course, followed by the hours of *usiku,* or the night. The complexities are not yet satisfied, however, in that before dawn, at say, five a.m. (Western) you're in the time period of *saa kumi na moja alfajiri,* or 11 o'clock in the period of early morning prayer. There are many opportunities for confusion. The oldest village on the coast north of Dar Es Salaam is called *Saadani,* which means the "inside hour" or "inside clock". This derives from the fact that an Indian trader, 200 years ago, had as his proudest possession a very grand ship's clock that people travelled from afar just to see. The aphorism that Europe has the clocks, but Africa has the time, is most certainly true.

***

Christmas morning arrives with a glorious sunrise. The warm red sun clears the distant palm trees which fringe the coast where Africa meets the Indian Ocean. The crimson glow seems to gain speed as it swiftly spreads upstream, covering the night's coal black river with a burning ruby gloss. As our guests arrive in the restaurant, we're offering mimosas or Bucks Fizz as breakfast appetizers. Chichi is dressed as Santa Claus, in the traditional bright-red costume, though his full white beard is trimmed close to his face in the Arabic style more favoured by our tailor, who made the outfit. Rose *Kubwa* is dressed slightly less traditionally as Mama Claus, in a bright red *darisha* dress, but sporting a very fetching Santa hat. The two weave their way merrily through the restaurant, distributing gifts to one and all. The few children present are absolutely delighted.

When the guests depart on their various activities, Candy and Soudi busy themselves with the final preparations for the gala Christmas dinner. By lunch time, all is ready, and Soudi announces that he'll rest before returning for dinner service.

It's now dusk—between *jioni* and *usiku*. The guests have returned from their evening game drives in the conservancy. Even the animals seem to have entered into the Christmas spirit, with our local pride of thirteen lions serving up a Christmas lunch of freshly killed Cape buffalo upon which they're all feasting at some two kilometres from the lodge. The ghastly sight of a lion cub completely inside the hollowed-out stomach chamber, covered from head to tail in blood and gore like some Devil's imp, is the star sighting. Ali and Juma have joined the rest of the staff in singing a selection of Christmas carols. Candy appears at my side.

"Come to the kitchen, quickly," she whispers urgently.

Inside the kitchen we find Soudi, spectacularly drunk. He's wielding a paring knife and chasing Saleem, a tiny sous chef, around the preparation table. Soudi is a big guy in every sense, powerfully built and imposing in height. I intercept his pursuit, allowing Saleem to escape, and wrestle the knife from his hand. He slumps to the floor and starts sobbing. The rest of the kitchen team are peering round the door jamb to check if it might now be safe to rescue the turkey from the oven. I call Mumbi, the giant *askari,* and instruct him to take Soudi to his room in the staff quarters. They're great friends, so I advise Mumbi that, for both their sakes, I'd better not see Soudi before tomorrow morning.

The other chefs and Candy leap to action now that the coast is clear, and start plating the food. The Roses, Abedi,

172

Chichi and the rest of the restaurant team are delivering the meals as soon as they're ready. I stroll around the restaurant, wishing everyone a Merry Christmas, and am delighted that all the hard work is paying off. The guests are universally enjoying their African Bush Christmas.

Suddenly, from the corner of my eye, I see a white-clad figure, staggering like a drunken spectre along the raised wooden walkway from the guest rooms towards the restaurant. Soudi has escaped. As nonchalantly as possible, under the circumstances, I amble from the restaurant in a slow-motion, yet frantic effort at intercepting Soudi, who is clearly intent on addressing the guests. In the middle distance, I can see Mumbi running towards us, hoping himself to divert Soudi from making his grandstand appearance. On seeing me, Soudi beams like a cherub and opens his arms to greet me with a massive bear hug. Unfortunately for him, it also gives me the opportunity and leverage to pick him up, tip him over my shoulder and launch him head-first into the bushes beside the walkway. Head-over-heels, he crashes through the bush and before he can rise to his feet, Mumbi wraps him in a s*huka* and departs towards staff quarters, the inert figure of Soudi slung over one shoulder.

As I re-enter the restaurant, a beaming Candy emerges from the kitchen, where everything is running like a Swiss watch.

"All okay out here?" she enquires.

"Sure, no problems this side. Can I offer you a glass of champagne?"

Blessedly, Saidi Saidi appears, as if by magic, with two flutes, chilled to perfection.

"Happy Christmas, darling," I murmur, as we take a seat

on the terrace where we bid *"sikukuu njema"*—happy holidays—to our guests as they drift past and are escorted to their rooms for the night.

There's a full moon, with not a cloud in the night sky, nor a drunken chef to be seen. We wander hand-in-hand towards our room. Chui, our resident leopard, is lounging on a tree branch next to the path.

"Just ignore her," I whisper to Candy. As we stroll past the tree, Candy wishes Chui *"sikukuu njema pia."* Chui continues gazing imperiously into the night, ignoring us entirely, and we meander confidently beneath her comfy perch, heading to our own cozy bed.

Life is good.

***

New Year's Eve is approaching fast, a new set of guests have arrived, and most of our Christmas revellers have moved onwards. The rhythm of the safari circuit never falters.

Jafari appears at the office door to inform me that one of the guests has requested that his wife be allowed to celebrate their wedding anniversary by serenading the other guests with a saxophone performance over lunch time. As I'm quite unsure whether or not either Jafari or I have misheard this, I seek out the guests to confirm. Oscar and Mathilda, who are from Leipzig in former East Germany, are found relaxing by the pool. As Candy and I approach, Oscar leaps to his feet and offers Candy his seat. This very gentlemanly act is somewhat unfortunate, as Oscar is wearing what are doubtless the smallest red Speedo swimming trunks ever constructed, and as we introduce ourselves, Candy is now seated at eye level with said tiny trunks—her cheeks blushing as red as the garment. Mathilda speaks no English whatever, so Oscar begins to fill us in on the details of his request. Candy is craning her neck at a painfully awkward angle in an effort to maintain direct eye contact with Oscar. He's oblivious to her embarrassment, and proceeds to explain that his wife is a bit of a local celebrity in the area surrounding Leipzig, and is in frequent demand to perform at weddings. He shows us an old-fashioned CD player which provides back-up music to the saxophone that Mathilda is cradling like a babe in her arms. The act, it would appear, is a well-oiled machine. They seem so enthusiastic about the idea of giving a performance that it would be churlish of us to refuse. We do have reservations about how our multicultural collection of high-end safari guests will react to this bush cabaret, but we agree—if for no other reason than to allow Candy to finally stand up and avert her gaze without seeming rude.

Come lunch time, I address the assembled guests and introduce Mathilda. Oscar presses play, and she launches into the first number of her set. The staff love it. The girls sway between the tables to the rhythm while serving the entrees, and the Maasai amongst the staff just cannot help themselves, as any time they hear a melody they are transported. Their shoulders begin to dip in time to the music. With the staff, Mathilda is a big hit.

The guests, on the other hand, seem somewhat less enthused, their reactions varying between astonishment and stifled amusement. This is, without question, the most appalling saxophone rendition anyone present is likely to have ever heard. Even I, weaned on bagpipe music, can tell that it's totally off-key. Oscar introduces each number with a quick explanation, and when he introduces the final tune of the set, he explains that Mathilda always finishes her wedding renditions with this number, as it is her very favourite. As she launches into ACDC's *"Highway to Hell"*, one guest, who has just sprayed his soup all over the table, has to excuse himself to rush to the toilets to clean up. The cheering and clapping as she finishes is finely balanced so as not to encourage an encore, and with a flourish and wave to one and all, Oscar and Mathilda retire to their seats to enjoy their lunch. I mingle with the guests as they finish eating, quietly reassuring them that saxophone will not feature in tonight's celebrations.

It's New Year's Eve at last, and the guests are drummed into the restaurant with great ceremony by the Bagamoyo college troupe. They make a spectacular appearance, with their multi-coloured headdresses and grass skirts. They've set up a levelled area on the river bank in front of the restaurant, and put on a simply stunning show. Fire-eating is followed by limbo dancing under a flaming bar set at impossibly low heights. Juggling and, of course, dancing and singing are highly interactive, and the guests are loving being dragged up to participate. I can see Mathilda playing along on her saxophone, but the actual sound is thankfully drowned out completely by the varied and very loud Tanzanian instruments. Unexpectedly, Sembuli appears at my side and whispers in my ear.

"We can hear gunfire nearby."

"What?"

I tell Candy, and then depart with Sembuli. We walk through staff quarters and towards the gate leading into the lodge grounds. Sure enough, now I can hear sporadic gunfire echoing through the pitch darkness.

"Where is the rest of the team?" I ask Sembuli urgently, and he gestures towards the staff canteen where I can see the heads of our security team peeking timidly from around the safety of the door.

I send Sembuli to patrol to the east, and rouse the unwilling team and instruct them to form a rough circle outward. I check that each person has his gun and a working radio.

"Do NOT, under any circumstances, fire at anything," I emphasize to them all, over and over again. I don't want this to turn into The Alamo. I grab my phone and call Stanley the Immigration Officer.

"Happy New Year," he bellows in my ear, but when I explain the reason for my call he mutters, "That's not good."

He tells me that he's in Arusha celebrating with his family but that he'll make a few calls. I can hear another burst of gun fire, and cut him off as he asks, "When can we meet for drinks, *kaka*?"

I check again that all the *askari* are in place, but cannot find Mumbi. Sembuli informs me that Mumbi is outraged at this, and has disappeared into the bush at a run towards the gun shots. This is not really what I need to hear. Mumbi could start a fight in an empty room. I run back to the restaurant and update Candy. Thankfully, the drumming and celebrations are so loud that the guests are blissfully unaware of any of our background drama.

As I return past the staff canteen, I see lights approaching along the road through the trees towards the gate. I can't see any *askaris,* and in desperation, I look about for a suitable weapon, settling on a hammer I find lying on a work bench. I take a deep breath and walk towards the lights. I can make out a *pikipiki* motorbike as it pulls up outside the gate, with two men in khaki trousers and T shirts. The driver has a Kalashnikov machine pistol strapped across his chest and his partner, who has dismounted from the bike, has another in his hand. With the hammer clenched tightly in my hand but held out of sight behind my back, I reach the gate.

Thinking confidence is the best approach I yell at the top of my voice, "What the fuck do you want?"

Our somewhat startled visitors look at each other and announce, "Stanley phoned us and asked us to rush here! We are the Tanga Police Department!"

"Happy New Year, guys." I beam at them, drawing breath at last, desperately stuffing the hammer down the back of my trousers. It's difficult to walk with a hammer in your trousers, but I open the gate and greet them with considerable relief, explaining the situation. A distinct burst of gunfire once again shatters the night, and we all turn sharply eastwards.

"Let us check it out," they tell me.

Just then, they're joined by the police Land Rover, a double-cab pick-up with four more heavily-armed officers seated in the open back. They all speed off in the direction of the gun fire. I return to the restaurant, taking care to remove the hammer from its hiding place down my pants, and give Candy the good news. The festivities are continuing full swing and I gratefully accept a Negroni cocktail from Saidi Saidi to settle my nerves. It's fast approaching midnight when my radio announces that the police Land Rover has returned.

I reply, "Roger that," and can only shake my head sadly when the voice from the radio says, "This is Sembuli, not Roger."

I make my way to the gate. Sargent Safari greets me

warmly. It's all okay, he assures me. They've discovered that an old man in the village has been celebrating the approaching New Year by drinking copious amounts of *Konyagi*, then walking into his garden and firing his machine gun wildly in the air. He's apparently retired from the army, and "forgot" to hand his weapon back in. Safari confirms that they've confiscated the weapon as well as his supply of Konyagi, and I can hear the old man singing happily from the back seat of the Land Rover, despite being manacled to two police officers. The Sargent further informs me that it was a very productive visit, as when they arrived at the old man's house, they were able to apprehend a Maasai whom they found beating three innocent neighbours with a stick. My horrible suspicion is confirmed as the Sargent pulls back the cover of the pick up to reveal Mumbi bound and handcuffed on the floor of the car. It takes me twenty minutes and a case of Kilimanjaro beer before a far from remorseful Mumbi is released into my custody, under threat of instant imprisonment should anything remotely like this be repeated. I call Stanley to thank him but cannot hear a word he says above the sound of background music. I instruct Sembuli to lock Mumbi in his room and return to the restaurant.

Ten, nine, eight... the countdown is on. The Rose twins, Saidi Saidi, Abedi, Jafari and the rest of the team are charging all the guests' glasses with champagne. Chichi lights the kerosene-soaked mattresses, and on the stroke of midnight from the deep, black darkness *2018* bursts into flame, illuminating the river in the background.

"Happy New Year!" echoes throughout the restaurant as guests from a multitude of different cultures hug, kiss, congratulate one other on survival in the bush, and welcome in the New Year. We all link arms and begin singing *Auld Lang Syne*, gently rocking back and forth. This congenial activity suffers a slight interruption as some of the Maasai join in, jumping high in the air, following their tradition, dragging everyone else completely out of rhythm. This then sparks off a jumping competition among the guests and the Maasai, which can only ever result in one result. No one on the planet can jump like the Maasai.

Gradually, the party winds down, and the guests are escorted back to their rooms. The staff clear up to make ready for tomorrow, and Candy and I sit, arm in arm, by the fire and reflect on another year spent in Africa. We agree between us that we now feel truly African—not because we were born in Africa, but because Africa has been born in us. Africa changes you forever like nowhere else on earth. Once you've been there, you'll never be the same again. At this moment of acknowledgment of time's inexorable passing, we hope the changes are for the better. But we feel, as well, that it's a kind of honour to be African. Africa has accepted us, we sense. A privilege. An honour.

***

Our Scottish Maasai Walk date is nearing, and we're delighted that our son, Kris, and wife, Kirsty, have arrived to join us. The staff go out of their way to welcome them, many arriving at the office to drop off gifts for their new *wazungu* friends: Maasai beaded cuffs and anklets with their names, misspelled, of course, but intricately and affectionately woven into the pattern. They're now identified as "Kiss" and "Christy," in much the same way as we remain forever known as "Cream" and "Mama Kandi."

Guests have been wonderfully generous, and by the morning of the walk, we've collected more than five thousand US dollars in donations. After the guests depart, Kris and I appear for breakfast in our tartan kilts, to be met with great hilarity by the staff.

Last year, Candy had noticed some of the Maasai children using a pile of building sand as a play place, and it dawned on us that they had never had the simple pleasure of a playground. So, we set out to rectify that in spectacular fashion, and together we designed and built a recycled playground for the school. We used all the old tires from the game drive cars, plus old metal fence posts, and managed to create an incredible, interactive play area with climbing frames, swings, balance beams and even a pile of old tires cemented together to recreate Mount Kilimanjaro, its top three tiers painted white to resemble the snows and topped by a flag pole flying the Tanzanian flag. The kids love it all, but unfortunately so do the teachers, and we have to constantly make repairs to the swings. They were designed for kids, not for two teachers at a time, and with their excess weight, they continually snap the ropes. I've told the Head Mistress she'll be put on the naughty chair if it happens again. I made clear that her *wowowo kubwa*— huge ass—is ill-designed for a kids' swing, an admonishment which receives only a huge roar of laughter and an entirely insincere promise to refrain in the future.

Candy feels like Mary Poppins each time we visit and she has up to ten children hanging on each hand as they drag her around the playground to demonstrate every new feat they've mastered. It's a joy to visit these kids. Nowhere else in Maasai land is there anything remotely like this. On one visit Candy kissed the back of a tiny girl's hand, leaving a clear imprint of her lips in lip gloss. The little girl stared at it in astonishment, then ran off to proudly display this weird piece of magic to her class mates.

We gather now in the car park, pre-walk. Our family has grown from Candy and me to include Kris and Kirsty; the chairman and chiefs from two villages; several elders; Ben, the walking guide; Ali, our head guide—who gravely informs me that someone has to keep me safe—several staff members; four guests; and Balloon Barry, a great friend of ours who is visiting with his wife and daughter from Canada and who wants to open a hot air balloon camp somewhere out in the wilds. We're waved off by remaining staff and exit the gate into the dense forest surrounding the rear of the lodge. I tell the guests that a bush walk is the only form of safari where you hope not to encounter a lion, but reassure them that they don't have to run faster than a lion—only faster than one of their companions. Old joke, but they love it anyway.

We leave the forest area without incident and begin to cross the wide-open plains. Dramatic umbrella acacia dot the landscape. Mount Kilimanjaro is in full view as she graces us with her presence. It's unusual for the peak to be so visible in the middle of the day, as most often she shows her face only in the early morning and late evening. The heat is also building. Zebra and Grant's gazelles eye us warily as we hike gently past them. A curious pair of giraffes pause from their morning browsing the acacia and watch every step as we wend our way down the dirt track. As usual, Ben and Ali see so much more than we do, and are constantly pointing out footprints, or "footy prints", as Ben calls them. Ali calls a halt, and stooping low, he eases up with a twig the flap of the trapdoor spider's lair. This ingenious spider lives in a hole in the ground that's covered by a hinged lid woven from its web. The vibration of any passing prey allows it to spring the lid and drag its prey down into the hole, to be devoured at leisure. On a walking safari, the little things that are impossible to see from a moving vehicle are astounding.

We pass next to a small village with goats grazing under the watchful eye of an eight-year-old boy. One male goat has the mud guard from a truck suspended beneath its belly and secured with a rope tied around its middle. When a guest questions the reason for this, we chuckle. Ben explains that the mud guard is "goat birth control" used to stop him "sexing the lady goats".

It's nearing midday when we finally reach the school. We're all delighted when a quick head count confirms that we're all alive and accounted for. There's much high-fiving. All of the children are gathered in the quadrangle, together with their teachers, to cheer our arrival. The Headmistress is enjoying one last turn on the playground swing before joining us, beaming with pleasure. She knows why we've come, and that a library with books and laptops will transform the learning capabilities for the children. She makes a speech which leaves us blushing. The chairman makes a speech, as well, and informs us that we are now truly Maasai.

I'm obliged to make a speech in return, which I end by presenting the chairman with my *Sgian-dubh* knife, which he has been eyeing throughout the walk. Just after cattle, goats and women, the Maasai really love a knife.

We promise to start the new library as soon as possible. Juma has arrived with two cars to drive us back, he has a cool box open, and we're all enjoying the coldest and most well-deserved beer ever. Once we manage to extricate Candy from the customary cloud of children vying for her hand and attention, we mount the cars and head back to the lodge. Not only have the guests enjoyed a unique experience of walking with some kilted madmen through the jungle, they've also experienced seeing the school, the children and the facilities— or, rather, lack of facilities. This can be a life-changing experience for some: both uplifting and upsetting. The guests pepper me with questions on the costs involved in schooling a child, and are astonished how little it represents for a person with a Western salary, but how impossible it can be for a Maasai with cows, but no income. We, as individuals, cannot change the world, but we can damned well try to make a dent in the poverty. I vow to Candy that we will always support this school and community, by hook or by crook.

The next day, Candy, Kris, Kirsty and I fly to Zanzibar. Kris and Kirsty are ending their visit with a few days on the Island, and Boss has managed to get us all two nights in The Park Hyatt in Stone Town. The hotel is a haven of air-conditioned paradise in the very centre of the hot and humid *Shangani* area. It's normally very much out of our price range, but Boss has even gotten us all upgraded to sea-view suites. He's a good man to know, our Boss.

We head for a drink to Mercury's Bar and, as expected, are accosted by *Mia Tano* (Five Hundred), an itinerant street vendor who doesn't actually even sell anything, but merely follows people, mumbling, *"mia tano"* repeatedly until he finally wears them down. I give him a thousand shillings, and he shakes his head vigorously, pointing at his chest, yelling *"Mimi, Mia Tano!"* ("I am Five Hundred!") and gives me my change before he stalks off. We've known him for years, but inflation means nothing to Mia. Kris finds this hilarious, and we retreat to the relative safety of Mercury's Bar, which overlooks the harbour and ferry port. As we sip our cocktails, it's slightly incongruous to watch the sun dipping red over the Indian Ocean, with the silhouettes of traditional dhows on the horizon contrasting with the Superfast Kilimanjaro IV ferry from Dar Es Salaam—sleek, ultra-modern, and, as the name suggests, super-fast, effortlessly passing them on its way to docking before us.

Kris and Kirsty are leaving very early the next day, so we try to spin out the hours, as we're greedy for their company. They'll return to the hustle and modernity of Shanghai, while we remain in the relative peace and simplicity of the bush. Back inside the lobby of the cool, sophisticated Park Hyatt, we hug each other tightly and confirm that we'll come to visit in a few months' time. We part with tears, and Candy and I walk to our room, hand in hand, missing them already. I wince a little as she squeezes my hand tightly. I look for the cause of the small pain, but there's only a small red dot on my wedding ring finger—an insect bite, most likely.

Candy hugs me tightly and whispers through her tears, "Remember what Old Mohamed once told us? 'Don't be dismayed at goodbyes; a farewell is necessary before you can meet again,' he said. Remember?"

Meeting again, after moments or lifetimes, is certain for those who are as close as we are, in our family. Just a temporary farewell until we meet again. Old Mohamed is a wise man, and always offers genuine comfort, a reliable easing of our small agonies. Nothing hurts, though, quite like goodbye.

CHAPTER 13
HOW CANDY SEES IT

Kris and Kirsty have departed from Zanzibar to Shanghai. It's always so hard to watch them leave. We ourselves were also scheduled to depart the Park Hyatt, but life is rarely that simple, and now we'll need to stay awhile longer. At least it's in paradise.

Sitting alone on the poolside with this dazzling view over the Indian ocean, my customary *"dawa"* cocktail in hand, I find myself reflecting on my life here in Africa. Coincidentally, Graeme has gone to have his own special *dawa*—the Swahili word for "medicine"—at the local hospital. His sore finger has turned out to be a bite from a violin spider, also known as the brown recluse, and toxic as hell. The bite has turned decidedly nasty—a tiny nibble from a tiny creature in the middle of the African bush, representing a level of danger we've so far managed to avoid while living among lions and hyenas and other large, perilous wildlife. Ironic, I muse. Africa supplies surprises every day, most of which are among the many reasons we've settled here in Tanzania, far away from our native Scotland. Some surprises, however, remind us that Nature is still in charge here, however much we may think we've brought our more "civilized" expertise with us into the bush. She challenges and tests us every day, and we live always at her convenience and at her mercy.

These musings lead me to an infrequent examination of

the complex feelings I experienced all those years ago when we first arrived here in Africa, and of the perhaps less complex feelings I have about our life choices now that this is well and truly my home.

I remember, as though it were yesterday, the night we landed at Kilimanjaro airport in Arusha. I was feeling somewhat apprehensive, not unsurprisingly. It had always been Graeme's dream to have more African adventures, and he wanted to share with me the sights, sounds and smells that up until then I had only been able to imagine from hearing his colourful stories. Movies like *Out of Africa* can give you an insight into what life is like here, but you have to actually be here to truly understand its magic. And, sometimes, its tragedies.

The intense heat hits me as we disembark from the plane. This is the first, most immediate contrast to my life in Scotland. There will be, I sense, many more to follow.

My very first impression upon entering the arrivals area of Kilimanjaro International Airport is the huge crowd of people, and the equally huge and reassuring number of smiles! Gordon's own unique, special smile is easy to spot, but, of course, his six-foot four-inch frame and shock of curly hair makes him pretty hard to miss. Hugs and kisses, and our bags deposited in his car, and we're off into the dark—to me, both literally and figuratively. Gordon proves eager to introduce us to his life and friends here. He's no doubt also eager for our help with the hare-brained scheme he's cooked up to buy tanzanite stones, about which he's been very light on detail. He chatters all the way to the hotel, thrilled that we've come.

***

Over the years I've often been asked, particularly by visitors from Western countries, what I miss most of the life I had before. Before Africa! That's an easy one, as I miss my family and friends tremendously. Missing those we love who live at a distance is one of life's most aching challenges, and so I'm deeply grateful for the modern technology which allows me to stay in touch with loved ones. Nothing, of course, can replace the hugs and the warmth of the face-to-face human interaction we used to share with people we've known all our lives—interactions we even took for granted. I'm aware, of course, that what I sometimes miss is a unique, private version of "home"—a massed collection of every happy memory of half a lifetime, of which I have so many. And so, when returning home for a visit, I sometimes feel vaguely disappointed, as things and people change, and time moves on. I am reminded that life is impermanent, that home really is the place we love and the people we love, and that we can have many homes in our lives.

***

Once we settle into our new home and new life, we quickly adopt our new Tanzanian family; the everyday problems, struggles, life stories, weddings, funerals and births of our staff members all now involve us. Issues large and small absorb our attention: Is Rose *Kubwa* in love? Jafari's little sister needs shoes. We are going into Tanga for supplies; could we please buy Saidi Saidi a bell for his bicycle? Soudi's mother has died. Zaina visited her husband in town and now she is pregnant! Strangely, other little things I miss at first seem to take on less and less significance as we slide inevitably into this new life, this new way of living, this new way of noticing as time passes by. What I saw as essentials at home have now become luxuries. Necessities evolve into mere niceties. We are learning resilience and the fine African art of resourcefulness.

One thing I realize pretty quickly is that life can be very tough here, and if I am to survive, I'm going to have to be tough, too. At first, especially, things and situations can be overwhelming when you don't know what to expect. I quickly learn to expect the unexpected every day.

It becomes obvious early on that, when Graeme enticed me out here, he had been a little economical with the truth. His description of Tanzania had strongly suggested that life would be "easy" since "everyone" spoke English. This was equivocation at its least defensible. As it turns out, almost no one speaks English, and I'm thrust into a world where I must navigate among Kiswahili, Maa, and their admirable, if often hilarious, efforts at English, which can determine the outcome of even the most insignificant events of my day.

Graeme's description of the local hairdressing options fell way short of my expectations, as well. I discover that the "saloons" are mostly staffed by people entirely unfamiliar with the needs of a blonde Scottish girl with far too little hair to plait, and of what they clearly regard as a puzzling texture.

I've been fortunate to travel to many parts of the world, but this has been my first time living away from my home country of Scotland, and I can see at once that the contrasts between Scotland and Tanzania are vast. Here, I have witnessed poverty of a kind one rarely finds elsewhere, and I've often been overcome with guilt and sadness at the realization that we in the West seem to have created a throwaway society, with access to an abundance of things and services, yet so many of us remain dissatisfied with our lives. We seem to constantly seek more, and then more, and the entire notion of *value* begins to lose its meaning. We seem always to be living for the future, for that bigger house or newer car, yet here I am living among people who have almost literally nothing and yet remain deeply grateful just for life itself. They embrace the day with a smile and with tremendous optimism. When things do go wrong—even when coping with the inevitable pain of human mortality—their sorrow, though real, is mitigated by the simple acceptance of the fact that some things are out of our hands, and are part of the circle of life itself. They say, at such moments, *"Maisha."* "That's life." They do not say this ironically, as we do in the West, but reverently, with gratitude and love.

What is a bit ironic, however, is that the first person I ever heard say, *"Maisha,"* in exactly this context, was Ann, a lady from Denmark who had arrived at our lodge, on Christmas Day. She'd been due to arrive at eight a.m. on a charter flight, and our driver/guide was prepared to collect her from the airstrip. Just as the vehicle was about to depart, we received a call from the charter company to advise us that the plane had already landed at our airstrip. It would have been helpful if we'd been given advance warning of this change of arrival time, as now the guest would be forced to wait to be picked up, which was not our normal practice. We were very concerned, especially, as the guest was a single female traveller. We dispatched the vehicle immediately and made quick preparation for Ann's arrival.

Ann arrived soon after, and we were there to greet her with a refreshing scented face towel and welcome drink. She was a very elegant, slender lady, in her sixties, with shoulder-length silver hair, wearing an olive-green chiffon dress and beige safari hat. We offered our apologies for not being on time to meet her, and she waved the apologies away.

"I grew up in Africa, and I was delighted to have that extra time at the airstrip just to soak everything in again. The smells, the sounds and the sights of the beautiful trees and plants and landscape. Please don't fret. Everything is perfect."

We gave her the usual safety briefing and said we would see her again once she had settled in. A few hours later I walked into the bar and found Ann lying across some chairs fast asleep. Poor soul, I thought. She must be exhausted from traveling, and must have been up early to catch the morning flight. As I passed by, her eyes opened and she gave me a faint smile. I crouched down beside her and asked if she was okay. Did she need anything?

She took my hand and told me in a gentle tone, "My dear, I am dying. I have cancer. I only found out six months ago, and I do not have long. It was my wish to return to the country where I grew up. I want to swim one last time in the Indian Ocean, to see the red soils of Africa and to hear the cries of the fish eagle. I do not want to spend my last days staring at the bland grey walls of a hospice in Copenhagen."

I had only known this lady for five minutes, and yet my eyes filled with tears.

"Don't be sad," Ann said. "*Maisha*."

She told me that she had been lucky enough to have enjoyed a wonderful life, and that now was simply her time to pass. She told me that her daughter and son-in-law would be joining her in two days' time. We took very special care of Ann, but could see that she was struggling. She went downhill rapidly after her daughter arrived, but we still managed to organize a trip for her to visit the ocean and feel the waves wash over her one last time.

It turned out that we had to arrange for an earlier flight than planned for her to return to Denmark. We had grown very fond of Ann, and admired her bravery and great spirit. Graeme had to carry her onto the plane. I came up behind them, as well, to say goodbye. She smiled, and wished us a long and happy life in Africa. Although we were very sad, we were comforted by the fact that Ann had finished the last chapter of her life exactly as she had wanted. I will never again swim in the Indian Ocean without thinking of her. Her daughter sent us a beautiful email to let us all know that Ann had died only one day after arriving back in Denmark. She had said goodbye to her beloved Africa, and it was indeed, as she had known, her time to pass. *Maisha*, Ann.

***

I remain cursed with a powerful urge to "fix" everything, and I suspect I always will. And yet I realize, as well, that one individual can do only so much, and I sometimes find myself slipping into a debilitating sadness. These moments are increasingly rare, as I'm learning my limits, and I'm coming slowly to terms with the new balance of values that Africa is teaching me. I have determined that if I can do one kind act a day, I can make a difference. And I'm finding that it is making a difference that matters, in the end.

One day when I was strolling along the beach, I came across an old fisherman casting his net from the shores into the sea. He was barefoot, and wore a blue t-shirt pocked with holes, and long grey shorts. We chatted for a while in Swahili, that lovely language with which I am at last beginning to feel comfortable. He brought in his small catch of the day, which consisted largely of leaves, sticks, general *takataka* (rubbish) from the ocean, and, amongst this refuse, a few *daga*, the small local fish similar to white bait. I noticed that his net was very old, and even the repaired holes in it were resulting in this fisherman losing a lot of his catch. I offered to buy him a new one from the village. The cost, at ten American dollars, was prohibitive to him, but nothing to me. His smile took my breath away. An African proverb has it that the cheapest way to improve your looks is to wear a smile. His face must have been, that afternoon, the most beautiful face on the planet.

I met this fisherman again two weeks later and he told me that not only was he catching enough fish to feed his family, but he was also now able to sell some, and with this extra income, he was sending his little girl to school. My small contribution had helped an entire family, and perhaps created a future for a child to which she otherwise would have had no possible access. In a place like Tanzania, poverty is often a matter of the little things: holes in a fishing net, a bicycle tire, a broken sewing machine. No individual can change a world, but one individual could compensate for the holes in a fishing net and send a little girl to school. The recognition of how easy it would be for me to make a genuine difference in people's lives here—far more easily and far more often than I ever could in my old life in Scotland—was a revelation. I had felt overwhelmed by the poverty, and suddenly I was overwhelmed with joy.

It's funny how often people will tell me that they feel more alive when they're in Africa. Especially since, in many ways, we're also quite often nearer death! But that sensation of being "more alive" is very real. I think our senses are heightened, that colours seem brighter, the smell of the earth after the rains is intoxicating, and all of the sounds of the wildlife and birds remind you that we're a part of their world here. And, since we're living in their world, we're not completely in control—we really do have to be alert, aware, tuned in. And fully open to the joy.

***

I'm thinking, suddenly, of Jafari, who, on our first day managing the lodge for Boss, walked into the bar from the beach looking for a job— "doing anything," he said. We were in need of some wait staff in the bar and restaurant and, after a brief interview, offered him a job there and then. We asked him to start that same evening, and assured him that he'd receive good training, and that all we asked of him is that he work hard and listen well.

On that very first night, Jafari displayed a talent for hospitality. He appeared in a borrowed white shirt and borrowed black trousers, and looked every bit the elegant waiter! He had a wonderful personality, a great work ethic and, of course, one of those beautiful, infectious smiles. I knew then that we'd found someone with a great future ahead of him, and, indeed, this turned out to be prophetic. He was a star, a natural. He soon became our most popular and efficient waiter. But this wasn't enough for Jafari; he had ambition, and he wanted to improve his future. During a visit with us, our son, Sean, gifted him a book called *Computers for Beginners,* and took some time to sit with him, and teach him the basics of computer use.

Not long after, Jafari asked us if he could train on reception and reservation duties. He did this in his own free time, and whenever you spotted Jafari in the lodge, this book was constantly by his side. When the opportunity presented itself, he became our Guests Relations manager, and did a truly superb job for us. In fact, he did so well interacting with many large international agencies, that it wasn't long before he was poached by one of them. With our blessing, and with a lot of coaching from us before his interview, off he went to Arusha to start his new career as a reservation consultant, tripling his salary. We were bursting with pride, as we remembered his first day wandering into the lodge from the beach on the off-chance we would hire him. He thanked Graeme for the opportunity he'd been given and told us that his family regarded Graeme as a prophet, dropped from the sky and sent to Earth to lead him by example.

Tearfully, I waved him off on his way to the big city. With a single, small act of kindness, we had made a major difference to yet another young life. We still stay very much in touch with Jafari, and when he got married, we gave him, as a wedding gift, a night in a five-star hotel in Arusha in the Honeymoon Suite. He and his new bride were blown away. It's great sometimes to be the guest, after so long serving. On one of Graeme's birthdays, we received the following message from Jafari: "Mr Graeme, *Bwana Mkubwa*, *Simba wa Nyika*, the Big Enchilada, a baron, an eminence, a leading light, prime mover, a magnate, a very happy birthday to you and all I wish is for you to enjoy the day *kama kawaida*, take care and be safe." We're still not entirely sure what all of it means, but we do get the drift, and enjoyed the sentiment. We love you, too, Jafari.

Living here has allowed us not only to help individuals,

but also to contribute to whole communities and—most importantly—to schools in the area. I'm thinking quite specifically of one of our first visits to a Maasai *manyatta*. The children were so excited to see us, and we were equally excited to be invited to witness our first Maasai wedding. One little girl, braver than the rest, approached me and took my hand. The *mzungu* Mama with the strange blonde hair was a little scary to some of the children, but not to her. She was particularly interested in the wing mirror of our 4 x 4, as in it, she could see her reflection, causing her to giggle and making me giggle along with her. I took my makeup bag out of my day pack, and produced my compact mirror, and was suddenly surrounded by an entire audience of tiny little girls taking turns with the mirror, sloppily applying my best lipsticks—though not always to their lips—and shrieking with delight at the results. As happens to me so often in Africa, I fell in love.

Now, whenever I return from our overseas vacations or visits home, I always bring back all the "freebies" from hotels we stay in. Small things like cotton buds, sewing kits, emery boards, shower caps, shampoo, tooth brushes, hair conditioner, shower gel, lotions and potions invariably cause great excitement when I give them to the girls, and a surge of pleasure for me. They chatter and babble for hours on end, and not infrequently invent new and creative uses for very ordinary items we westerners have never contemplated. It brought, for example, a new meaning to fashion when Rose *Dogo* turned up on duty one evening festively sporting a plastic shower cap. Somehow, she managed to make it look beautiful and elegant, as she wore it with a confidence which entirely stifled my every urge to giggle.

One evening, three female guests from Boston were

sitting in the bar discussing earnestly and in great detail the relative merits of Jimmy Choo's over Manolo Blahnik, and I overheard them asking the Rose twins what would be their favourite shoes? This kicked off a long and heated debate in Swahili between the twins which ended when Rose *Kubwa* pronounced, "We both agree we would best like red."

***

I discovered early that our guests were eager to hear how I've adapted to living here. They're curious about the daily challenges I face, and what differences I've noticed between the two cultures. They basically want to know how I have managed to fit into African ways.

One of the first and biggest set of challenges and obstacles I had to face, I always tell them, was management of the male staff. Most of these guys are Maasai or Muslim, and they simply didn't take kindly to being bossed around by a woman. I'd managed male staff before, in Scotland, and had never had any problems or issues with respect to hierarchy, even in that bastion of European macho. I had witnessed, on the other hand, many other female managers who constantly screamed at their staff and were in a permanent state of stress. And so, I had deliberately determined that my own style of management would not be that one. Here in Africa, with a large staff which was predominately male, I knew I had to find a way of being able to get the guys to do what I needed from them, without driving either them or myself crazy.

I had instructed one of our *fundi*s to quickly repair some window shutters, as new guests were arriving soon for that room. Thirty minutes later, I returned to discover that the job had still not been done. I waited another thirty minutes, checked again, and was dismayed to find the job still unfinished. At this point, I asked Graeme to instruct him to do it, and—unsurprisingly—it was done within five minutes! How frustrating! I was livid, but again realized that I alone am not going to change a culture. The male staff liked me, and, indeed, I was "Mama Candy" to them all, but to be their boss was going to be tough. I had to find ways of getting the jobs done with the least possible stress for everyone.

One trick was simply to say, "Graeme needs this job to be done today," and—hey, presto—the job was done! Another useful tactic was to tell them that I couldn't work out how to do something, knowing all along what I needed done. They'd be wonderfully enthusiastic, even competing with one another to help Mama Candy solve her little problem. They'd make suggestions and we'd then discuss solutions, and somehow, I'd get what I wanted, as long as I allowed them to believe it had been their idea or plan all along. They have no issues with work, as such, or with showing off their "superior" abilities; it's only acknowledging a woman as holding a higher "rank" that they find objectionable! I do, however, still try to do my bit for "girl power", especially in lending as much support as possible to empower the girls and ladies who work beside us at the lodge, encouraging them to join our committees to represent the "gentle" sex.

And representing the "gentle" sex was Halima—perhaps the gentlest, most reserved young lady I'd ever known—who joined us for a time at the lodge. The very first day I met her was when she appeared for an interview in the manager's office. She introduced herself with a trembling voice and downcast eyes. So nervous she was physically shaking,

Halima was dressed in a long black robe, complete with hijab. A perfect young Muslim daughter, shy and gentle and lovely.

This would be a new experience for her—to be out of her village, mixing with terrifying *wazungu*. However, before long she began to settle in, and slowly gained confidence. She started out in the Housekeeping Department, showing real enthusiasm and an impressive willingness to learn. We'd soon discover, however, that she was willing to learn a lot more than her work duties. We noticed that one of our carpenters had taken to giving Halima a transfer on his *pikipiki* anytime she needed to leave the lodge for her days off. He was married, so we thought no more about it, considering that Halima was such a sweet, gentle, innocent girl.

One day, the two Roses approached me after one of our committee meetings. They asked if I had the time to discuss something that they had not wanted to raise at the meeting.

"Of course," I said. "What's the problem?"

They told me that they were having problems with little Halima. She was sneaking out at night to have *jigi jigi* with the carpenter, and then disturbing their sleep when she arrived back at four or five a.m. and crawled back in through the window. This was not acceptable, they pronounced solemnly. *Jigi jigi* was one thing, but waking them up was just unacceptable. They had therefore locked the window, and she was now very angry with them. So angry, in fact, that they were now scratching all day! This had me completely baffled.

"What on earth do you mean?" I asked.

"Well," replied Rose Mdogo, "She has been putting itching powder onto our underwear as a punishment for us being so mean to her."

"Okay," I thought to myself, "how am I ever going to deal

199

with this one?"

Fortunately, Halima was due for a few days off, so I decided to deal with her when she returned. I'll never know for sure exactly what happened, but Halima never did come back. I was sad about this, as she had a lot of potential; she was learning a lot. It may be that she'd been learning too much, as it happens. In the bush, the staff may sometimes have their own courts of law, which does not always involve us. We have learned not to interfere.

It's not only the local men with whom I've had my challenges, I tell my curious guests, remembering with glorious amusement an incident which occurred while we had some repeat visitors from Arusha who were spending a few days with us.

Maddie was a lady with her mobile phone constantly in hand, and constantly ringing, as she directed her Arusha business loudly and fiercely in the tranquillity of the bush. Between calls, she asked for a mojito, which Saidi Saidi, our magnificent mega mixologist, could make with his eyes closed and which he produced in mere seconds with his customary flourish. Maddie, however, did not judge our mint leaves to be of a quality fresh enough for use as the garnish for her cocktail, and demanded they be changed! We knew from past experience that it usually took this perpetually stressed and uptight woman a couple of days to relax from the routine worries and problems of managing her design business in Arusha. It always took her some time, along with a few mojitos, to wind down to the pace of the bush life, where things are done at a more relaxed and *pole pole* pace.

This was as fresh as she was going to get from us in the matter of mint leaves, so I decided to check with some of the neighbouring lodges and villages to see if they might have any fresher ones available—a tall ask in the middle of the African bush. I called around to a few friends and acquaintances, with no luck. When I spoke with Alex, a nice man from Germany who, together with his wife, ran a lodge reasonably nearby, he seemed a little annoyed at my asking him if his mint leaves were very fresh.

"Of course," he replied indignantly.

Assuming I'd offended him, I asked if we could borrow some and, mollified, he agreed, saying he'd have it ready at Reception for pickup. Delighted with this success, I asked Graeme to drive over quickly to collect the mint leaves so that Maddie could properly enjoy her mojito, pre-dinner, garnished with appropriately fresh mint leaves.

After what seemed like an eternity, Graeme returned with a great, big smile on his face, carrying a large cool box containing packages of minced beef which Alex had proudly presented him. Between my Scottish accent, a bad phone signal, and Alex's somewhat intermittent understanding of the English language, a certain miscommunication had occurred, resulting in Alex instructing his chef to sort out, not "mint leaves," but, rather, some nice, very fresh "minced beef."

I sought out Maddie.

"You have a choice, it seems," I told her. "We can give you a mojito with the very best mint leaves we have available to us here in the bush, or, if you prefer, we can prepare one with some very fresh minced beef courtesy of the owner of our neighbouring lodge."

When I explained what had happened, Maddie roared with laughter, sudden tears streaming down her face. She had started to melt. Her big city standards were at once replaced by the simplicity of the bush, and in her immediate future appeared a mojito thoroughly enjoyed as much for the joy of its setting as for its flavour. *Pole pole.*

***

"Wow," exclaimed my guests. "Tell us more! How do you get your hair cut? Where do you go for facials or to have your manicures?"

I laughed. I had forgotten what "essentials" were back home. Here, they had become luxuries in my mind—rather at the bottom of my list of priorities. Niceties, as opposed to necessaries! And so I gave them an account of my first experience at a Tanzanian "Hair Saloon" in Tanga.

Graeme had been getting his hair cut there for some time now and the "stylist" had always done a great job. He was known as the "Burnt Barber," as he had once set himself on fire in some bizarre sort of protest, after discovering his wife was being unfaithful to him. He was now badly disfigured, but still wielded the fastest scissors in Tanga.

So, I bravely asked, "Can you cut ladies' hair too?"

His reply, of course, was, "Of course."

I should have asked, "Can you cut ladies' hair well?" but would likely have received the same reply. My hair was styled in a shoulder length bob, and I asked him to simply follow the lines and just trim an inch all the way round. I was horrified when he chopped at least 4 inches from each side of my face! STOP I screamed. He looked hurt and insulted. I didn't care. This was no time to be diplomatic. Was I about to be given a bowl cut? Graeme helpfully suggested that I looked like an East German football player from the 1980's. I was, for many

202

months, somehow able to tie my hair up and disguise the amputated parts with grips, and I vowed that my visits to local "Hair Saloons" were permanently over. Hair appointments would have to wait until my days off, when I would be able to visit somewhere more suitable. Fortunately, I eventually found a great place in Dar es Salaam where they give great haircuts, and offer manicures and pedicures, as we know them, as well—all carried out while I sip an ice-cold Sauvignon Blanc. Heaven!

I still laugh whenever I recall receiving a parcel via Boss's office in Dar Es Salaam a few months later. He'd told me that someone had posted me a package from the United States. I was so excited. What could it possibly be? I wondered.

It turned out to be, in fact, a kind of "care package" from the lovely three ladies to whom I'd recounted my hair saloon visit. They'd felt such pity for me that they'd sent some fabulous lotions and potions to help me get through my bush days. How very sweet of them. I always love to chat with my female guests. I miss my friends at home a lot, since discussing girly things with Graeme simply does not afford the same level of satisfaction, and cultural differences prevent the local women, however much we do have in common, from understanding some of the issues which bind the friendships of western women.

Graeme is mostly great company, as it's virtually impossible to embarrass him, though he never quite knows what to say when I ask, "Does my bum look big in this?" He does try his best, though, to deal with a wife who lacks sufficient outlets for her girly instincts, and is tolerant enough even to join me often in watching "chick flicks" without ever sighing in impatience or exasperation. One of a kind, my Graeme.

I've been thinking a lot lately about the death of our dear friend, Gordon, after we'd been with him here for only three months, and how strange it seems that his death had been the real beginning of my love affair with Africa. The way the local people supported us and helped us in our hour of need made a powerful impression on me, and I knew then that I was not ready to leave these African shores. Hemingway once said that he envied the man who had not yet been to Africa as he has much to look forward to. Now I get it. I understand him so well. It was the start of a new chapter for us, and that was exciting as we began our new adventure. I can still hear the moving words so many of the local villagers said to us on the day we buried Gordon: *"Tupa pamoja."* We are together.

Even after all this time I am alternately overwhelmed and inspired by the fortitude of the African people—especially of the women, who carry such a large part of the burden for the well-being of the family. If wealth were the inevitable result of hard work, then every woman in Africa would be a millionaire. I drove recently through a very poor area and was overcome with a compelling sense of the injustices inflicted on our world, and when I returned to the lodge, I retired to our house, and took pen to paper:

They have the money,
Therefore, they have the power,
We are quickly losing it -
Hour by hour.

We post, we "like" we "share,"

But how much do we really care?
Our charities, our NGOs,
Our donations end up where?
No one really knows!

The billionaires grow richer,
Politics—a dirty word,
People are dying, children are crying,
But they are never heard.
So where do we go from here?
We could love, instead of hate,
But we need to do it quickly,
Because the planet will not wait.

Sipping my cocktail, I watch the distant dhows sail slowly past the lodge, with the moon's glow reflecting on the still ocean, and I wonder what the next chapter of our African adventure has in store for us.

Graeme returns now, hand bandaged and supported by a sling. He orders two margaritas for himself and another *dawa* for me, and sighs. When I enquire how his hand is, he reaches for his margarita before replying that what little confidence he'd had in the doctor had evaporated when he spun the doctor's laptop around on the desk to discover the doc had googled "what is this?" with a photo of Graeme's hugely swollen hand. I then hear how Graeme had directed his own operation, with only a pain-killing injection, as he refused to be put under anaesthesia, insisting that they cut open his hand to release the venom while he watched. Following this, the doctor had inserted twenty-six sutures and re-bandaged the hand. While relaxing, enjoying an intravenous drip of a cocktail of antibiotics to counter the onset of necrosis, Graeme had received a mobile call from his South African friend, Shaun. Shaun is an expert on insects and snakes, and using a photo I'd sent him earlier, he was able to diagnose the problem as a bite from the potentially deadly violin spider. The recommendation from Shaun was that it should be cut open immediately and the venom drained. Under no circumstances, however, should the wound be stitched closed, as this could lead to complications up to and including the need to amputate.

Suppressing the urge to throttle the doctor, Graeme returned to the surgery to have all twenty-six stitches removed. This time without the painkiller as his hand was now too swollen to inject one.

"What else did he say?" I ask, when he has disconnected from the call.

Graeme chuckles. "He advises me to have three large margaritas," he says, signalling the barman and holding up three fingers.

I sigh, and reflect on a typically African bit of wisdom: "She that beats the drum for the mad man to dance is no better than the mad man himself."

CHAPTER 14
STORIES FROM AROUND THE CAMP FIRE

We finally made it back to the relative safety of Mashetani Ridge Lodge after an unexpected week's delay. My spider bite had seemed determined to resist every antibiotic thrown at it, resulting in a need for seven days of intravenous drips, morning and evening. As I refused to stay in the hospital overnight, and Boss had kindly extended our stay at the Park Hyatt, I commuted each morning and evening in a three-wheeled *bajaji* taxi and was waved off and greeted back from each trip by the entire Hyatt staff, who were uniformly fascinated by my predicament. *Mzee Mkono Makubwa*, or "Sir Big Hand", as I had been dubbed, was required to give a detailed daily briefing on the day's procedures to the assembled staff crowding around me in the hotel foyer, and who, in their excitement, would be completely ignoring their waiting guests at Reception. I felt I had to oblige my audience, despite being fairly certain that overhearing my gruesome tale did little to fortify their overseas guests' sense of the relative safety of this island paradise.

Candy took advantage of this unexpected holiday extension and the rare opportunity to relax for hours by the pool or in the spa—at least, when she wasn't called upon to trawl the pharmacies of Stone Town in search of the day's latest antibiotic that "Dr Google" was frantically prescribing. Naturally, the hospital pharmacy did not stock any of these, so

Candy, with the enthusiastic assistance of the *bajaji* driver who was delightedly earning a relative fortune from my misfortune, explored the back streets of the downtown Shangani area in search of my ever-changing daily fix. Candy will now and forever have a taxi driver's intimate knowledge of the tiny back streets of Stone Town.

It was, then, a great relief when my hand gradually returned to a semblance of normal size and colour, as eventually the good doctor struck lucky with his most recent prescription. They say that even a broken clock is correct twice a day, so it is with satisfaction and gratitude that we've now finally waved a fond farewell to the staff, carefully avoiding the ritual shaking of hands, and made our way to the airport to journey back to the lodge, hopefully in time for the afternoon guest arrivals' flight and sundowners by the fire.

***

Flying the plane once again is our Belgian friend, Benji. Often, when he's with a charter group, he'll stay overnight at the lodge and then continue on with his guests as they weave their "flying safari" through the hot spots of all the Tanzanian and Kenyan safari destinations. Occasionally, he'll join us for sundowners by the fire, or dine with us and our guests in the evening. While this can be entertaining, it's always slightly fraught with danger, as Benji has lived and flown in Africa so long and in such exotic and often dangerous places that the bizarre has become normal to him. Moreover, he has absolutely no filter or recognition that what he says may frighten someone with limited exposure to the less advertised delights of the African bush.

I should perhaps explain that the "sundowner" is a uniquely African safari experience, a revered daily ritual which should be more widely adopted throughout the world, as it's the perfect way to end a day. Candy is fond of advising guests that, "Sunrises and sunsets are absolutely free. Please make sure you see as many as possible. You can never get them back."

At Mashetani Lodge we usually gather for sundowners around a fire pit that's been dug into the river bank a little in front of the restaurant, expertly positioned for a beautiful view of the river as well as the spectacular sight of sunset over Mount Kilimanjaro. An hour or so before the sun sets, at the end of another day full of fantastic safari experiences, the staff place the safari camp chairs—wooden folding chairs with green canvas seats—in a semi-circle around the fire pit, facing the river and the setting sun, and here we all gather to enjoy our own favourite sundowner drinks. On offer will be everything from the classic gin-and-tonic to the dawa safari cocktail to the beloved ice-cold beer served in a frozen glass. We always have small snacks or "bitings" as they're known in lodge-land. It's a rare moment on a safari vacation where you're not being offered food and drinks—a holiday experience like no other. And during the traditional sundowners, guests will have the opportunity to share their experiences, not only of the day's sightings, but of their extended safari or even their lives. Africa has a kind of spiritual aspect, often triggering introspection. It can combine a sense of peace with a simultaneous and contrasting thrill of suspense or anticipation in a way few other places in the world can produce. There's no question but that it has a remarkable effect on many people. Some save their entire life to have one safari experience. Others will succumb to the bite of the safari bug and will return to Africa time and again, at every opportunity. But very few are indifferent to the safari experience. For many people, Africa engenders a response capable of profoundly changing their worldview.

Candy once observed a single lady traveller from Germany dining alone at lunch time, quietly crying. Approaching the guest, Candy asked if she was okay or needed some assistance. Heidi, a doctor from Berlin, smiled and replied that this was the thirtieth anniversary of the reunification of East and West Germany. She had been a trainee doctor on the east side of the wall, and remembered that day very clearly. She was now recalling her feelings that day, and how before then she could never have dreamed of being free to visit Tanzania and to witness the stunning natural beauty of Africa. She hugged Candy, explaining that she was feeling so blessed and fortunate that she'd been overcome with emotion.

***

Africa has the power to leave you speechless, but it has the potential, as well, to turn us all into storytellers.

The show isn't over when we return to the lodge after sundown, and the animals don't just conveniently depart for the day. Our *askaris* are always on patrol, and constantly have an eye on the river, particularly at this time of night when hippos become more active. Though appearing clunky and awkward, hippopotamuses are responsible for more deaths in Africa than any other creature, save for the mosquito. They are the angry vegetarians of the bush, and it's not uncommon for us to have to quickly grab our drinks and run to the restaurant if hippos decide to come out of the river for an evening stroll.

Indeed, this evening we can see a pod of seven hippos heading our way. I advise the guests that we should head in before they arrive, and one guest argues that, "Surely, they'll be afraid of the fire? Don't all animals fear fire?"

"Well," I reply, "why not just stay seated and test out your theory? You'll find me in the safety of the bar, though." Then, thinking better of the potential danger that he'd take me seriously, I added, "I'd really recommend you follow my advice."

Reluctantly, he follows me inside, and as we turn to watch from the bar entrance, the hippos march straight through the seats we'd just occupied, knocking them in all directions, totally unimpressed by the fire. Happily grazing in the lush riverside grass, they represent a massive wall of powerful flesh, fearing absolutely nothing. We watch for some time as they nibble delicately at the grasses before waddling awkwardly onwards. These comical killers may look clumsy and ludicrous, but they can outrun a man and snap him in two with one mighty bite.

"Well, I will be damned," I hear the guest mutter.

"Aye, *The Lion King* has a lot to answer for," I reply, not a little amused. "I think the lion may be overstating his position in the hierarchy."

With the coast clear once again, we all return to pick up our seats and settle back in around the fire. Benji joins us and I make introductions, explaining that he works as a bush pilot. Almost all our guests fly between camps and lodges throughout the northern circuit, coastal and southern Tanzania due to the distances and terrible roads. Our guests present a flurry of questions, as few people have ever really had an opportunity to chat with a bush pilot. The inevitable questions begin:

"Are these planes safe?"

Not many people have prior experience flying in four, six, or twelve-seat planes, let alone landing on grass strips cut from surrounding jungle and bush, and often populated by herds of wild animals.

"Sure," replies Benji. "Fuck, I've only crashed once or twice in my life," he asserts proudly, reaching for his beer.

I try to fill the uneasy silence by ensuring that everyone has full glasses, and then attempt to steer the conversation onto safer ground. While Candy and I have heard all of Benji's tales before, despite the initial alarm they first produced, we've found his stories overall very reassuring, as all these charter companies offer extremely safe and professional operations. The guests, however, have no way of determining Benji's reliability, making for entertainment even beyond the stories themselves.

"Pray, tell us more," says a slightly flustered and clearly sceptical retired accountant from Washington DC.

Given the green light, Benji launches into his tale about the time he was flying from the Serengeti to Arusha in a six-seater Cessna 206 when the one and only engine had cut out mid-flight. Aboard was a single, sweet, French honeymoon couple, and he turned to instruct them to ensure that their seat belts were tightly fastened.

"I'll be busy for a little while, so please try not to disturb me," he advised. "I need to concentrate a bit. But don't worry—it's all under control."

He turned back to his controls, initiating a downward

212

glide, slowly losing speed as he also lost altitude, and scanning below in the hope of spotting one of the many bush airstrips that dot the landscape throughout Tanzania & Kenya. Spotting one, he approached in ever decreasing lazy circles in a tense, absolute silence, with the only sound the wind rushing past the windows. When he was confident that he'd slowed enough for approach, he lined up and, losing speed all the way in, landed gently, "with hardly a fucking bump!" he boasts.

The Cessna coasted along the bush strip, bumbling quietly along the runway until some convenient bushes finally snagged and dragged it to a complete stop. Turning to grin over his shoulder Benji announced, "This is Captain Benji speaking, welcome to somewhere in the bush! I hope you've enjoyed your flight. Seats one and two may now disembark using the side door."

"They were a weird couple," he concludes, signalling the waiter for another beer. "She kept kissing me, while her new husband was kissing the ground!"

They only had to wait an hour or two before another plane, alerted by radio of Benji's predicament, arrived to collect them to allow them to complete their journey. Repeatedly extolling Benji's astonishing courage and skills, they left him sitting under a tree awaiting his own ride, due shortly.

"Only doing my job," Benji claims he replied, with unconvincing humility.

He follows with another story about a less than appreciative guest who reported him to his head office for being extremely rude to her. Benji had flown in to Katavi to collect four ladies in a very remote part of southwestern Tanzania in another Cessna 206, which had only five passenger seats. As it transpired, these turned out to be four

213

very large ladies. Benji tells us that he made a mental calculation of their weight and that of the extensive luggage arrayed around the landing strip, and concluded that he would be unable to safely take aboard all four ladies and their luggage. Considering wind direction and the short landing strip, it simply wouldn't be possible to gain enough altitude in time to clear the trees at the end of the runway. He explained this and suggested it would take two trips which he would organize immediately with his Dar office.

The largest of the ladies demanded, "How dare you! Are you calling me fat?"

Benji considered this for a few seconds, then replied, with what he claims was a charming smile and a typically Gallic shrug of his shoulders, "Not at all, madam, but your luggage is fucking obese."

This rather clueless attempt at discretion resulted in a written warning from his employer, which continues to baffle him. If he is to be believed, this was a clear case of "Was it something I said?" I usher the still laughing guests through to dinner, leaving Benji nursing both his beer and an apparent sense of grievance.

**

Joining us this evening is a young English honeymoon couple who seem completely overawed by the entire safari experience. Benji's banter has done little to reassure them in that respect, but then again, even their arrival had proved a little traumatic. Ali drove them from the airstrip together with a charming Australian couple, Ashley & Derek Ashley. The honeymooners had arrived directly from their wedding in the

U.K. to Dar Es Salaam, and from there on to Mashetani via Pemba Island where they picked up Ashley and Derek. Their bush plane then arrived at the lodge in the late afternoon, as *alasiri* gently faded into *jioni.*

On arrival, Alice, the young bride, proudly announced, "We saw a tiger on the drive here!"

Ali, who was helping with their luggage, smiled and corrected her. "I believe it was a leopard, Miss Alice."

"That's right. A big cat thing," she exclaimed loudly.

There's some further confusion at check-in, as we have never had a guest named Ashley Ashley before. But Ashley confirms that this is, indeed, her name. It seems that love really does conquer all, even the prospect of forever having to explain her name at every hotel and airport check-in, hospital, credit card company and other identification-sensitive organizations, as a result of surrendering her maiden name back in the day, when Ashley McDonald fell for Derek Ashley.

For Ashley, it was a small price to pay, and I suspect she rather enjoys the mayhem it inevitably causes.

As I carry out the safety briefing, I ask if this is everyone's first visit to Africa, eliciting a very definite "yes" from the wide-eyed honeymooners and a definite "no" from Ashley. It turns out that she's a former war correspondent, who had covered multiple incidents in Congo, Rwanda, Sudan, and Mogadishu.

"How was Pemba?" I ask.

"Well, action-packed, actually," Ashley replies, by way of introduction to her story.

On the second night in their beachside diving lodge on Pemba Island, she explains, their sleep was disturbed by shouting and loud noises. Ashley and Derek emerged from their room only to find the lodge manager lying on the floor, bleeding profusely from a wound to his head. Three masked robbers stood over him, demanding the key to the safe and brandishing their Panga bush knives threateningly. Before Ashley and Derek could retreat, a fourth bandit grabbed them from behind and marched them to their rooms, where he looted everything of value from their luggage and dragged them back outside.

By this time, the manager had sensibly handed over the keys, and two of the gang were filling a pillow case with the safe's contents. As this was happening, the only other guests staying at the lodge appeared from their adjoining rooms. These were two grey-haired Italian ladies of a certain age, clad in rather revealing negligees, and accompanied by two naked Maasai boys in their early twenties. The two Maasai lads instantly and correctly assessed the situation, and took off, buck naked, down the darkened beach. *Jigi Jigi* with someone old enough to be your mother is one thing, but being murdered during an armed robbery wasn't part of the contract! As the two valiant members of Africa's finest and most noble fighting tribe disappeared into the distance, Derek managed to catch one lady as she fainted, and Ashley attempted to calm the second while the gang ransacked their room. Their goals met, the men turned and ran, prudently taking the direction opposite to the one towards which the Maasai lover boys had so hastily made their escape, and vanished like smoke into the night.

At this point in the story, Candy emerges from the office, having overheard my earlier somewhat truncated safety briefing, and suggests that she escort the honeymooners to their room. As she leads them off towards the honeymoon suite, I can hear her assuring the white-faced and somewhat shaken young couple that Ashley's experience had been an incident pretty much unheard of, and how extremely safe it is here at Mashetani. She tells them, as well, that we've been able to upgrade them to our honeymoon suite complete with infinity swimming pool, at no extra charge, as a wedding gift, and that Mumbi will be their personal security officer for the duration of their stay, so they should be perfectly safe. I have a momentary thought regarding the suitability of the extremely combative Mumbi perhaps not being the best choice, but then turn my attention to our remaining new arrivals.

"Oops, do you think I've scared them?" Ashley muses.

"Not at all, not at all," I reassure her. "I'm sure it was watching *Blood Diamond* at the movies that prompted them to visit Africa on honeymoon in the first place," I add, grinning.

Derek hoots with laughter and apologizes for Ashley.

"Once a war correspondent, always a war correspondent," he explains.

***

I make it a point to ensure that we give the honeymooners private dining experiences throughout their stay, lest Ashley have any more tales of the unexpected with which to terrify them. Indeed, Candy remains on chaperone duty for the remainder of their visit, and a much more relaxed and confident couple departs than they were when they arrived.

This leaves me free to dine with Ashley and Derek during their stay, and they prove to be amazing company. I learn from our many dinner conversations that Ashley is actually The Right Reverend Bishop Ashley Ashley, and she produces her passport to prove that it is, indeed, true. My sceptical expression obviously prompts further explanation, and while downing another large G & T she confesses that, along with a fellow war correspondent, she joined the clergy by taking an online course offered by a U.S.-based "Midwestern School of Divinity." She told us that the small course fee has more than repaid itself ten times over, since they've both enjoyed multiple flight upgrades when they travel together.

Ashley finds that, for all the benefits of her profession, it's a small price to pay to answer the many and frequent requests she receives to issue blessings—both prior to and during flights, from check-in to the departure lounge to the main cabin. Once, however, on a flight from Mogadishu to Johannesburg, only her quick thinking in disavowing ordination in the Catholic faith prevented her from having to administer the Last Rites to an unfortunate fellow passenger who'd suffered a heart attack. She promises to wear her dog collar, which she never travels without, tomorrow evening at dinner.

They actually are also currently working from and living in Shanghai, living less than five kilometres from our son and his wife. We make a promise that on our next visit we'll meet up for dinner in the French Concession and introduce them to our son and his wife: a small world, indeed.

There seems to be something about living in the bush that makes highly improbable or coincidental things like this occur regularly. Candy and I once hosted a retired Dutch couple from Amsterdam who had opted not to go on game drives, as the husband, who was nearly eighty years old, had very limited mobility. During lunch one day, they told us they'd worked for thirty years in Angola, he as head brewer for a large Dutch brewing company, before moving to Kuala Lumpur in

Malaysia. Indeed, only the previous week they'd returned to Kuala Lumpur to revisit the brewery he had established there, and were delighted when the new head brewer took them out to dinner. I looked at Candy and laughed.

"Was it, by any chance, a Scots guy called Bill Mathers?" I enquired.

"How on earth did you know that?" his wife exclaimed.

"Candy and I both went to school with Bill as children in Scotland, and I knew he had recently transferred out there."

The drinks were on the house while the elderly couple regaled us with their memories of Africa—new friends somehow brought together by destiny thousands of miles from our respective homelands. Also, sometimes the best safari experiences seem to fall on the righteous. We were delighted, the next morning, to witness them enjoying a coffee from the lounge when five enormous elephants chose to walk through the river and directly into camp, spending an hour munching happily on a marula tree not fifteen feet in front of our new found friends. A truly unique and very personal safari experience.

***

The constantly revolving door of the safari circuit provides an ever-changing array of dinner guests, as on average, most guests will spend only two or three nights at each lodge. So, we meet an astonishingly wide cross-section of world travellers. During the rainy seasons, we normally have very few guests. This allows us the luxury of time to spend in the company of often very interesting people. We once had the great pleasure of spending an extremely entertaining evening with three very elderly Tanzanian residents. Our staff had set up a table overlooking the water hole, complete with starched white linen, crystal glasses, and the romantic kerosene lamps, providing a lovely ambiance. Brothers Henie and Johan, along with life-long friend Glen, shared with us stories of Tanzania as it had been long before we knew it.

They'd all been born in Tanzania, of South African and Welsh parents, respectively, just around the time of the Second World War, into a very, very different world from this one. Tanzania was, at the time, Tanganyika—a British protectorate in what was then German East Africa. The men had all grown up and attended school in Tanga before being sent to London for secondary education, and had then been apprenticed to different London firms to learn their chosen professions. Glen told us that he had trained as a pilot, returning to Africa as soon as he could. The typically cold weather in the U.K. was not for him.

An early introduction to big city life while he was still in London, however, provided a lesson that the world had become a smaller place than he'd previously believed. He laughed at his bad luck at making derogatory remarks to his brother in Swahili, his native tongue, regarding the size of a rather large woman struggling to fit into the seat directly in front of them on the London tube. He'd been astonished and chagrined when the furious lady rounded on him and clipped his ear, shouting in equally fluent Swahili that he needed to learn manners and respect his elders.

"Assume makes an ass out of U and ME," he laughed, proffering the ancient joke.

He went on to tell us how he'd worked as a private charter pilot for many rich and famous people, George Bush and the

Aga Khan numbering amongst the list of clients he'd ferried throughout East and Central Africa.

In the 1970's, while working in South Sudan during the first Civil War there, he'd been flying aid charters for MSF (Médicins Sans Frontièrs), when the base he was operating out of came under attack from one of the warring tribes who ruled these lawless lands. He could have flown to safety, but couldn't contemplate abandoning his heavily pregnant German wife and his many colleagues. Moreover, there was every chance the rebels would have surface-to-air weapons, so any attempt at escape could prove deadly. He was taken hostage along with almost fifty other people—a sorry group of admin workers, accountants and field workers who were sadly only there as volunteers to help alleviate pain and suffering. They were marched off into the desert, Glen pushing his heavily pregnant wife on a bicycle, as there was no way she could walk in the sand and heat.

The table fell silent as Glen described how, each evening, anyone who could not keep up with the column would be savagely beaten with canes. If they couldn't move out the next morning, they were summarily executed where they lay: shot in the head and left for the hyenas and vultures. The group endured this ordeal for two months until news arrived that the German government had agreed to pay the demanded ransom, though only for the German nationals among them. Glen had watched, helpless and silent, as his wife and several others were driven off to safety, while he and the remaining hostages continued their forced march through relentless heat towards uncertainty and a town called Nasir, near the Ethiopian border.

Glen is a big, heavyset guy, and he tells us that he never misses a meal after having survived a further six additional months on a diet of geckos and insects—anything to sustain himself to battle on. He had vowed that if he survived his ordeal then, in the future, whenever food would be available, he would eat. He lost three stone during his forced march, a cruel but effective personal Weight Watchers program.

Eventually, the French government brokered a deal and agreed to pay a ransom. The hostages were informed by the bandit leader of the group that the next day they were to cross a river into Ethiopia, where they would be free to leave unmolested. He told us that wading through that river with these ruthless bandits behind, training machine pistols on them the entire time, was the longest walk he ever endured in his life. He was actually astonished when they reached the far river bank to turn and find that they were alive and totally alone. Eventually, they were collected by a United Nations contingent and evacuated to safety. He never saw his wife again, nor was he ever able to hold his baby in his arms, as by the time he was freed, she had divorced him. I can see in his eyes that, while he makes light of the story, the pain remains, never too far below the surface. Candy hugs him and he leaps gamely to his feet and charges everyone's glass. By the time he retakes his seat, we sense that he has returned to the present time, his memories once more firmly in the past.

Johan enters into the void left at the dinner table by Glen's tale, and relates his own story of how, as a young man serving an apprenticeship in a London engineering office in the 1960's, he fell madly in love with a close friend of one of the young secretaries in the office who also worked part-time as a dancer. He dreamed of whisking her back to the family farm, high up in the Usambara Mountains near Lushoto to grow cabbage and eggplant. One morning, however, as he was travelling on the tube to his London office, he opened his newspaper to discover photos of his prospective wife and future Tanzanian farm assistant, splashed sensationally over the front page. She was headline news, as she and another acquaintance of Johan's—a certain Mandy Rice-Davies—had brought down the U.K. Conservative government single-handedly as part of what became known as The Profumo Affair.

"Well," he observed ruefully, "I suppose it wasn't *single*-handedly. More than one hand must have played a part in the scandal."

We all join in the loud laughter around the table, as Johan wistfully observes, "To tell the truth, even then I suspected Christine Keeler was perhaps a bit too lively for me. With hindsight, I must acknowledge that she never really showed too much interest in step farming techniques."

All eyes around the table fall on me, as the host, to respond with a story of my own. How on earth do I follow that? I'm saved almost at once, however, as Henie casually takes up the challenge.

He, too, had studied engineering in London. With a pointed glance at his elder brother across the table, Henie tells us that he'd confined his studies to plain engineering—not acrobatics—and had returned home to Tanzania, where he continued his work in mining and heavy engineering. After Tanzania gained independence in 1961, he'd been tasked by the government minister for mining, to put a stop to the corrupt exporting of emeralds.

He was working at an emerald mine near Lake Manyara and observed oil drums full of uncut emeralds being welded shut and disappearing by the truck load. Johan interjects that he had visited the camp on one occasion, and found that the

223

paths between the tented accommodations were made of gravel taken from the mines. He collected a dozen small emeralds in only one hour, picked directly from the path to his tent; such was the extent and richness of the emerald pipe they were working that the gravel was considered worthless.

Henie reported to his superiors what he'd seen. Less than a week later, a trusted friend arrived breathless at his tent in the middle of the night. He told him to grab what he could carry and depart with him immediately. He'd heard that the government official profiting from the stolen emeralds was less than happy at what he saw as interference. With his friend driving, they left camp immediately, cutting directly through the bush and avoiding the only road into camp, Henie hidden in the back of his pick-up under a tarpaulin sheet, wearing only the clothes on his back, and clutching his passport and the small stash of cash he had on him when they ran. Mere minutes passed before a squad of gunmen charged with his arrest had burst into camp in search of him. Sometimes, it seems that telling the truth in the wrong place at the wrong time actually isn't the best course of action, he learned that night. It would be many years before he could safely return to Tanzania again.

"And would that old bastard even share his emeralds with me? Like hell!" he roars, pointing at Johan. Johan chuckles, throwing his hands up in mock horror.

"Remember what the Maasai say, Henie?" he grins. "If something is not truly yours, then don't be surprised when the owner returns and takes it back."

We're dining under the stars under a waning moon, a family of elephants quietly drinking at the waterhole and silhouetted against the dense bush. A gentle breeze from the river sways the acacia trees, and we can hear the night sounds of the bush, the call of the nightjar, hyenas jabbering far in the distance in the dusky black darkness of dim moonlight. Great food, excellent wines, fabulous company—a perfect end to a perfect safari day. I raise my glass and mutter, "S*hikamoo, wazee*," as I offer my warmest thanks for a great evening of sharing their highly-entertaining and often moving memories. These brief moments of true intimacy among perfect strangers are among the highlights of the unique experience of managing a lodge in the African bush, and we treasure them. And sometimes, strangers turn into forever friends.

The next day, the three amigos depart. We exchange contact information, and there's never been a time since that night when Candy and I have visited Arusha and failed to visit Glen and his generous, charming wife, Mamie. We stay in their quaint guest cottage at the very foot of Mount Meru. This has become a tradition for us—one which has afforded us hours of joy and for which we remain deeply grateful.

***

Our elderly visitors are not only confined to guests. We have a permanent lodge resident who answers to the name *Mzee* or "Old Man." He's an aged Vervet monkey who has lost his position of power within his troop and gets bullied by the younger, more dominant males. We first noticed him when he came to hang out with us on the viewing deck at our house, using the proximity of humans as his safety net. I was sitting crossed-legged one evening, reading a book, when Candy started laughing.

"Look over your shoulder," she said.

I did, and was greeted with the sight of Mzee, totally

relaxed, sitting with his legs crossed exactly like my own. As a strict rule, we never feed wild animals, as it interferes with nature, but Candy has made an exception with our new friend, and very soon Mzee began to appear at the office, always checking nervously over his shoulder to ensure that none of his tormentors were around, then walking on his two hind legs into the office. Gently holding one of Candy's hands to steady himself he will pick cut pieces of tomatoes (his favourite dish) from her open palm, and enjoy his breakfast or mid-morning snack. He likes to sit perched on the *makuti* thatched roof of the garage directly opposite our office. Candy can walk out to Reception and shout, "Mzee, Mzee!" and, rather in the manner of a Labrador puppy, he'll scuttle down the roof, bound up the walkway and march into the office to receive today's offering.

Famously, once, when receiving new guests—a charming elderly British couple—while giving them an orientation tour of the lodge, as Candy was leading them to their room, she encountered Mzee up a tree next to the walkway. As she was introducing the guests to our celebrity monkey, she stepped backwards to better point him out and cartwheeled off the raised walkway into the bushes. She boomeranged almost at once back onto the walkway, twigs and grass sticking out from her hair, but in as professional and dignified a manner as possible under the circumstances. Calmly, she informed them, "I can now show you to your room," and beckoned them onwards. The guests gave no indication whatever that this was even remotely out of the ordinary. She later admitted, however, to being slightly flustered, and so, preoccupied with removing twigs from her hair, apparently failed to explain in sufficient detail all of the room's amenities.

The next time we met these guests was when an alarm air

horn blasted deafeningly from their room at three a.m. Candy and I arrived simultaneously, accompanied by the *askari*s, Mumbi and Sembuli, shotguns at the ready, to discover a rather dazed elderly British gentleman collapsed backwards on the bed. It transpired that while trying to deter a particularly persistent mosquito, he had reached for the compressed gas air horn in the mistaken belief that it was mosquito spray. His wife was berating him loudly as an "old fool." We assured them that it was no problem at all, and that we were just happy that it was in fact not an emergency. Candy told them to relax; it was a common mistake. Certainly, no more of an issue than one of our regular resident guests, who, each time he visits, uses the air horn to attract attention whenever he wants a fresh gin & tonic, despite our repeated reminders that it's for emergency use only. His illogical reply is always, "You may not consider an empty glass an emergency, but I certainly do!" He has an impressive, booming voice and is pretty much impervious to reason.

One morning, we found Mzee on our terrace. His arms had both been badly bitten and he could not even lift them to take the food Candy offered him. We both sat with him, and he ate, very gently, directly from the palm of my hand, using only his mouth, occasionally looking directly up into our faces. This continued, morning and evening, until he recovered. I think we have a friend for life.

***

We occasionally have celebrity guests visit the lodge— sometimes movie stars, politicians, singers—but none has thrilled us as much as when we received a booking for Dr Jane

Goodall and her family. Dr Jane's family mostly still live in Dar Es Salaam, so we have a multi-generational visit which includes her son and grandson.

This exciting visit, however, does present one dilemma. Kissy, our resident common genet, has refined her act to such an extent that she appears every evening, parading around the bar/lounge area, adopting seductive poses, standing on her hind legs like a meerkat, and generally playing the audience to ensure that a decent proportion of the guests' evening bitings of chicken drumsticks or beef kebabs will inevitably come her way. In addition, Mzee is not averse to making the odd cameo appearance in the restaurant, looking for titbits from Candy. How will this be greeted by the world's foremost primatologist and animal conservationist?

We need not have worried. Dr Jane and family have joined us on an evening game drive—or, I should say, "safari drive," as she doesn't approve of the word "game", implying, as it does, hunting. We have sundowner drinks on a hill with a glorious view to Mount Kilimanjaro, and return as night begins to envelop the lodge for pre-dinner drinks and snacks in the bar/lounge area. When Candy and I return from duties in the kitchen and restaurant, we're horrified to find Kissy standing to attention next to Dr Jane's table while munching scraps of chicken taken right from her hand.

"Oh, eh, I see you've met our resident genet," I mumble. "I didn't think you'd approve."

Dr Jane laughs and pats my hand.

"My dear Graeme, of course I don't disapprove. How on earth do you think I managed to make friends with my chimpanzees at Gombe Stream?"

She goes on to explain that at the beginning of her

research program, for months she'd made no progress at all in interacting with the chimpanzees or in earning their trust. They wouldn't approach her or interact in any way, until one day, having lunch in the bush, she threw some food towards a nearby chimp. Cautiously, he came forward and collected the scraps, before disappearing at speed into the safety of the bush. Each day, she repeated the exercise until, after a short while, she had a veritable chimpanzee's tea party going on, as each lunchtime would find her surrounded by an-ever growing circle of more and more confident new friends. The rest, as they say, is history.

We join the family for dinner, and even Mzee appears and sits on a tree directly next to our table; it appears that news of her arrival has spread. It's impossible to imagine that this remarkable lady is over 85 years old; her energy and enthusiasm radiates from her, and we easily believe her when she tells us that she travels three hundred days every year, spreading her words and wisdom, and encouraging the world's youth to take care of planet Earth.

As we're sitting around the table after dinner, listening to this humble and fascinating lady, her grandson excitedly points towards the bar. We all look over and can only see the large furry tail of a bush baby sticking up out of an ice bucket which Saidi Saidi uses to store his cocktail garnishes. I take her grandson by the hand over to the bar in time to watch our furry friend re-emerge from the ice bucket with a pineapple slice clutched firmly in his paws. It's not every day you get the opportunity to introduce the grandson of a legendary primatologist to his first-ever in-person encounter with a greater Galagos—one of the cutest primates you could ever hope to run across. The adorable little guy lazily strolls the length of the bar before hopping, kangaroo-style, across the floor to a comfortable, open spot where he leisurely finishes his snack, much to the delight of his young exclusive audience.

The perfect end to a perfect evening.

Like many people, especially when young, we occasionally make the mistake of dismissing elderly people, forgetting that they have passed through a long journey and along the way have gained great experience and wisdom. There is an African proverb that comes to my mind: "The death of an elderly man is like the burning of a library."

I have long been of the opinion that those who respect the elderly, and who listen attentively when they speak, may be paving their own road toward success.

CHAPTER 15
AMBULANCE CHASERS

Boss had made one of his sporadic contacts with us, requesting that we visit Tanga for a few days to pay for some licenses, and to renew permits for the lodge. We never need to be asked twice to visit Tanga, so we make hasty plans and depart in the morning, as soon as the first blush of dawn starts to lighten the sky above the distant palm trees. Guide Ali is driving. Saiber, our normal supply run driver, is already in Tanga, confined to the dubious luxuries of Bombo Hospital with a severe bout of malaria.

Riding with Ali is a joy, as he always spots so many things we might otherwise miss, and some things, of course, no one could possibly miss. For example, directly outside the lodge gates we have to pause while more than a hundred elephants emerge from the bush and wash around us, our vehicle caught like a pebble in a stream as they amble, in their own leisurely time, on their way. We could reach out the window and touch them, they're so close. Completely relaxed, they pay scant attention to us. Only the occasional mother with a small baby in tow stops and flares her ears at us as a stern reminder that we're near enough, and no further movement towards her darling baby will be tolerated. Ali talks to her in a gentle tone, assuring her we mean her baby no harm, and with a final, haughty toss of her head, she turns and moves to the other side of the track, her little one tucked beneath her legs and nearly impossible to see. Within minutes they've disappeared into the bush on the far side of the road. Without the branches dropped while they were eating and the steaming piles of dung that have littered the road, you'd never know they were here.

I remark to Ali that it was such luck to be here at this exact time to witness this. Ali smiles and replies, "Yes, the more I guide the luckier I get," and we all laugh.

We're continuing through the conservancy, heading towards the main road, when Ali stops and reaches for his ever-handy binoculars. He's spotted a secretary bird that has killed a spring hare. He points it out, but advises us to watch carefully. A lurking black-backed jackal appears suddenly and, with lightning speed, steals the hare from the unfortunate secretary bird. Before he can enjoy his triumph, however, a spotted hyena, in one swift move, swipes the hare from the jackal! The bush pecking order is summarily demonstrated in a matter of mere moments, right before our eyes!

Ali's excitement at witnessing this confirms that it's a truly unusual sighting. You can always assume that if the guide's excited, you're getting a gem of a sighting!

Action over, we continue onwards. It's great spending some time with Ali and catching up as we drive, as we've all been very busy over the preceding two months, with little time for socializing among us. Ali updates us about a horrific sighting they'd had when he was dropping off an English honeymoon couple at the airstrip recently. They'd come across the gruesome spectacle of a hippo, injured in a previous territorial fight, being devoured—while still alive—by a hyena pack, right in the middle of the track to the airstrip. The poor creature was being consumed from the hind quarters forward. Ali had thought Alison was going to faint, so he detoured around them, and they made their way in a stunned silence to the airstrip. Ali muses, rather sadly, that the couple will certainly remember vividly the last few minutes of their honeymoon.

I can overhear Juma McLean's voice coming through on the radio, though not clearly, as he's speaking Swahili, very fast.

We're aware that he's guiding some guests, and they've apparently come across an injured wildebeest, standing on its own in a waterhole with several hyenas patiently watching it from the banks, awaiting their chance. Juma's speaking Swahili quite specifically so that his guests won't understand what he's asking Ali.

I overhear Ali replying, again in Swahili, that "the alternator and battery have gone but the engine is still running."

I'm naturally concerned that Juma's vehicle appears to have a problem, but I can see Ali's shoulders shaking as he laughs out loud and turns to explain. The previous night, Ali had witnessed the same unfortunate wildebeest under attack by some hyenas. The injured and terrified animal had escaped into the waterhole, but not before the hyenas had managed to castrate him and rip off his tail. Ali chuckles, repeating his macabre joke: the "alternator" and "battery" have gone but the "engine" is still running. I suspect the engine won't be running for much longer given the persistent ring of gathering hyenas, those giggling killers of the bush. We marvel at the wildebeest's unwillingness to submit to its predicament. Life is stubborn, and living things will often suffer much to cling to it as long as possible.

We arrive at the main road and turn towards Tanga. It's

pleasant to be on a surfaced road for a while, and we glide along, glorying in the ever-changing scenery. Fish eagles, with their haunting calls, sit proudly atop the palm trees that fringe the coastal forest which shields the shimmering Indian Ocean. Through breaks in the forest, we catch tantalizing glimpses of the sparkling aqua ocean. We pass villagers on push bikes stacked high with grass cut to feed their cows—piles so high they resemble hay stacks on wheels. We pass the bizarre sight of a tree full of goats, balanced precariously on seemingly tiny branches as they climb ever higher to enjoy the freshest leaves.

The Mombasa Express bus thunders past us in a cloud of diesel smoke, heading for the border, hard-core motherfucking rap music blaring loudly from ancient, oversized speakers. Stacked high on the roof beside the ubiquitous caged chickens and goats in baskets, as well as water containers, mattresses, and piles of all types of fruit, are a bundle of flat-screen televisions. Ali confirms that the TVs are imported from Dubai to tax-free Zanzibar, then shipped over to the mainland by old Arabic dhow sail boats and deposited onto deserted stretches of pristine beach, where the smugglers gather them up and transport them north for sale in Tanga, Mombasa or Nairobi.

Seeing the bus reminds us of a journey our son Kris and his wife, Kirsty, once took from Arusha to Tanga. The bus was predictably over-stuffed with passengers, three for every two seats. Kris was jammed into the aisle seat, with Kirsty pressed hard against the window. To his left sat three Maasai, each with a goat trussed on his lap, heading to market. In the seat directly in front of Kris was an autistic teenager hanging over the seat staring directly into his eyes, repeatedly slapping the chair back with enthusiasm, sometimes even in rhythm with the extremely loud Swahili gospel music blaring from the speakers. I still treasure his text message to me, sent six hours into the eleven-hour journey:

"If I snap and murder Rain Man before I reach Tanga, will you visit me in jail?"

We pass children selling bags of fresh mangos in baskets made from leaves they weave themselves. If you don't have a bag, in Africa, then make one—or buy one from an enterprising child. Ten children here are all selling the same thing, and when we stop to spend a few dollars to buy some fruit, we're swamped by ever more kids with ever more mangos, and we have to explain, firmly but good-naturedly, that we can't buy them all.

We pass baboons seated cross-legged on the road verge, patiently awaiting scraps thrown from passing vehicles. Gas stations are surrounded by wrecked vehicles, the detritus of the casual "Inshallah" attitude taken by most road users. Bars line the road, each with a wonderfully imaginative name tacked onto its side: "The Honeymooner Bar," "The Country Club," "The Come Back, Please Bar." Almost every shop or store sports a brash, bright red Coca Cola sign with the name of the store printed in black below. The Coca Cola rep tasked with raising the brand profile had signs made for everything on the coast even remotely resembling a shop, whether it sold cold drinks or not. He also insisted that each shop should have a name, and so we now have stores proudly sporting Coca Cola signs with names such as "My Father's Shop", "Fish Shop," "Cow Medicine Shop," and—my all-time favourite—"Bishmillah Butcher and Haberdashery Store."

Our idyllic journey comes to an abrupt halt when our front

drive shaft snaps and we coast quietly and serenely to a stop by the road side. We're still a good forty-five minutes' drive away from Tanga. A quick inspection confirms the damage and the fact that there's nothing we can do to make a temporary repair.

I slide out from under the vehicle on my back as my phone rings. "*Habari, kaka*," Rasta Ali's voice rings in my ear. "Let's meet for a beer when you get to Tanga," he continues.

I look at Candy, and she bursts out laughing. Ali shrugs his shoulders and chuckles. How on earth does Rasta know we're heading to Tanga? This is, however, truly opportune, and I explain our predicament with the car.

"*Pole fucking sana, kaka*," Rasta sympathizes, and continues, "Worry not! I am on my way to help! This is an emergency!"

We push the car to the side of the road, and the three of us seat ourselves under the shade of a huge mango tree to wait. We have some water from our cool box and some chapatti, so enjoy our impromptu roadside picnic. Children selling cashew nuts appear miraculously from the bush, and we buy some, sharing our water and sodas with them.

Every single vehicle that passes us stops to offer assistance: Do we need a lift? Do we need water? Can we call someone? No one would ever consider not offering assistance. Rural Tanzanian hospitality is never far away, however remote you may feel from civilization.

After some time, we spot an ambulance with its light flashing speeding towards us—a more unusual sighting than even this morning's secretary bird. As it passes, the driver jams on his brakes and, in a cloud of burning rubber, screeches to a stop. The beaming face of Rasta Ali, haloed in dreadlocks, appears out the window.

"You said it was an emergency, *kaka*. Rasta Ali and Dr Yusuf at your service!"

Once we complete our greetings and confirm that there is, indeed, an ice-cold beer available for Rasta in our cool box, we position the ambulance and attach a tow rope. I overhear Ali stressing to Doctor Yusuf that he does not want to be towed at one hundred kilometres per hour.

"It does not matter how slowly you go, as long as you do not stop," is Ali's sage advice.

We set off quite sedately towards Tanga, with Ali, Rasta and Yusuf up front while Candy and I recline on the twin stretcher beds in the rear of the ambulance. Rasta informs me through the hatch that he was having a beer with Yusuf when he heard of our plight, and so they rushed to our aid in the best possible emergency vehicle available. Yusuf cannot resist having his light flashing but, to be fair, it does a splendid job of warning any approaching traffic, and we arrive without incident into Tanga town.

Since the siren is blaring from the ambulance as we arrive, it's not an understated entrance. In the happy chaos of Tanga, an ambulance towing a car is hardly worthy of a second glance. Children are selling boiled eggs, the trays balanced perfectly on their heads. The change they collect for their sales, loosely clutched in their hands, rings out a jingling rhythm that's both enjoyable and an attraction for further business. Young girls sit outside the "hair saloons" having their extensions fitted by the stylist, who carefully uses a candle and melted wax to create the most exotic looks in the latest fashion, while they all chatter excitedly with their gathered friends. The street-side cafes, fashioned from old tarpaulins or brightly coloured cloth to create a bit of shade, are full of old men smoking shisha pipes and enjoying their very sweet tea.

We drop Ali and the car at the garage of Mzee Rashidi al Haji, who promises a quick repair. He never moves from behind his desk, never picks up a tool or looks under a car hood, but he can prepare an invoice quicker than any man I have ever met. We climb once more aboard the ambulance and proceed to the town centre and the comfort of the Ocean Breeze to repay Rasta and Yusuf for their efforts in rescuing us. We're not even remotely surprised to see the bulk of Stanley, the immigration officer, in his customary corner, crammed onto a stack of four plastic chairs. He greets us warmly, signalling frantically to the waiter for more beers. Candy comments that he is now using four chairs rather than his customary three, but other than a muttered, "I had an incident recently with three chairs," he doesn't expand on the subject.

It's great to catch up, and particularly great that Stanley is around, as he's always a big help with officialdom. Proof that the jungle drums are playing loud and clear, Old Mohammed shows up, grinning madly, joining us to share a meal of chicken curry, chapatti, rice, *michicha* (spinach) and *ugali*, the stiff maize porridge that is a staple of any meal in east Africa. A local councillor appears in the restaurant, shaking hands and greeting everyone with politic good cheer. He's seeking re-election in the upcoming month and is therefore particularly gregarious today, busily distributing free caps and T-shirts to his potential voters.

Rasta whispers, "We may as well take the shirts and hats. Once he's elected, these will be the last things he gives away for free."

On seeing us all seated at our table and mistaking us for persons of importance, the beaming politician approaches and offers to buy us another round of beer. Then, noticing Mohammed, cigarette in mouth, his Muslim kufi hat, and white flowing kanzu, he exclaims, with studied chagrin, "Oh, so sorry, *Mzee*! May I offer you a soda? I did not wish to offend you!"

Mohammed takes one long drag on his cigarette, and nonchalantly tosses his hat behind the bar before announcing, "Make mine a beer, please, with a Konyagi chaser!" He grins wickedly at the astonished councillor, and settles comfortably back in his chair.

My phone rings at this point, and I step outside so I can hear the call above the laughter. It's Greta, from the dive school down the coast past Pangani.

"Are you in Tanga, Graeme? I really need your help!" Her words gush, her tone agitated.

"Sure. I'm at the Ocean Breeze with Candy and Rasta, Stanley and Mohammed. What can I do?"

"Can you meet me at Bombo Hospital? I've been in an accident, and I'm on my way there. I should arrive in fifteen minutes!"

I can hear the underlying note of panic in her voice. I try to calm her, and assure her that Candy and I will be there to meet her. I tell her that I'm actually with Dr Yusuf, and that he'll come with us. I confirm that I'll meet her at the main entrance.

It's usually chaotic at the hospital, as almost every patient arrives with what seems like their entire family, who spend the duration of their relative's hospital stay either at the foot of the bed, outside shading under a tree, or at the gate where vendors sell them everything from food and water to medicine and syringes—items often not actually available inside the hospital.

I re-enter the bar and inform everyone about Greta's accident. Rasta and Dr Yusuf offer the ambulance to transport us, and, joined by Candy, we pile in the back of the vehicle and speed to Bombo Hospital. Situated on the banks of Tanga estuary in the east part of the city, the hospital is set in magnificent grounds, with baobab and flame trees, and broad, green lawns—a deceptively lovely setting.

I don't like hospitals under any circumstances; I guess most people hold the same opinion. But I don't like Bombo Hospital in particular. I can't even drive past it without being instantly transported back in time to the evening when I had to bring my friend Gordon here and leave him dead in the mortuary. All alone. I can somehow even taste the hospital smell. Candy, sensing my change in mood, hugs me, and we turn as we see a Tanesco—Tanzania Power Company—pick-up truck pull up at the gate. The driver, who knows us, calls across with urgency straining his voice, "Come quickly."

We rush over and he says simply, "In the back."

I pull the tailgate down and there is Greta. She has climbed or crawled inside a large cool box, which was full of ice she'd planned to use to store the meat purchase from her weekly supply trip to Tanga. I jump in the back.

"Greta! What happened?"

Through clenched teeth, she explains that she was driving to Tanga when her truck overheated. Her old truck's engine is beneath the front seats, and without thinking, she'd opened the radiator cap and was instantly soaked with boiling hot coolant. I can see the skin on her right arm hanging off like a loose shirt

240

sleeve.

"My face!" she sobs, but I can see no damage, and assure her she's okay. Rasta jumps in, and with the help of the Tanesco driver we carry her, still in the cool box, towards the doctor's office, bypassing Admissions. We hurry past the curious stares of the multitude of chattering families and the kids playing chase in the corridors. Candy and Dr Yusuf run ahead to prepare. As we reach a ward, Yusuf's head appears out of an office and he orders us in there. Rasta and I, as gently as we can, place her on the ground, still curled up like a drowned kitten in her cool box.

Yusuf has a pain-killing injection ready, and quickly administers it. It takes effect almost immediately, which must be a blessed relief for Greta, who escapes her immediate pain into a glassy-eyed daze. Yusuf tells us that she's in shock, and begins to peel away her clothes from the affected areas. Her right arm, back, and neck seem the most affected. Candy is holding her hand and talking softly to her, their heads close together as she desperately tries to reassure and calm her. Yusuf applies some ointment to disinfect the burns and applies dampened loose bandages to her arms and back.

When we step outside, leaving Greta with Candy, he explains that she has full and partial thickness burns, and that Bombo is not equipped to treat an injury such as this. Speed of treatment is essential, he cautions, as she can't afford to become infected.

The Tanesco driver tells us that he'd been driving behind her, and had arrived on the scene in time to see what happened. He'd immediately offered his assistance to drive her directly to the hospital. He's distraught, as well, because, while trying to help Rasta and me as we carry her inside, he found himself slipping on the wet floor, had kicked off his sandals, and somebody had stolen them by the time he returned outside. I promise to buy him a new pair.

Greta must have also called her boyfriend Johan, as he suddenly appears and we bring him up to speed on what has happened. While he rushes to her side, I send Rasta to engage the help of a friend who has an air-conditioned people carrier. Yusuf phones a doctor colleague at KCMC hospital in Moshi, who advises that we send her there for immediate treatment.

KCMC is an international standard hospital, but it's a six-hour drive away, a long drive in any circumstances and a marathon in Greta's condition. Rasta Ali arrives with the car, and Dr Yusuf agrees to travel with Greta and Johan. He packs a bag of all and anything he thinks he may need to treat her on the journey. Candy emerges from the hospital, pushing Greta in a wheel chair, with Johan holding her hand. We settle her as best we can in the car with Johan, Yusuf and the driver. Her face, on one side is starting to darken to a charcoal colour. None of us mention this.

They drive off, and I look once more around the immaculate gardens and grounds. My eyes fall on an old auto shock absorber hanging from one of the trees by a length of rope, with a spanner attached to it. A huge Mama walks over to it and uses the spanner to beat the shock absorber. The improvised dinner bell announces that lunch is ready. Or perhaps, I think sardonically, it's the end of Round One. For all its beauty, I really do not like this place.

I reflect that only one hour ago we were having an early lunch in the Ocean Breeze. The improvised Tanga Rapid Response Team have acquitted themselves well. She is now in Fate's fickle hands. We've done what we can, and hope it's enough.

When spider webs unite, they can tie up a lion. Africans have a pithy epigram for everything, it sometimes seems.

We're delighted when Johan calls later that evening to say they arrived at the hospital safely and Greta is doing well. The burns on her face are thankfully superficial, and she should have no lasting damage. There was a reason, we believe, that we found ourselves in the right place at the right time to assist Greta. Maybe God, maybe Fate—but we know it wasn't just an accident that she found us.

***

Candy and I are to spend the next few nights at the Mkonge Hotel, close by Bombo Hospital. It was once the home of the Greek Sisal Farmers' Club when, in the 1950s, the sisal industry employed thousands upon thousands of workers while the industry enjoyed boom years. It's a grand building, with stunning gardens overlooking Tanga Yacht Club and Tanga Bay and the eerily impressive Toten Island, where it was rumoured, that prisoners were once abandoned and left to their fate on the heavily jungled and snake-invested island. Their ghosts are still believed to walk there at night, and the Island is avoided by all but the foolhardy.

The sisal industry went into serious decline after independence, and was nationalized by the government at a time when synthetic products also dramatically reduced demand. The Greeks left, and the club, which had at one time been described as the Las Vegas of Africa, where owners lost and won entire plantations over a game of cards, slowed back down to the sleepy pace of Tanga and morphed over the years into a lovely and picturesque hotel.

We have an early dinner in the gardens, at a table under a giant baobab tree. We order drinks, and Elias, our waiter—who appears as if by magic each and every time we visit here—delivers them in record time, along with an array of samosas and *chevra*, the hot and spicy fried chickpea flour mix much favoured in Tanga. Candy excuses herself to visit the ladies' room, dodging past the several vervet monkeys gathering in an opportunistic manner in the branches of our tree and surrounding bushes. It seems they like snacks as much as we do.

As Candy returns, she reaches the table simultaneously with Elias. Elias hands me back both my shoes, which he has retrieved from the bushes, and I thank him and place them on the adjacent empty seat.

Candy sighs, "Please tell me you haven't been giving the monkeys The Shoe again."

The truth is that when dining here, it's become somewhat of a tradition for me to throw my shoes at the monkeys whenever they get too close. I've become remarkably proficient at it, and it allows us to enjoy our meal unmolested by monkeys. I admit it does cause some consternation amongst the other diners, but the staff seem to find it rather amusing, and when I arrive wearing boots rather than say, flip flops, Elias will often comment, "Ah, I see you've brought the heavy artillery today, Mr Graeme."

The calls to prayer start to fill the evening air with their beautiful, mystic chants. The sun is a red, burning coin, slipping down the sky towards the far horizon. The silhouettes of the yachts and dhows in the bay paint a magical batik. As the prayers fade, a tranquil silence falls over the gardens, and we sit contentedly, hand in hand, in the deepening darkness. Elias places kerosene lamps discretely around our table. Where there's love, there is no darkness.

My mind drifts back to a visit to Tanga many years ago, when Candy and I spent one memorable New Year's Eve with Gordon at the Tanga Jazz Club. The building is somewhat dubiously named, as it's more of an open roofless quadrangle, loosely tacked onto the Tanga Hotel, which still somehow retains an International Rotary Club sign proudly hanging outside its once grand, but very faded, façade. We were to stay here the night after seeing in the New Year, following a festival of jazz music.

I can't think of any other establishment in my memory which requires on the registration form that you state not only your name, profession and sex, but also your tribe. Any official in the future, tasked with checking the records of that evening, will no doubt be perplexed to learn that Charlie Chaplin, double bass player with Hoffmann's Flying Circus, male, and a druid, stayed the night of December 31st, 2009, accompanied by Marilyn Monroe, sex symbol, female of the Sioux Nation, occupying room twenty-three on the first floor, overlooking the jazz arena. Nor that Che Guevara, ballet dancer, male, Hottentot, was their neighbour in room twenty-one. The fact that the receptionist never blinked an eye at these statements is itself testament to the quality of the establishment.

Here, many years later, the "jazz" club doesn't, in fact, offer any actual jazz music, but presents instead an ever-changing group of musicians whose sole purpose seems to be to exterminate music as an actual art form. While "The River of Babylon" is being tortured to an early death on stage, we enjoy a few drinks in the almost complete darkness of the bar area. The waitress who has delivered our drinks takes the seat next to me and stares directly into my eyes.

"I love you," she states, taking my hand and beginning to gently caress it. Candy, two feet to my right, is slightly perplexed by this development. Whilst somewhat bemused by this, I am quite enjoying the attention. I tell Candy that I think this young lady is under the impression that I'm a Hollywood film star.

Candy instantly brings me back to earth with her smart-ass quip, "Aye, I heard her tell her friends she thought you were Danny DeVito."

***

As dawn breaks the next day, we enjoy an early morning coffee under a giant mango tree in the gardens. The dawn chorus is breaking into full, splendid voice. Square-tailed nightjars give way to the gorgeous song of the spotted morning thrush, who is itself competing with a host of myriad different types of weavers, the mournful, agitated call of the white-bellied go-away birds and the shrill shrieking of the yellow-necked spurfowls. A red-and-yellow barbet joins us on our table and happily pecks away at crumbs dropped from our morning mandazi snacks. The vervet monkeys are having a lazy start to the morning, so my shoes remain firmly on my feet. The ferry departing Tanga slips lazily past, through the treacherous Pemba Channel on its voyage to Pemba Island.

We've promised Saiber we'll visit him at Bombo Hospital, where he continues to fight his serious attack of malaria. We often say that the first symptom of malaria is denial. It's easy to convince yourself that you are just overly tired, run down, been too busy, or simply feeling the flu coming on. Quick testing for malaria, however, and instant treatment can stop this killer disease from getting a real grip on your body. Without early treatment, one can deteriorate quickly. Saiber's denial, followed by homemade "cures" and no doubt spells from a witch doctor, have resulted in him becoming seriously ill. He's currently being administered quinine by intravenous drip.

When we arrive at Bombo, the gate is already thronged with the usual brightly-attired crowd of mostly women. Every shade and hue are on display in the glorious array of Kanga dresses and head gear adorning these women, the colours glowing in the morning sun. The birds in the Mkonge gardens pale into insignificance against this beautiful display. Children flit about in their school uniforms, the girls with flowing white headdresses that make them look like a swarm of butterflies chasing one another and playing under the trees. The shrieks of innocent laughter deflect from what lies beyond the ward doors. We weave our way through the crowds and head towards Ward Six. As I pass by the shock absorber still hanging from the tree, I bang it furiously with the hanging spanner. Like Doctor Pavlov's dogs, several people start forming a queue with plates under the tree.

We find Saiber, asleep and tied to the bed by two large, thick leather straps. We pull up seats and deposit the fresh mango juice and fruit we've brought for him on the bedside cabinet. A doctor approaches and we exchange greetings. He explains that Saiber is not in good shape, and has been hallucinating, and trying to run out of the ward. He tells us that these problems are caused by Saiber's extremely high fever, and that they really have to get the fever down and the parasites

247

in his blood under control.

At this point, Saiber awakes and is delighted to see us there. He seems coherent, so the doctor takes off the leather straps. We sit together and chat, and we entertain him with all the lodge gossip. We swap jokes, stories, memories, make plans.

He's entirely lucid until we tell him we have to leave and he announces cheerfully, "Okay, let me bring the car round."

I gently explain that it's okay, that Ali is with us and will drive, and that he must stay and rest.

"Sure, I understand," he agrees before leaping buck naked from his bed and sprinting straight out the door.

In the ensuing silent, pregnant pause this produces, we exchange stunned glances, at one another and then towards the door. Flanked by two orderlies in white uniforms, an extremely reluctant Saiber is dragged back into the ward, the elderly ward Sister holding a bed pan roughly over his groin area and berating Saiber loudly.

"My nurses have more to do than chase stupid naked young men around the hospital grounds! This is not The Jazz Club," she yells.

One of the young nurses turns and wistfully asks her colleague, "Do you remember the time Danny DeVito visited The Jazz Club? Oh my God, I wish I'd been there!"

Candy can't look at me for laughing.

Saiber is coaxed back into bed, the sister insists he be strapped in, and Candy and I sit on either side of the bed and re-engage with him to calm him down. Candy holds his hand while Saiber and I reminisce. We laugh about the first time we ever met, the day he helped Gordon and me escape pursuit from the local police by hiding the *pikipiki* we were riding on in the back of his Land Rover pick-up and driving us over the Pangani River ferry to avoid having to pay the multiple fines Gordon had racked up for riding an unlicensed bike. It's great to hear Saiber laugh.

The Sister returns and hooks him up to yet another one-litre bottle of quinine solution; this is the nineteenth bottle of his treatment. When the sister departs, I tap the bottle and announce "I don't think this is going in fast enough," and both Saiber and Candy immediately yell, "Don't you dare touch it!"

Saiber knows well the tale of Candy's bad bout with malaria, and neither relishes my medical attention. I laugh, but leave well enough alone. We stay with Saiber until he drifts off to sleep. Candy leans over and gently kisses his fever-hot forehead, whispering, "Sleep well, Saiber, *tutaonana kesho*." (See you tomorrow). I ruffle his hair, and we tiptoe out of the ward, leaving him sleeping peacefully.

Saiber never woke in the morning; he passed away sometime during the night. His body was not strong enough to cope with the malaria, nor with the treatment. We make plans for Ali to transport him home to Pangani, and inform his many friends at the lodge. They vote for Ali to be staff representative at the funeral, along with Candy and me.

We drive to a local shop in Tanga and, after sifting through the beds, garishly upholstered sofas, and coffee tables, the owner pulls out a coffin from under an ornate double bed. Handy place to store a coffin, I observe wryly. I must remember that.

On our way back to Bombo Hospital, Candy makes the point that Saiber was very tall, pushing six foot four inches, in fact. "Do you think the coffin is big enough?"

Ali pulls over to the side of the road, and we manhandle

the coffin onto the grassy verge of the road. I climb in, stretch out and cross my hands over my chest. Ali blesses me, which, as he's Muslim, seems somehow inappropriate. My position inside the coffin, however, does give him the opportunity to confirm that there's ample room to accommodate the long legs of Saiber. Candy gets out of the car in time to witness my resurrection. As I pull myself to my feet and give myself a shake, a passing *bajaji* taxi veers off the road and crashes into the dense bushes. The driver jumps clear of the vehicle and runs screaming off into the trees. Ali is of the (probably correct) opinion that the driver thinks he's just seen a man rise from the dead.

We quickly reload the coffin and head onwards. Ali and I drop Candy off at the hotel and then collect Saiber's body from the mortuary and gently place him in the coffin. I screw the lid shut and we look at each other.

"This is becoming a bad habit," Ali sighs.

He has agreed to drive the coffin to Pangani Town where Saiber's family lives. Candy and I are to follow in a separate car. The funeral is to take place later today, following tradition.

When we arrive, Saiber is in the place of honour, his coffin lying on the dining table outside the family house with the lid open. Inside the house, all the women of the family are gathered, supported by friends and neighbours, and there is much wailing. The men are arrayed around the garden under the trees in small groups. The contribution book is discretely passed around, and we pencil in our own offering of help. Without any discernible signal, everyone starts to move towards the graveyard—only a short walk through the village. Ali and I take our turns carrying the coffin. Following a brief ceremony, the coffin is lowered into the grave and covered by the rich, red soil of Africa.

Another child of Tanzania taken long before his time.

His grave is marked only by four broken tree branches, placed at the four corners of the plot. I look around and can see many more tree branches withering as they stand in solemn guard over recently departed friends or relatives.

Candy and I greet Saiber's mother and sisters. His wife is too distraught to even make it to the graveside. They take some consolation in hearing that Saiber will be missed by all his friends in the Mashetani family. Finally, we depart for the long drive home, Ali leading the way. They say that life is the beginning of death, but that the grave of a good person will always be loved and cared for. We are comforted by the knowledge that Saiber will be very well cared for.

It is late afternoon by the time we reach the lodge. We've called ahead and arranged a staff meeting to brief the staff on the funeral, and during the meeting we're deeply touched to discover that the entire staff have agreed to send this month's tips to Saiber's family, in a moving gesture of affection and respect.

Tired from the emotional toll from the long day's events, Candy and I walk along the wooden walkway by the river towards our house. I look up, and at first glance it appears as though a party is in full swing in our lounge. Figures are dancing with their hands waving in the air. As we get closer, however, I can make out the unmistakable silhouettes of baboons. They've broken through a net window, and have emptied the fridge, eating everything they could find. Worse, they've opened or broken several cans of beer and a bottle of gin!

I approach the door gingerly, and they become even more

agitated as they can't find their way back out. They charge the door as I try to open it, teeth bared and barking in alarm. I slam the door shut and retreat hastily, trying to think of a Plan B. At this precise moment Mtoro, our five-foot-two-inch house girl, strides confidently past, pushes me not too gently aside, throws open the door and leaps through, brandishing her broom.

A veritable flood of baboons charge past us, shrieking loudly as Mtoro bats them around the head and ass. They evacuate the lounge in a frenzy and disappear in ignominious disarray into the bush. There's one final shriek as the last baboon is discovered on our bed, and Mtoro deals with him in the same efficient manner. An all-night student bash couldn't have left wreckage as great as that produced in their wake by our furry neighbours. We begin to help Mtoro upright the furniture, but she shoos us away, and sets about rectifying the damage. As it happens, we have to stay overnight in a guest room, as the destruction is pretty thorough—even for the supremely efficient Mtoro!

The next day at breakfast we're surprised and delighted to discover that Brigitte, the lovely Belgian gems expert, has arrived. She tells us she's discovered a sudden window in her busy schedule and just caught a flight at the last moment, arriving yesterday. We join her for coffee and a catch up.

She and her husband have been trying very determinedly to buy some land on the coast for over a year now. Every time they think they have a deal completed, one or another problem arises, or another "rightful owner" of the land appears out of nowhere.

Unknown to Brigette, she has earned the sobriquet, "The Body," since when visiting the lodge, rather than taking part in the customary safari drives, she prefers instead to lounge by the pool in a micro string bikini displaying a seamless, perfect tan. Being European, she thinks nothing of walking through to the bar in this state of near undress to order another cocktail. Candy has subtly tried to advise her numerous times that, on the mainly Muslim Tanzania coast, it's best to adopt a somewhat more modest mode of dress, but her only nod to decorum has been the concession to wearing a hat. When she's in residence, Candy finds herself regularly having to monitor the staff, manually returning the jaws of Saidi Saidi, Chichi, and Abedi back into their proper position as they gape in astonishment at this unaccustomed view. The two Roses register only as mutely dumbfounded. Once, when Boss had tried to introduce new housekeeping uniforms that included a skirt reaching four inches below the knees, there was a near riot, as the girls point-blank refused to wear the uniform of a harlot!

***

During coffee, Brigette exclaims, "Oh! I have a present for you," and hurries off to her room, returning with a small box that she presents to Candy. Inside is the once rough, uncut Tanzanite stone I had given her during her last visit. It has since been polished, cut, and set into a stunning pendant with matching ear rings. She explains that she had it examined and learned that it was an Investment Grade stone, its quality among the top 1% of all tanzanite stones mined. Once cut, she says, it produced a two-carat pendant and one-half-carat-each stones, for earrings. Purchased in Brussels, the polished and cut stone would retail at roughly six-thousand U.S. dollars.

"It's really beautiful," she continues. "Do you have a

certificate for it?"

It's my jaw Candy needs to push back into position this time, as I sit gaping at this information.

"I bought it from a friend," I mumble, omitting the fact I had purchased five kilos of similar stones from my old friend, Bahati Mbaya, and that they're currently luxuriating in a shoe box under my bed. "Is the certificate important?" I ask, in as nonchalant a manner as I can muster.

"Well, of course. Otherwise, it would be illegal. Or, at best, nobody would purchase them from you," came her disappointing reply.

"Ah. A bit like blood diamonds," I manage, crestfallen.

I leave the girls chatting together, joined by the Roses, who never miss a chance to involve themselves in something as exciting as this new addition to Candy's jewellery collection. Back in our house, I fish the shoe box out from under the bed, remove the lid, and stare forlornly at the admittedly unimpressive sight of what would appear to most as nothing more than a box of gravel. Given that they were mined by the father of Bahati Mbaya, who virtually lives in a cave half-way up a mountain, I'm not very optimistic about the prospect of his having kept strict records or issuing certificates. I am even less optimistic that "Bad Luck" would even comprehend what my problem is now, let alone be able to assist in resolving it. I plan to call him tomorrow, in any case, but this does seem more like a job for Stanley. I resolve to visit him as soon as possible.

Over dinner that evening Brigette confirms that if I had more stones, complete with the certificates, then she would be happy to broker them for me in Belgium.

"Just FedEx them to me, along with the certificates and

customs clearance, and I'll do the rest."

I can see Candy rolling her eyes, and this is before I have even mentioned introducing Stanley as my solution. I'll clearly have to play this carefully.

The next morning, I try calling Bahati Mbaya, but his phone is out of service. I call The Spotted Zebra in Moshi, where he seems to spend so much of his time, and the owner sadly informs me that "Bad Luck", true to his name, was killed a few months back. While leading a walking safari for another group of Eastern Europeans in Tarangire National Park, he was charged by a lone buffalo and badly gored. While he was being rushed by ambulance to hospital in Arusha, there was a head-on collision with a cement truck on the highway. Bahati Mbaya is no more.

I phone Stanley, and we arrange to meet at the Ocean Breeze in Tanga, next week.

Brigitte departs the next day. Candy and I drive her to the airstrip, and we're all delighted that when the plane lands, we discover that Benji, her fellow countryman, is the pilot. They board the plane, and we wave them off, wishing them *safari njema* (safe travels) and *bahati njema* (good luck).

We drive slowly back to the lodge. Candy breaks the silence, asking the question that's preying on both our minds. "Do you really think that pile of gravel could possibly be worth so much money? Can you get certificates for them?"

I glance over at her and smile gamely, quoting an old African proverb: "When bad luck chooses you as a companion, even a ripe banana can remove your teeth."

Candy sighs.

"Let's hope that Bahati Mbaya choosing me as a friend

has no dental implications," I joke, lamely. "Maybe if I can keep my teeth, I'll be able to keep a great deal more."

Discretion being the better part of valour, I resist any urge to mention Stanley.

CHAPTER 16
BLUE BLOOD DIAMONDS

If I tell you my dream, you may forget it. If I act on my dream, then perhaps you'll remember it. But if I involve you, then it becomes your dream, too.

In Africa, dreams are what you hope for, but reality is what you plan for. Putting my dream of the "blue diamonds" unimaginatively concealed under my bed firmly at the back of my mind, I try very hard to focus on the present.

This morning, at this moment, the present is Jafari. He tells me that one of the guests wants to talk to me about one of our resident pussy cats. We have two cats who live around the lodge, and who occasionally deign to favour us with their company. Eartha is jet-black, with exquisite deep green eyes, missing half an ear and most of her tail. It's pretty clear that she can't have many of her nine lives left. Candy has treated her for various bites, or when chunks have been removed by predators or other cats from her ample body, and she always seems to bounce back. Candy feeds her sausages every morning after breakfast, which she delicately consumes in a grudging manner. If I try to proffer this same small gesture of friendship, however, she'll take the sausage and then, hissing furiously, try to scratch me.

Snowy is the diametrical opposite of Eartha. Admittedly not imaginatively named, she's soft, pure white, and spends most of her day reclining in Reception, usually on top of the guest laptop. She has an imperious look about her, lying like a queen expressing her clear assumption of ownership of that intended-as-communal laptop. Recently, though, she's been especially—even uncharacteristically—quiet.

I wander through to Reception with Jafari and discover that the guest who wants to see me is Andreas, a regular resident guest who's a veterinary surgeon from Dar Es Salaam, having a few days away from the madness of the city to enjoy the bush with his family. After the elaborate ritual greetings which are part of every encounter with a Tanzanian, he informs me sadly that Snowy is in a bad way. His kids love cats and always fuss over her when they visit, and they've been worried about her, he says. He shows me her pink ears, which are very badly infected, and points out how thin she is. He has taken the trouble to make a full examination of our lovely Snowy, and since his last visit three months previously, sees a huge deterioration in her condition. She has cancer, very advanced cancer, he tells me, and says she must be in great pain. It's true that over the last month, we've noticed that she has rarely moved from Reception, and is looking very scrawny, but we've never been able to get close enough to her to check her out. Cute and docile as she may seem, she's every bit as capricious as Eartha.

Andreas informs me that she should be put to sleep as soon as possible, as she's suffering badly. Candy arrives in Reception, and we update her. While we're both shocked and upset, Candy and I know it is the only humane thing to do, so, with heavy hearts, we give our consent. Andreas does what must be done. We call Tano and Omari, the gardeners, and ask if they will bury her in the garden near our house, under a beautiful mango tree. They disappear to carry out our request, and we can hear the dogs howling in the background. Somehow, they seem to know. It's weird and uncanny, but animals seem to know these things. They may periodically ferociously turn on the cats and chase them up a tree, but they seem to still recognize them as part of our one, beloved lodge family.

***

We have a hectic schedule this day, with multiple check-ins and check-outs. Running a safari lodge with guests mostly on a once-in-a-lifetime trip, we're in the "smile business." Guests want everything to run smoothly, so no matter what's going on in the background, we can't let it affect the guest experience. In fact, guests often comment that we're always on duty, always happy and smiling. Candy usually laughs and explains that we're like swans. The guests see us floating serenely along the surface, while under water our legs are kicking furiously to get us where we need to be.

I recall one morning at six a.m., standing with a coffee in hand and chatting with a retired accountant and his wife from the UK while escorting them through to their waiting guide and immaculately prepared safari vehicle. The accountant looked around at the nearly empty parking lot.

"What are you going to do all day while the guests are out on game drives?" he asked.

Behind my smiling eyes, my brain was contemplating the seventy members of our staff, the maintenance issues, the vehicles, supplies, reservations, arrangements with authorities, interactions with local communities, management of the airstrip, food budgets, KPI's, health & safety concerns, and a hundred other things we have to undertake daily to ensure our guests enjoy a seamless five-star experience.

"Well, my hammock's not going to adjust itself," I replied. "That should keep me busy until you return."

He departed, laughing appreciatively and muttering to himself, "What a life."

Today, when I return to my office after lunch, Jafari and Moses are patiently waiting outside for me. I invite them in and go through the ritual of inquiring about their respective families, how they slept, and if their goats or cows are prospering. Eventually, we get to the point of the meeting.

Moses coughs, pauses, and then blurts out, "The staff have requested I come to see you to ask why you murdered our cat!"

A pregnant silence ensues as I digest this.

"I did not murder the cat," I splutter. "The vet said that she was in great pain, that she was dying, and that it was wrong to allow her to continue to suffer."

Jafari and Moses exchange a glance, and then Jafari replies, "But only God can decide when any creature should leave this earth! Who are you to overrule God?"

I explain that if we had done nothing she would have suffered very badly and, in any case, she would have died very soon, according to the vet.

"Then why did you interfere? This must have been the path God chose for the cat," is Jafari's stubborn reply.

I ask what they thought I should have done, and they explain that we should have put the cat in a box and taken it deep into the bush and left it in a shaded place under a tree there.

"But it would have been eaten by a hyena or jackal in

minutes," I protest.

"Then that would have been God's decision."

I cannot argue against such determined illogic, though it does occur to me to ask if they think that all doctors are interfering with God when they treat an injury or illness. I decide not to press the issue. Instead, I apologize for offending them. I was only trying to follow the best, kindest course of action, I tell them, and promise that in the future I will discuss something like this with the Staff Committee before deciding what to do.

Slightly mollified, they thank me for my time and depart.

Candy, who has been listening from next door, enters the office, bends down, puts her lips to my ear and, as I expect a warm consoling kiss, hisses, "Murderer," and walks back out.

***

We're expecting a high-profile group of VIPs in a few days' time. They'll be arriving in their own helicopter, and the charter company has been in constant contact with us for landing instructions. I've supplied the airstrip GPS coordinates, and a Google Earth photo of the turning circle at the end of the airstrip which will improvise perfectly as a helipad. We've stressed that they can't land anywhere else, as we're in a controlled conservancy and, moreover, we don't wish to disturb our other guests.

They've requested permission to do a trial run, and we're expecting them to arrive at any time. Sure enough, we can just hear the helicopter approaching low over the trees as it comes into sight and circles the lodge. Then, rather than continuing onwards to the airstrip as agreed in great detail and via numerous emails, we watch incredulously as it slowly descends towards staff quarters. I run in that direction, furiously trying to wave them off, but by the time I reach their position, the helicopter has landed—directly in the middle of staff quarters and the parking area for our safari vehicles, and adjacent to all the solar panels and laundry, all of which are now covered by two inches of fine dust. The laundry ladies are extremely incensed, as all their morning's work is now a reddish-brown rather than white, and everything must be re-laundered. The guides' cars, freshly washed after the early morning game drives, look like they've just completed a rally drive. The solar panels are a blur through the slowly settling mini dust storm.

The moronically grinning pilot appears through the haze, aviator shades pushed back on his head, love beads prominent around his neck, and with his hand outstretched in greeting.

He's somewhat taken aback when I explode, "Why the fuck did you land in the middle of my camp you fucking idiot?"

"Oh, eh, one of your staff directed me to land here," he replies.

"What staff member?" I demand. "The last time I looked, I didn't see any fucking airfield ground crew here!"

"That guy over there in a uniform!" He points calmly at Omari.

"The gardener? He'd be waving at you, thinking you were a creature from heaven! He has never even seen a helicopter before!"

"I may have been mistaken," the pilot sputters.

"If he had waved you towards the river, would you have landed in that? Get back in your helicopter and fuck off before

I make you wash every sheet, solar panel and car in sight! When you return, VIP onboard or not, if you attempt to land anywhere but on the agreed landing zone, Sembuli and Mumbi will open fire on you!"

At this, both Sembuli and Mumbi jack a round into their respective shotguns and point them at the pilot. Mumbi is silently tracking an imaginary helicopter along the tree line with his gun, and making soft "bang, bang" noises.

Employing discretion rather than valour, the pilot sprints to his chopper and makes an emergency take off, leaving us all covered in a second layer of dust. He circles the camp and, with a cheery wave out of the window, departs.

I stalk back to the relative safety of our office, leaving the entire staff complement involved in a mass clean-up. I arrive at the office in time to overhear Candy on the phone assuring the owner of the helicopter company that Graeme was only joking with the pilot and, yes, we're fully prepared for the VIPs' visit. She hangs up and looks inquisitively at me.

"All sorted," I assure her, and slump into my seat.

Just at this moment, Jafari and Moses arrive, knocking at the door. I invite them in. Once seated, they advise me that they've had a long meeting with the entire staff contingent at breakfast this morning in the canteen. They tell me that the staff are all in agreement regarding the cat incident. I had rather hoped this was already in the past, but I smile bravely, take a deep breath and ask for the outcome.

"Well, we discussed it all in great detail," Moses explains. "Then we took a vote which was unanimous. Every single person was as one voice. If you had to murder one cat, we all wish that you chose Eartha and not Snowy. Nobody likes Eartha; she always tries to bite us."

I am sitting with my head in my hands. Candy has had to leave the room, unable to contain her laughter.

Eventually, I set about explaining that killing Eartha would not bring back Snowy, and that I once again apologize. We were acting only on expert medical advice, I assure them, once again. Satisfied at last, it seems, they depart. Eartha, who's been watching the proceedings from the top of a cupboard, hisses at their retreating backs, yawns, and goes back to sleep.

***

I make a phone call to Stanley. The lodge is pretty quiet this week, affording me a window of opportunity to try to get some certificates for my tanzanite hoard. When I finally get through to him, he tells me that he's in Dar Es Salaam. Someone has complained about his work—something to do with the cost of a visa extension, he explains. It had perhaps been paid in cash, he mentions. He assures me, of course, that it's all nonsense, but it means he's based at headquarters in Dar until he proves his innocence. So maybe, he allows, it's not the best time for him to help me get tanzanite certificates. Before he hangs up, though, he suggests I try asking Faithfully. She knows so many people. She can help.

I had already thought of Faithfully as Plan B, as she does know almost everyone. She may be "only" part owner of a small bar on a deserted beach, but there always seem to be ministers and dignitaries visiting. In fact, her daughter is married to Zulphi, and he's involved in a mining company in Mwanza up near Lake Victoria. I remember once sharing a beer with him in The Beachcomber and listening as he recounted the tale of how, despite having an eight-foot electrified fence around their compound, they had big problems with yellow baboons getting inside, stealing food supplies, and generally causing mayhem. The mystery of how they were getting in was resolved one morning when he was driving out of camp and witnessed a huge alpha male grab a small juvenile baboon by the arm and throw him bodily into the fence. As the unfortunate youngster took the full force of the electric fence and grounded the current, the rest of the troupe, as one, scrabbled over the temporarily disabled fence and inside. Baboons are ruthless.

I try Faithfully, and she answers at once. I explain what I am looking for, without mentioning my five-kilogram stash of uncut stones, and she says that Zulphi will be able to help. In fact, he's staying for two weeks with the family, arriving tomorrow. Why don't Candy and I come down at the weekend, when she's sure we can sort it all out? What an offer! We're overdue some days off, so after a quick call to Boss to confirm it's okay, we arrange to drive down on Friday and return on Monday.

That evening, we're having a sundowner with Andreas and his wife, Martha, by the fireside and I see a discarded bottle that a baboon has stolen from the restaurant and deposited in the bushes nearby. As I retrieve it, I snag my trousers on a thorn tree and rip them across the knee. Candy and the guests laugh and I tell them I'd better go change, and, in any case, as it's getting dark, I need to collect my torch.

Walking in an unfenced lodge at night without a torch is definitely not advisable. With a torch, you can pick out any predators that may be lurking about, as their eyes reflect like mirrors in the torch beam. As an added bonus, the light unsettles them, as they can't work out what it is, and generally they'll retreat from the light to seek concealment in the dark of the bush where they can await their prey.

It's only a short walk to our house, and I jump off the wooden walkway and cut through a sand path that we and the kitchen staff use as a short cut, or "shortykut" in Swahili, from our house and staff quarters to the kitchen and restaurant. As I round the corner, only twenty-five meters from our house, I can see movement in a large bush adjacent to the path. Bloody baboons, I think. As I approach, a male lion rises up perhaps ten feet in front of me and lets out an almighty roar. I freeze—which is a good thing to do, given the circumstances. We stand and stare at each other. Eyeball to eyeball. I raise my hands above my head and roar back at him. A second male raises his head above the long grass. I can't run, as to run from a predator will make their hunting instinct instantly kick in. So, arms still outstretched I start to slowly Michael Jackson-moonwalk backwards. One lion sits back down, apparently perplexed, but the other still has his glare locked on my eyes. I continue my moonwalk and, incongruously, given the situation, I suddenly picture Saidi Saidi winning last year's Christmas staff dance, doing this same manoeuvre while wearing the Rose twins' wig and silk shirt and one marigold rubber kitchen glove on his left hand.

As I manage to slither further and further away, my dance partner sits back down and becomes once again invisible in the long grass. Still moving backwards, I reach the camp fire. Candy looks up.

"I thought you were going to change your trousers."

"I bloody need to, now," I declare, and explain what happened.

They are all horrified.

"Are you serious?" Andreas asks, incredulously.

I grab a double Scotch that Saidi Saidi has delivered unrequested, with his customary mysterious ability to anticipate my needs. I down it in one, and make a radio call. *"Askari Askari, simba wawili ndani camp! Karibu nyumbani na mimi, njoo haraka haraka."* (*Askaris*! There are two lions in the camp near my house; get your asses here quick!)

"Tango," replies Sembuli.

"May Day, over and out," replies Mumbi, with professional calm.

They do both arrive in unison almost immediately— praise where praise is due—and when I point to the spot, they instantly illuminate the area with their powerful Maglite torches. We can easily make out the four eyes glaring back at us from the bush in the now almost total darkness. Before I can utter a word, Mumbi lets out a blood curdling yell and leaps off the walkway, running straight towards the lions. Gun above his head, torch in hand, he crashes through the bush with the diminutive Sembuli only feet behind him.

The lions turn and bolt in the opposite direction. Andreas, standing next to me on the walkway, turns slowly and regards me bemusedly.

"Well, I suppose that was one way to deal with the problem," I grin.

Still laughing, we return to the restaurant and the waiting Candy and Martha. I explain what has happened and Candy giggles nervously.

"Oh my God, Mumbi will end up in Kenya sometime tomorrow morning, still chasing them."

As they are tonight our only guests, we're dining with

Andreas and Martha. Their two delightful kids are currently being extremely spoiled by the two Roses, who are having great fun looking after them in the Family Suite.

Mid-way through the meal, Martha suddenly asks me, "Does this happen often? Lion encounters, I mean?"

As my heart has recently returned to a more normal rate, I can be a bit more nonchalant about the entire affair. I explain that normally predators like to keep as far away from humans as possible, since we're by far the most dangerous predator on earth. History shows most animals seldom prosper from the experience. Our usurpation of their habitats alone places entire species in peril. But occasionally predators do stray close by, especially leopards. Indeed, we have a female leopard who has grown up around the lodge and is incredibly adept at living amongst us with very few actual sightings. She did once run directly under my feet as I was walking on the raised timber walkway late one evening after everyone had gone to bed. The very same thing happened the next night to Jafari, who almost had a heart attack. This resulted in mayhem on the radio, but no actual damage, other than to his dignity. You can never say never, but in general, a leopard is unlikely to attack an adult human unless cornered or startled.

"So always use your torch," I caution.

Candy relates the story of the time we were radio called in the office from the *askari* on the gate. A villager wanted to talk to us urgently. We asked him to be shown to Reception and when we arrived, he was standing there with a huge, gaping wound on his ass, and his arm badly mauled. When we asked what had happened, we learned that a female lion had been sheltering in long grass with her young cubs and he had innocently walked past too closely. She'd rushed him, mauled him, and then swiftly returned to her cubs. He'd made his way to our lodge for assistance. Candy went into full trauma first aid mode, and staunched the bleeding. She bandaged him as much as she could, and Ali helped us load him into a car before driving him to Bombo Hospital in Tanga. The big danger with any wound from a predator is infection, so it was imperative to get him hospitalized as soon as possible.

The next day, elders from the village passed by to thank us for our assistance, and assured us that he was recuperating well in the hospital. The crazy part of the story for us was how calmly and without any apparent pain or fuss he dealt with the entire situation. We guessed he must have been in shock. Weeks later, two very heavily armed Maasai Tanzania Park Authority rangers visited for a soda one morning. I asked them how our mutual friend was recovering, as they all live in the same loose community structure.

"Who cares? He is a coward! If he got bit on the ass, then he must have been running away. That will teach him," came the unexpected, but typically Maasai reply.

One of them wagged a finger in my face as he admonished me, "When faced by a lion, always run towards him!"

Suitably reprimanded, lest I consider flight when faced by one of the world's most fearsome killers, I promised that in the future, should the occasion arise, that is exactly what I would do.

Just as Candy is finishing her story, Sembuli returns to the restaurant to report that Mumbi was last seen still in hot pursuit of the two lions somewhere to the north of the lodge towards the Kenyan border. He further reports that the remains of a Grant's gazelle have been found in front of our house. It seems I had inadvertently disturbed the lions' supper; no wonder they

269

were upset. But all is now safe within the lodge, he confirms with a smart salute.

Andreas offers Martha a moonlight stroll to watch the stars by the swimming pool, but Martha makes it very clear that she prefers the option of a heavily guarded walk back to the safety of her room. As she departs with Andreas, flanked by Sembuli, gun at high port, she smiles and says her grandmother always told her as a child, "A fly that dances carelessly in front of a spider's web, risks the wrath of the spider's teeth."

Spider. Lion. Close enough.

Andreas and Martha are departing after breakfast, and we've agreed to drive in convoy as far as Tanga where they'll stay on the nice, beautifully surfaced highway via Segera and onwards to Dar Es Salaam. We flash our lights and wave them off as we cut off and drive through Tanga, taking the extremely bumpy but extremely scenic coastal highway towards Pangani Town.

We're both still laughing about comments from the two Roses as Martha departs the lodge. She's a strikingly beautiful woman and, as befits such a stunning African lady, married to a wealthy and successful husband. She's a very large woman, as well, with an ample figure and extremely large bottom. As she makes her way down the walkway from Reception towards the car park, the Rose twins look at each other. Big Rose sighs, wistfully.

"If only one day I could have a *wowowo* (ass) as big as that, I would be truly thankful to God," she says. Little Rose nods solemnly, in perfect agreement.

The twins are almost model material by any western standard, but once again we're reminded of the amazingly

270

divergent cultural standards that we encounter here in Africa almost every day. The grass truly is always greener on the other side, I remind myself.

***

As we bounce along the road heading southwards, we have the Indian Ocean to our east and acre after acre of endless sisal plants rolling into the distance to our west. The symmetrical fields are broken by a multitude of giant, ancient baobab trees around which the sisal has been randomly planted, giving a haunted look to the landscape. There's one particularly huge baobab adjacent to the road, and if you look at it closely, you can see graffiti stretching back to the 1700s. It has been used as a look-out tree to watch for ships approaching the shore, a punishment tree where people were hanged, and a local meeting spot where great debates took place in its shadow.

Local legend has it that this was the tree where the distraught widow of a German sisal plantation owner used to take her revenge on any passing British troops during the First World war. Her husband had enlisted as an officer in the German East African regiment to repel the British troops invading from Kenya, and had been killed in battle. His widow refused to believe this news. She took to sitting high in the tree, on the edge of their plantation, armed with his hunting rifle, and would shoot at any British troops who had the misfortune to come within range. After wounding two soldiers in separate incidents, and in a more civilized era than now, the British commander made an exclusion zone around her property, forbidding troops to venture within a two-mile radius of her home. She was thus left to grieve in peace, guarding their property, and ever awaiting his return.

It was very near this tree, as well, that Greta had her accident when she was burned by the coolant from her car, and we agree that we should go visit her, since her dive centre is only a kilometre north of The Beachcomber Bar on Ushongo Beach. As we near Pangani, we begin to see more cyclists on the road. One has the most colossal swordfish we've ever seen hanging forlornly over the handle bars, tail trailing through the dust behind him. We stop adjacent to a stretch of beach. School children returning home for lunch from school are walking along the shore. They're picking mangos from the trees and chattering and laughing. Every now and then, a group breaks away and they dive headlong into the bathtub warm waters of the Indian Ocean, only to reappear seconds later, shaking themselves like wet puppies, and skipping their way homeward. It's not a bad "school run," we conclude.

As we pass the police road block, we're waved through, as we're well-known to the local police. We still laugh whenever we remember the story of an elderly friend of ours named Shirley Bishop, who, along with her charming husband, own a stunning house between Pangani and Tanga hidden directly on the beach. When they first arrived in the area, Shirley was stopped by the police, who asked for her driving license. She duly produced it, and it stated her name as "Bishop, Shirley."

The police sergeant studied it carefully, then jumped to attention and saluted her. "Please accept my apologies, Your Excellency. I did not know you were a bishop of the holy church! Please proceed with God's speed."

Shirley quickly grasped the situation and the opportunity, leaned out the window, and made the sign of the cross. "Bless you, my sons. Go in peace."

That was the first and only time either she or her husband were ever stopped by the local police.

We reach the first houses on the edge of Pangani and the small stretch of tarmac finished road, which is a blessed relief from the bone jarring "coastal highway." We pass the petrol station and turn right, having enjoyed a full fifty metres of smooth road, and bump again through the dusty narrow streets of Pangani towards the bus stand, or "station," as it's locally known. Every house is fronted by a covered porch with a built-in concrete seat on which someone is invariably fast asleep. Chickens scrabble around, goats wander past, ever more bicycles weave among the pedestrians, and we suddenly burst out into a large square filled with shops and stalls on all sides: a riot of colour and noise as the traders laugh and joke with their customers. Buses from Tanga and Muheza, and even from Dar Es Salaam and Lushoto, disgorge people out into the square. Engines are gunned, creating thick clouds of diesel smoke as buses prepare for departure. Conductors hang out of windows yelling their destinations, as if they might persuade a passer-by to suddenly feel the urge to head in their direction. Nets of cabbage, mangos, oranges, onions, watermelon, spinach, corn, beetroots, and lemons are delivered via every bus roof, to be quickly replaced by fish and prawns, cashew nuts, and anything someone thinks they can sell. I cannot witness this sight without silently vowing again never to eat fish or prawns anywhere where I cannot see the sea. I dread to think what a basket of fresh caught prawns will be like after a ten-hour-long drive on top of a bus roof, in temperatures nearing forty degrees centigrade, by the time it reaches Arusha or some other inland city.

We park in the corner of the square in the shade of a mango tree, and enter Valentine's Bar. Zaina, the barmaid, greets us warmly and fetches two ice-cold Kilimanjaro beers. We order chips *mayai* (a potato omelette) with chili and *kachumbari* salad. Through the chaos and pandemonium that is the bus stand square in Pangani, we can see Faithfully weaving her way towards us, waving furiously, a beaming smile lighting up her face. We jump to our feet and all hug our greetings; it's been too long since we last met.

She informs us that she knew we were coming and, as the captain of the Pangani River ferry told her we had not yet crossed the river, she concluded that we'd be in Valentine's. She is delighted her detective work has proved correct. We order more food and a beer for Faithfully, and she catches up with us on all of her news. Rasta Ali appears with his impish grin, as if from thin air, and flops into a plastic seat, joining us.

"How is my brother from another mother?" he queries, high-fiving me and grabbing, without even asking, the ice-cold beer Zaina has just delivered for Faithfully.

"Aren't you guiding this week, Rasta?" I ask disingenuously. I know he's been suspended by the Pangani Tourist Board for inappropriate behaviour with a young, female, German tourist. We had been sent an email at the lodge stating that Tour Guide Rasta Ali had been suspended indefinitely, and was not to be engaged in any guiding activities until further notice. This was followed a week later by another email stating he had been reinstated after apologizing to the Tourist Board. It even included a copy of his grovelling letter of apology which, given the almost criminal and ludicrous misspellings, could only have been penned by Rasta himself.

"Next week, *kaka*," he replies, grinning. "I had a misunderstanding with a group I took on a bicycle tour from Pangani to Ushongo, with an overnight stay at The Beachcomber. But it's all resolved now."

Faithfully shrieks with laughter. "The only misunderstanding was you thinking that young girl was remotely interested in you. I hope you have learned a big lesson."

Rasta grins, and Candy opines, "You actually look embarrassed, Ali! I didn't know that was even possible."

Abruptly changing the subject, Rasta tells us there's a big ceremony just about to begin outside the main government building a short walk away towards the ferry crossing, and he suggests we should all visit, as it will be very interesting. It turns out that the councillor who bought us all drinks in Tanga when Greta had her accident had won his election, and is being invested today. There's to be a band and some entertainment, Rasta tells us, so we agree to make the short walk over.

A huge crowd of maybe a thousand people have gathered, and a stage has been set up, with rows of chairs for the various dignitaries already in attendance. The crowds are held back by a temporary rope fence, and an area the size of a small football field is clear in front of the stage. We take our place by the rope under the shade of a massive Jacaranda tree in full, spectacular bloom. Most of the area is under the shade of these majestic old trees. They're everywhere throughout the town and in season offer fantastic shade from the sun. The setting is truly magical; the purple-blue petals fall occasionally like snow in sunlight, and give the scene an almost spiritual softness.

Just as we arrive, the Tanzania Defence Force have just finished a marching exhibition, and a group of twenty sisal workers are filing onto the field. They're all stripped to the waist, with red ochre daubed on their chests. Their feet are bare, and they sport wigs made of sisal leaves woven through their hair. Most spectacularly, they are wearing "skirts" of beer bottle tops tied in row after row from ankles to knees, so that when they walk, the bottle tops jangle loudly like hundreds of small bells.

Faithfully is clapping excitedly and hopping up and down. A police officer suddenly appears at my shoulder, informing us that the Honourable Councillor has requested we be escorted up to the stage to join him to watch the show. Candy and I would much rather stay exactly where we are, but Rasta and Faithfully propel us firmly by our arms onto the stage and usher us to four seats directly next to the Councillor that have miraculously become vacant. There's a pause as we take our seats, followed by a round of applause. We wave somewhat sheepishly to the crowd.

The huge speakers burst into life, and the strains of *Jerusalema* begin to blare out, but then go quickly silent, as the dancers leap into action. They begin an impressive high-kicking dance routine, lifting their legs shoulder-high with precise coordinated timing, before stamping ferociously onto the packed red earth beneath them. The effect is incredible, with the bottle tops resonating with a crashing sound in perfect unison. The crowds roar their approval, as another group of twenty sisal workers enter the field. They're also stripped to the waist, with white chef hats on their heads, but are wearing gum boots with bottle tops tied to them. They begin what looks like a dance challenge, and when they stamp their feet, they make a different but equally loud jangling. The gum boots seem to have a life of their own, and the crowd is jubilant at this development. The two groups face off and the dance reaches a crescendo, with each participant from each team virtually chest-to-chest with their "adversary." The dance culminates with a thrillingly high simultaneous leap, for one last stamp.

Faithfully, seated between Candy and me, breathlessly explains that this is a dance developed by the sisal workers many years ago to keep themselves amused when the industry employed tens of thousands of men. She tells us that they used to compete, plantation against plantation, and it was a great honour if the workers from your area won. Today, the Mwera Sisal team have done themselves proud. As they leave the field to thunderous applause, Faithfully informs us that the ceremony is now reaching its climax. The dignitaries file off the stage, leaving us in splendid isolation, and form a loose circle around the newly re-elected councillor, who is parading around the field with something in his hands. Faithfully, pausing from her enthusiastic clapping, explains there's going to be a "chicken chase."

Before I can even register this Candy exclaims, "Oh look! The Councillor has a rubber chicken in his hands!"

Alas, if only.

It's a large male cockerel, and very much alive. The Councillor is displaying the poor fowl above his head, one hand firmly gripping its feet together while the other stretches the neck to its furthest extreme. The cockerel emits a strangled cock-a-doodle-doo while making a futile attempt to escape. With a final flourish, the Councillor throws the bird in the air and the crowds roar once again in anticipation. The cockerel lands on its feet, and then takes off like a demented rugby fly-half. Dodging left, then right, screeching to a halt, executing deft about-face turns and jinking between unsuspecting legs, he avoids every attempt to catch him. The crowd is roaring with laughter as the once-dignified council officials dive head-long after the cunning cockerel. Matronly assistant regional commissioners are pushing account clerks out of the way in a futile attempt to catch the cockerel. At last, the private secretary to the Regional Commissioner launches himself full length, sliding in his three-piece suit through a ruck of legs and emerges in a cloud of bright red dust triumphantly holding the poor beast above his head with its feet in a vice-like grip.

The crowd, including Faithfully and Rasta Ali, are on their feet screaming their approval. The private secretary does a lap of honour as he jogs around with the cockerel above his head to an enthusiastic round of applause. We use this distraction to escape the stage, dragging an extremely reluctant Faithfully and a laughing Ali with us as we jump in our car and head for the nearby ferry. If we stay until the very end, the queue for the ferry will be monstrous.

"My, oh my! He'll be eating chicken and eggs for many years to come now," Faithfully finally exclaims, with not a little envy in her voice. I must assume he has hens at home.

The ferry is waiting, luckily, on the Pangani Town side, and we drive straight on. Or rather, I do, as they never allow passengers inside the cars once it's on the boat, so Candy, Faithfully and Rasta Ali jump out as I drive aboard. The only time I've ever driven onto the ferry with a passenger in the car was the day Gordon died and I was taking his body to Pangani Hospital. The captain had been adamant that *all* passengers had to get out of the vehicle.

"No exceptions accepted under any circumstance," we were told.

"Ask him yourself," I had testily replied. "I, for one, will be fucking delighted if he wakes up and walks out."

This had left the captain totally confused until someone whispered in his ear that my "passenger" was dead.

"Just this once I shall allow this," he had graciously conceded, before shuffling off, dignity intact, and climbing the steps to the ferry bridge to prepare for departure.

Today, we reach the *Bweni* side of the Pangani River with only one seamless pirouette, as still only one of the two diesel engines is operating. The captain has become an expert in this manoeuvre, and we are perfectly lined up to drive straight off the ferry. Everyone jumps back in the car, and we roar off up the hill heading towards Ushongo Beach and The Beachcomber. We fork left and proceed along towards Kikokwe Village. The road is lined on both sides by ancient flame trees, which form an arch as the branches of trees on opposite sides of the dirt road intertwine thirty feet above our heads. All are in full, glorious bloom, with their vivid red hues creating the impression that we're driving into a red tunnel.

We emerge into an area of small farms or *shambas*, where the villagers grow a large variety of vegetables, to complement the rich harvest of fish they catch every day from the shallow waters surrounding the reef at the edge of the Zanzibar Channel. As we pass out of the village, we encounter a small group of laughing children staring and pointing up into a mango tree. Closer inspection as we pull to a halt reveals they are pointing at Karim the Rasta, who makes the most amazing furniture, candle holders, napkin rings, place mats and drink coasters from coconut wood. He seems to be hanging with his knees over a branch, fast asleep with his long, Rasta locks and braided, beaded hair hanging beneath him like a colourful mini-waterfall.

Rasta Ali advises that we leave him to sleep, as he seems happy enough, so we restart our journey. I ask where Karim's twin is today, and Rasta just starts laughing. Every time we've attempted to buy from Karim in the past, he has produced great quality goods, but virtually always a totally random number of them rather than the quantity we actually ordered. Sometimes, our delivery would even include items we'd never ordered in the first place. If I called Karim to complain, he'd inevitably blame his twin for messing up the order. If I called in to his workshop in person, then his twin would claim that Karim had failed to properly take down the order. Finally, Rasta Ali had clued me in to the fact that there is no twin, and that Karim had merely invented one in an attempt to have someone to blame for errors—or a little cheating here and there—in his business dealings. Having just seen Karim hanging sleeping from a tree with a discarded joint lying beneath him, I finally believe him.

We continue the short drive to Ushongo Beach, approaching through the thick coastal forest fringe, and enter the palm tree stands that line this seemingly endless beach. We pull into The Beachcomber car park and all jump out of the car. It really is an idyllic setting. The strong, cooling onshore sea breeze rustles the palm trees, reducing the ambient temperature to perfection. As our cases are carried off to our room, I make certain, once again, that my shoe box full of tanzanite stone is still safely locked in the tool box compartment of the car, secured under heavy padlock.

We enter the bar to find Tony holding court; thankfully there's no sign of his guitar. He does, however, have a gleaming set of new pearly white teeth to replace the ones that he still thinks "that bastard fish ate."

The bar is busy, as a young guy from the fishing village, Ushongo Mtoni, is to marry a very exotic looking young lady from Zanzibar. Many of her family and friends have sailed over to celebrate the occasion, and a Tarib band has set up in the corner. Many are dancing and all are drinking, and we've hardly sat down before Candy and Faithfully are dragged up to join the dancing by the Zanzibari ladies. The men are pressing Tony and me to accept glasses of Konyagi and brandy from bottles they've carried with them from the island. I'm delighted, as Zulphi has joined us and he, too, has drinks pressed on him from all sides. His wife, Suzie, and their children are on a snorkelling trip with Greta to Maziwe Island Marine Reserve and will return later as the tide rises.

"Oh, before I forget, Mama Faithfully told me that you needed some certificates for some tanzanites you have," Zulphi remarks.

In as nonchalant a manner as I can muster, I confirm this is, indeed, the case.

"Give me a moment," he says, and runs to his car. Returning, he hands me an A4 *kitabu* (book) with the logo of the mining company he works for emblazoned on the front. I open it and find six certificates per page, each numbered and stamped with the company official stamp and signed by Zulphi. There are more here than I will ever need.

"You just have to weigh each stone and record it. Write in the area in Tanzania where it was mined—which, with tanzanites, is the Mererani Hills region—and put it and the stones in a box, and that is you, sorted."

He points to a large carton on the floor next to the bar, and tells me that he's even brought me a load of boxes. I ask how much I can pay him for this, and he refuses point blank to even

281

consider taking any money from me, no matter how hard I press him.

"My wife is always telling me how you and Candy looked after her when she was young, and even helped pay for her brother, Matty, to attend pilot school when Faithfully didn't have the means to send him. If Mama Faithfully heard that I took money from you, she'd cut my bollocks off!" He roars, laughing heartily.

The subject is closed. I carefully store the certificates and boxes in our car, and then join Candy and Faithfully in dancing. There's a happily festive air throughout the bar. Greta and Suzie and the children appear, back from their snorkelling trip, and we all hug. Greta's looking great, a total transformation from the last time we saw her. There are no scars at all on her face. She tells us that her arm is still tender and very sensitive to the sun, but since she spends the vast majority of her day in a wet suit, it's not an issue. The only scars she says that are raw are those emotional ones from "that bastard, Johan."

She tells us that one day she had returned from her morning dive trip on the island to find him packed up and waiting for her outside the dive shop beside a taxi with the engine running. He stated bluntly that he was leaving her. She could keep the dive gear, he said, and with a perfunctory "*kwaheri*," he was gone.

Tony, sensitive as ever, yells across the table, "Fuck him! He was a miserable bastard, anyway!" and we all laugh, Greta more than any of us.

He never returned or contacted her again. But she seems to be blossoming. She's a strong girl, indeed. Single-handedly, she established and continues to run a charity to protect the

Green Sea Turtles that traditionally nest on Maziwe Island. The island used to be much bigger than it is today, and was once covered with palms and trees of various species. Old Mohammed, the fisherman, has told us many tales of how as a teenager he'd spend days, if not weeks at a time, living on the island and fishing the rich waters that surround it, only venturing back to Ushongo Mtoni to hand over his catch to his mother and sisters, who would transfer the fish balanced in baskets on their heads all the way through the bush to the market at Pangani.

In the 1970s, the Tanzanian government, convinced the island was being used by Uganda to spy on Tanzania, cut down all the trees. The fact that Uganda is land-locked and doesn't have sea-going boats was regarded as irrelevant. This foolish act, of course, resulted in erosion, and now the island is only a sand bar that appears majestically out of the surrounding pristine waters of the Indian Ocean when the high tide ebbs. There are nearly thirty kilometres of unspoiled coral reef walls around Maziwe, and it's a haven for a multitude of exotic fish, dolphins, reef sharks and, during their migration, humpback whales.

Greta visits the island every morning to collect any eggs that the turtles have laid. Like salmon, turtles return to where they were born to lay their own eggs. If they're not collected, the eggs will die when the high tide returns to submerge the entire island. To protect them, Greta takes the eggs to the mainland, carefully digging a hole in the sand well above the high- water mark and placing them in the same pattern as she found them. Approximately sixty-five days later, the eggs will hatch. It's a dramatic and moving event: more than one hundred tiny little turtles struggle out of their shells, circle until they can smell the sea, and then scurry towards it as fast as they can fight their way through the heavy sand. In this way, Greta has hatched over fifteen thousand turtle eggs, and the project now employs six young guys from the fishing village full-time to carry out the work. The entire village is now seeing the benefit of nurturing these amazing creatures rather than thinking of them only as a source of eggs or meat. Tourists visiting the beach lodges invariably want to witness a hatching, and Greta never misses a chance to try to get them invested in sponsoring the turtles or to visit the local school. She is a one-woman ecological miracle, and thriving herself in the joy of service to nature and the people she has come to love.

The dancing and merriment continue until after dark, and just as we're about to make our way to the restaurant, three men from the Zanzibari wedding group approach our table. They call for silence and then, leading Candy out into the middle of the floor and seating her on a bar stool, they gather around her and begin to sing, *Malaika* (My Angel). Their beautiful, strong, melodious voices rise in impressive and poignant harmony. Everyone is captivated. The lead singer is on one knee, with his backing duet at either shoulder.

Malaika, nakupenda Malaika
(My Angel,I love you, My Angel)
Ningekuoa mali we, ningekuoa dada
(I should've married you, mama, I should've married you, sister)
Nashindwa na mali sina we
(I am defeated, as I do not have wealth)
Ningekuoa Malaika

I should've married you, My Angel
Nashindwa na mali sina we
(I am defeated, as I do not have wealth)
Ningekuoa Malaika
(I should've married you, My Angel)
Pesa zasumbua roho yangu
(Money disturbs my heart)
Pesa zasumbua roho yangu
(Money disturbs my heart)
Nami nifanyeje, kijana mwenzio
(And what should I do, fellow boy?)
Nashindwa na mali sina we
(I am defeated, as I do not have wealth)
Ningekuoa Malaika
(I should've married you, My Angel)
Nashindwa na mali sina we
(I am defeated, as I do not have wealth)
(Ningekuoa Malaika
(I should've married you, My Angel)
Kidege, hukuwaza kidege
(Little Bird, you don't know, Little bird)
Kidege, hukuwaza kidege
(Little Bird, you don't know,Little bird)
Ningekuoa mali we, ningekuoa dada
(I should've married you, mama, I should've married you,
sister)

Nashindwa na mali sina
(I am defeated, as I do not have wealth)
Ningekuoa Malaika
(I should've married you, My Angel)

285

Nashindwa na mali sina
(I am defeated, as I do not have wealth)
Ningekuoa Malaika
(I should've married you, My Angel)
Malaika, nakupenda Malaika
(My Angel, I love you, My Angel)
Malaika, nakupenda Malaika
(My Angel I love you, My Angel)
Ningekuoa mali we, ningekuoa dada
(I should've married you, mama, I should've married you,
sister)
Nashindwa na mali sina we
(I am defeated, as I do not have wealth)
Ningekuoa Malaika
(I should've married you, Angel)
Nashindwa na mali sina we
(I am defeated, as I do not have wealth)
Ningekuoa Malaika
(I should've married you, My Angel)

The bar erupts into a boisterous round of applause and cheering as the last sorrowful note hangs in the still, balmy tropical night air. Candy is overcome with emotion. She stands, and solemnly, sweetly kisses the back of each singer's hand. The Zanzibari songsters are absolutely delighted with this, and the effect that their performance has had on their audience. I order drinks for everyone and receive a cheer almost as appreciative as the one for the singers. Tony appears with his guitar, but Faithfully and I manage to wrestle it from him and divert his attention back to Greta, who is still being bombarded with questions regarding the whereabouts of

Johan, the turtles, and her plans for the future. She's beaming with smiles and laughter, happily savouring the party atmosphere and comradery.

"*Hapa kazi tu,*" she declares. "I am here to work, and this is my home. A boyfriend won't change any of that." She's very much an integral part of this coastal community, and intends to remain so.

It's a very late night, and only the first night of the wedding celebrations, which will last for four more nights. Candy and I excuse ourselves and retreat to our lovely beachfront bungalow. We sit on the terrace, staring out below the stars, towards where Zanzibar lurks somewhere in the distance. There's a full moon, and it is so bright we can see the palm trees silhouetted against the dark coastal forest kilometres away on the very edge of this stunning curved bay. I tell Candy what Zulphi has given me and that he refused to even countenance any form of payment, and she's stunned by his generosity and kind-heartedness. When we helped Faithfully with the fees for young Matty's pilot course, we did so to help a friend, and give an opportunity to a young boy brimming full of potential who we hoped would grasp it and literally soar skywards. We did not do it in the expectation of personal gain. We've always tried to help people we've met along life's journey. When a river flows, does it ever count the villages it passes by, and then say, "That's it; I've completed my daily quota of providing people water?" It doesn't. It simply keeps flowing, without keeping count of how many people are blessed by its water. We vow to continue to always be like the river, and to do good where we can, without keeping count.

We will, though, take full advantage of those fortuitous certificates. I mean, wouldn't you?

CHAPTER 17
IF YOU THINK YOU'RE TOO SMALL TO MAKE A DIFFERENCE, YOU'VE NEVER SPENT A NIGHT WITH A MOSQUITO

We're just approaching the hill and about to descend towards Bweni and the Pangani Ferry, when Candy's mobile rings and the display indicates that it's Faithfully. We'd left very early, before the first pink fringe of dawn had started to lighten the eastern sky. The trees are still only silhouettes against the morning's fresh glimmer of light.

"Hi, Faithfully," chirps Candy.

"Where are you?" Faithfully demands.

Candy replies that we're on the road from Mwera near Bweni, about sixteen kilometres from The Beachcomber.

"Can you come help please? Right away? Astrid is very sick," pleads Faithfully.

Astrid is a mutual Danish friend of us all, an eccentric, lovable, slim, sexy, sixty-something, blonde, hippy chick. She lives in the house next door to the one we initially rented from Crazy Thomas, directly on the beach. She constantly has a cigarette or joint in one hand and a vodka or white wine in the other, and hints heavily at a more than passing friendship with Mick Jagger, although when pressed on the subject, she confesses that she can't remember last Thursday, let alone Ruby Tuesday or the 1960's.

"We're on our way," I hear Candy confirm, as we do a sharp about-turn, narrowly missing a donkey carrying timber to Pangani, and roar off back towards the beach.

"We'll meet you at Astrid's house," Candy tells Faithfully.

It's called *"Peponi,"* her own little "heaven" away from her penthouse apartment in downtown Copenhagen. She once told us that her downstairs neighbour used to complain about her loud music and her anti-social hours, so she had purchased his apartment from him and now uses it as a buffer zone between herself and the other residents in the city-centre apartment block she calls home. Money never seems to have been a problem for Astrid, but we've never once heard her talk directly about money, and she lives a very basic life in complete contentment on the beach.

We turn into her drive and pull up outside the house. Faithfully is waiting by the door. Astrid, doubled over in pain, is very pale and sweating. Candy goes into first responder action, and tries to examine her, concluding that the problem is her appendix. A big problem. We call Upendo—Dr Love— the doctor at the nearby clinic, and he agrees that with these symptoms, she needs urgent hospital treatment.

We're on a very remote stretch of Tanzanian coastline, and it's a four-hour drive to the dubious charms of Bombo Hospital in Tanga, and at least a nine-hour drive to either Dar Es Salaam or Arusha. While the girls sit with Astrid, I take out my phone and call Benji, the pilot. We need an alternative plan and have to think outside the box.

He picks up on the first ring. "Hey Benji, is Coastal flying into Mashado today?" I ask.

"Not today, bro. I'm at the airport in Dar right now, getting ready for my flights," he replies. "I am flying Dar, Zanzibar,

Saadani, Arusha at nine thirty. Why do you ask?"

"How many PAX on the Saadani to Arusha leg?" I enquire.

"Just two. Why?" I can tell he's getting impatient.

I explain the situation with Astrid, and ask if he could please land at Mashado, the airstrip that serves Ushongo, only fourteen kilometres from where we are. If he could collect her and fly her to Arusha, it could prove to literally be a lifesaver.

"No problem, brother. I'll be there ten thirty and no later. Get her there and leave the rest to me."

I tell him to put the cost for the flight on the Mashetani Lodge account, and he replies, "Fuck paying! This one's on me!" Benji has such a delightful grasp of English idiom.

I'm extremely relieved, and before I go to tell the girls, I pause for a moment to reflect and gaze out over the beautiful, panoramic view from Astrid's terrace. This is a place where we've all enjoyed so much carefree fun. My mind checks that we've covered all possibilities. The tide is receding fast down the deserted beach stretching in front of her property. Fishermen are already far out to sea gathered around the reef. Their tiny *ngalawa* canoes -- simple, hollowed-out mango tree trunks—glide smoothly before the horizon, their small sails or *tangas,* from which the city takes its name, luffing gently in the light early morning breeze.

Today, however, the beach looks odd. Something isn't right. As I focus, my view falls on not one, not two, but at least eight dead cows lying at the high-water mark. They're spread all along the beach from here right on past The Beachcomber Bar: massive black and white Ankole-Watusi, the indigenous local cows, with huge horns much prized by the Maasai. "How odd," I think, but I have other more pressing matters to deal with at the moment.

Re-entering the house, I tell Astrid that we need to help her pack. I explain the plan to everyone, and that we have to be at Mashado by quarter past ten at the latest. Faithfully calls Rashid, who drives for Crazy Thomas and also, sometimes, for Astrid, as well. He's based mostly in Arusha. Thomas fires him every month or so for real or mostly imagined slights, and then re-hires him the next month, since nobody else in Arusha will work for Crazy Thomas. Luckily, we know that Rashid's in Arusha at the moment, and he confirms he'll collect Astrid at the airport in Thomas's car, and take her directly to AICC hospital. He promises to be there, ready and waiting when the plane arrives.

Faithfully, using her encyclopaedic knowledge of everyone in Tanzania, calls the hospital and speaks to a doctor she knows, and he promises in turn to be waiting for Astrid and Candy at the emergency room arrivals with a full team, set and ready for surgery, if that's indicated. He also confirms Candy's suspicion that the problem is most likely her appendix.

We've finished packing, and it's now quarter to ten, so we have to hurry. We help Astrid into the back of our car, flanked by Candy and Faithfully, making sure that she has her passport, cash and credit cards. I'm not even remotely surprised that, at Astrid's direction, we have to stuff over ten thousand US dollars in cash, which I found in the safe wrapped in a head scarf, into her bag.

"Small change, my dear," she grins gamely. "One never knows when one might wish to purchase a small gift or trinket."

I ensure that nothing is left in the safe, and Zaina, Astrid's housekeeper, promises to lock up and look after the house. It's in good hands, between her and Sunti, her diminutive Maasai *askari*. Sunti is perpetually lurking in the garden, day and night, armed with a bow and arrow. You feel he daydreams of being able to attack an intruder should the chance arise. She will have no need to worry about the house's security while she's away.

We head off to the Mashado airstrip at high speed. In an attempt to take everyone's mind off Astrid's predicament, I mention that there seem to be a large number of dead cows on the beach, a report which is met with much scorn and disbelief.

"Have you been smoking my home-grown cigarettes?" asks Astrid.

I insist that it's true. For verification of my claim, Faithfully phones the Beachcomber for an impartial view from Tony. To my relief, Tony confirms that there is indeed a fresh harvest of cows adorning the beach. He tells her that a dhow sank last night crossing to Zanzibar, and the unfortunate beasts drowned and were washed ashore. Of the crew, there's no news.

Faithfully is aghast, as she has a VIP group from the United States arriving in time for lunch, and they'll be anticipating a deserted beach and a special family vacation—certainly not a visit to a cow morgue. Tony assures her that he'll deal with the problem before she gets back, so with Faithfully somewhat mollified, we continue on our way.

This interlude has somewhat lightened the mood of everyone but Faithfully. Astrid and Candy tease her that she can simply tell her guests that the animals are African sea cows, and, as nocturnal creatures, they're just sleeping until nightfall. Faithfully is less than impressed with their sardonic advice. Candy and Astrid think it's hilarious.

At Mashado Airstrip, we park up under the boabob tree that traditionally serves as both the arrival and departure lounge. Half of an old *ngalawa* canoe has been nailed to the boabab's trunk as a sign proudly proclaiming, "Welcome to Mashado International Airstrip." The airstrip itself is set atop a hill in the middle of a sisal plantation, and provides a stunning panorama of the Indian Ocean and the mouth of the Pangani River. In the distance, shimmering through the beginning of the heat haze, we can just make out Nungwi, the northern tip of Zanzibar. The sea is dotted with tiny fishing craft, and waves crash against the reef wall far out to sea.

Astrid claims that she feels much better now, but then vomits suddenly, instantly disproving her claim. She asks for wine and a cigarette, and we give her some water.

"Oh, my gracious me, I really must be sick… water? Yuck. Don't you know fish fuck in it? I never touch the stuff."

"You stole that from W.C. Fields," I reprimand her.

"Borrowed," she replies. "Borrowed, my dear, merely borrowed," she replies.

We first hear, and then see Benji approaching: a small dot high in the sky. He's coming from Saadani National Park, a hundred kilometres to the south, and is flying at about eight thousand feet, directly up the coastline. We watch the plane as it performs a lazy curve and lines up for final approach. He begins to descend and finally thunders up the grass airstrip, turning with a flourish directly in front of our tree at the "Arrivals Hall." A spray of leaves, twigs, and debris showers us, along with a light coating of red African dust.

Benji exits the cockpit—engine still roaring, propeller still whirling, strictly against all standing operating procedures—ducks under the wing, and opens the rear door. I steady the tail, which would normally have to be supported by a metal stand to allow for boarding. He must have already briefed his two guests, as they've moved to the front of the plane, and Benji has fashioned a kind of bed along the back row of seats. Candy has offered to go with Astrid, so Benji and Faithfully help them on board and close the door. I drop the tail and, with a final wave, Benji is taking off, less than five minutes after landing. Faithfully and I stand watching as the plane disappears into the haze, heading directly for Arusha. I silently pray it gets there in time.

Faithfully murmurs, "Inshallah."

In silence, we climb back into the car.

When we reach Beachcombers, Faithfully asks the housekeeper to set up my room for me. If everything goes to plan, and once Astrid is in good hands, Candy can fly back down with Benji tomorrow, and I can collect her at Mashado or Tanga. I'll stay an extra night with Faithfully and Tony while we wait.

Faithfully and I walk through to the bar and find Tony strumming quietly on his guitar. The beach is completely cow-free, which is a massive relief to Faithfully. Tony tells us he was able to quickly organize a group of *vijana* (young men) from the village, and it's now all sorted.

"No problem, *hamna shida, hakuna matata*. Relax," he reassures her. "Tony's here."

Faithfully disappears momentarily and reappears, bringing with her a bottle of "Robert", or, as most normal people would call it, red wine.

"I think we deserve this," she proclaims, pouring us each a generous portion.

We three sit in silence, sharing a luscious cabernet sauvignon from the Paarl province in South Africa. I'm staring into the rich, ruby red wine in my glass, but my mind is elsewhere. All of us have one eye on my phone as we anxiously await an update from Candy on Astrid. The plane should have landed by now.

Tony breaks the silence, recalling the late morning years ago when we were all enjoying yet another Sunday brunch on the terrace of Astrid's house. Astrid loves nothing more than entertaining at home. Suddenly, a speck had appeared in the sky way, way south on the horizon. Soon we could hear a buzzing noise, not unlike a swarm of bees. As we stared south, the speck had grown in size ever so slowly, until we could at last make out some sort of tiny aircraft. Our curiosity engaged, we all drifted down onto the beach, and watched as the dot transformed into a tiny microlight aircraft suddenly buzzing directly over our heads. We all ducked instinctively, frantically waving at the pilot, who turned the micro light out to sea and then flew back in, barely fifteen feet above the beach and directly over our heads. Tony was gesturing with a beer bottle in his hand to indicate to the pilot that he could land on the beach, as it was at low tide point. The pilot did three or four fly-overs, gave a thumbs-up out the window, and then smoothly landed directly along the deserted expanse of the beach, neatly coming to a stop in front of Astrid's house.

"Welcome to Ushongo," declared Tony, as a leather-clad figure with flying goggles descended from the contraption.

"Can we offer you a beer or a wine?" Astrid offered, always the consummate hostess.

"Hi! I'm Max," announced our newest lunch guest, removing his helmet and goggles with a dramatic flourish before accepting an ice-cold beer from Tony. Astrid led us to the terrace where Zaina had the table, groaning with food and drinks, waiting for us all. An additional chair had magically appeared.

Max proved to be a German who owned a hot air balloon company in Europe, and who was attempting to fulfil his dream of flying the entire coastline of Africa in the microlight he had built by hand himself from scratch. He'd started his amazing journey in Cape Town, South Africa. Following the spectacular coastline north from there, he had leapfrogged through South Africa onwards into Mozambique and north again to Tanzania. We warned him about the peril of accepting any future lunch invitations like this once he passed through Kenya and arrived in Somalia. Lunch in Mogadishu may sound exotic, but we doubted it would be cold beers on offer.

While we wait for news from Candy, we recall, laughing, how much Max had enjoyed his impromptu lunch break, accompanied by three or four cold beers. The morning had turned to afternoon, though, and the encounter had to end before the tide could come rushing back in to strand his plane. He'd informed us that he was bound for Tanga, where he had planned to overnight—presumably after landing at the airfield rather than the main street. We waved him off cheerily, as he taxied down the beach and vanished into the blue distance.

My phone rings loudly, and it's Candy, and we're abruptly very much back in the present. Astrid has had an emergency operation to remove a ruptured appendix and is in the recovery ward. No complications. Rashid was waiting as promised, and the medical team were ready and prepared at the hospital. Candy has arranged to stay overnight and fly down tomorrow afternoon once she is certain that Astrid is on the road to recovery.

Crazy Thomas is also around in Arusha, and while that in itself is not particularly reassuring news, some other of Astrid's Danish friends have invited her to stay with them while she is convalescing. Candy says the doctors have told her it had been a close thing. If she'd stayed on the coast, the consequences could have been fatal. While I chat with Candy, Faithfully proclaims that this good news calls for yet another bottle of "Robert" to celebrate, and, of course, we're all delighted. It's amazing, we all agree, that so many things had come together at just the right time to enable us to get Astrid the treatment she needed.

I suggest to Candy that she fly to Tanga the next day and I'll meet her there off the Coastal Aviation flight. We can stay at the Mkonge overnight before returning to Mashetani Lodge. It's an irresistible offer, and she readily agrees. I'm very aware that Candy hates flying in these small planes, and I hope Benji will be the pilot to help reassure her. Benji may be crazy, but there is no doubt he is a superb pilot. I tell her to sleep well and I'll see her tomorrow.

***

Faithfully, with occasional help from Tony, is juggling the highly contrasting needs and expectations of her VIP group and the Zanzibari wedding party celebrations, and valiantly trying to accommodate both. Music is blaring in the background from the local bar in the village where the wedding celebrations are in full and very loud progress. Faithfully, by contrast, has prepared an amazing Swahili dinner for her American VIP's. She has a table set outside on the deck of a dhow that had been under repair on the beach in front of the bar, and which she has cleverly transformed. It's now lit with myriad brass kerosene lamps, and she has converted the sail into a subtle shade. The dining table is set on the main deck, and decorated with candles in multi-coloured glass shades in the Zanzibari style, almost like miniature stained-glass windows. The table is draped in kanga material, and the overall effect is very exotic. The wind is a gentle whisper through the surrounding palms, with the high tide lapping gently only feet from the prow of the dhow. Nature also lends a hand as there's a supermoon this evening, and the entire beach is bathed in its majestic, buttery glow.

Before her VIPs arrive for dinner, I bid her and Tony a good night, and retire to my room. Sitting on my terrace, enjoying a glass of Faithfully's superb red wine, I let my mind drift. Tomorrow, I plan to leave after breakfast and drive to Tanga to meet Candy. The following day, I need to weigh and certify our tanzanite stones, and then put my trust in the postal service of Tanga's FedEx branch and send them onwards to Brigitte in Belgium. I'm not convinced this is the safest route, but I decide I have no other choice, so I retire to bed and drift off to a content and dreamless sleep.

The rays of sunshine gently flickering through my mosquito netting wake me, as the first signs of dawn struggle to creep above the distant horizon. I walk out to the terrace. Slowly at first, and then with a suddenness that still constantly surprises me, the red orange ball of the sun appears above the Indian Ocean. The sky is streaked in a dramatic mixture of reds, golds, bronze, grey and black as the night is banished once more. In t-shirt and board shorts, I wander barefoot through to the bar and help myself to a green tea, settling on a sofa to enjoy the dawn. It's perfectly quiet, with only the distant, muffled sound of the sea at low tide to disturb the silence. I'm on my own, and I savour the solitude and opportunity to dawdle.

As the light gets stronger, I can pick out some objects along the beach. My eyes focus, and I can see first one, then two, and then—unbelievably—eight large cows' heads protruding above the sand, for all the world like hunting trophies mounted on a wall in an old English Manor house. I'm astounded, and discarding my tea, I get up and walk slowly down the beach, approaching this bewildering spectacle, barely able to believe my eyes. The first cow has its lips pulled back and appears to be grinning at me. These are the black-and-white Ankole-Watusi cows with huge horns which had drowned when the ferry capsized.

"Oh my God," I muttered.

Tony must have just dug shallow holes, I realized, and stuck each cow in each hole right where they lay. The Super Moon and the unusually high tide last night have just washed away most of the loose sand, leaving the heads of eight creepy, surreal animals staring blindly, forlornly inland.

I look back towards the lodge. No one has yet stirred. The place still seems deserted. I know that Faithfully is planning a champagne breakfast for her VIP's with a private setting under the palm trees on the beach. I don't think the VIP's will appreciate the decomposing Dead Daisy and her crew joining them for breakfast. I go and find Faithfully. She is predictably horrified when confronted with the sight on the beach. She stares at Tony.

"I didn't expect that," he mutters.

I quickly decide I have to intervene before Faithfully

explodes. I remind her that when she and Tony visited us at the lodge, we took them for a bush breakfast as a surprise and just how much they loved it. I think I have a solution, I tell her.

"Faithfully, here's an idea. How about you intercept the VIPs and tell them you've organized a special bush breakfast on the hill at Mashado? Tell them that it overlooks Zanzibar in the far distance and is a spectacularly romantic spot. You can take the food-and-beverage team; if they head off now, they'll have loads of time to get ready, and you can use my car to drive the guests up there. Then Tony and I can somehow get rid of the herd of cattle on the beach."

With a yelp of delight, she turns like a dervish, leaping into action. Soon chefs are loading gas bottles, portable gas cookers, tables, chairs, crockery, cool boxes full of food and ice, champagne, glasses. Faithfully is a mini-whirlwind, cajoling the staff into instant action. I grab two waiters, and we set up a coffee station out of sight of the beach under a stand of flame trees, with a table and six chairs. We intercept the VIPs as they emerge from their cottages on their way through to breakfast. The cars with the breakfast team have left for Mashado Hill already. As I guide the group away from the beach, I chatter distractedly. They are a charming family of six, mother, father, and their four sons, aged from late teens to early twenties, all hailing from Texas.

I am myself the very essence of graciousness. "I believe Mama Faithfully has a special breakfast planned for you guys this morning, but first you must try some of our famous Tanzanian coffee."

They all seem very excited at this prospect, and I keep them chatting, answering countless questions about Tanzania, the Swahili Coast, Zanzibar, and, of course, why such a charming Scotsman is in the middle of nowhere chatting to them about all matters African. I can see one or two of the kids are struggling to understand my Scots accent, and so I make a concentrated effort to speak more slowly and clearly. I explain to them that when growing up in Edinburgh, English was not my first language. I explain that if they're confused, Faithfully can translate. They're content, laughing, entertained and excited at what adventure today holds ahead of them.

I see Faithfully waving from my safari vehicle as she reverses into place neatly beside where we are all enjoying our coffees.

"I think your chauffeur awaits you," I advise my new friends, and usher them towards the car.

"Enjoy your breakfast!" I shout, waving as they drive off.

I stroll back through to the bar to where Tony is sipping a cold bottle of beer.

"That all went rather well," he observes, and I burst out laughing. Nothing much fazes Tony.

We now have approximately two hours to perform Ushongo Beach's first and, hopefully, last rodeo roundup-cum-mass-funeral. I take Tony's beer from his grasp and throw it behind the bar, and in minutes we have gathered together a dozen young guys from the village, Tony's old Land Rover, and several ropes appropriated from the fishing boats beached nearby in the sand. I lasso a rope around each cow's head in turn and I tie the first rope to the tow bar on the Land Rover. The *vijana* dig around the unfortunate beast's neck and body in an attempt to release the revenant from its temporary grave. Then, gunning the engine, tires spinning in the wet sand, I manage to pull the first cow free. It makes a loud popping noise and I am relieved to find it did not fire like a rocket into the air. I am also rather relieved that its head remained attached to its body.

As the boys move to the next head, I drag my trophy down the beach behind the Land Rover and into a stand of trees where the villagers maintain a huge hole in which they burn their rubbish. This will make an excellent improvised mass grave. One cow down, seven to go! We repeat the process, and by the time we're on the fourth cow, we have our system down pat, to pretty much expert level. Each time I drive past The Beachcomber, Tony salutes me from the terrace with a beer. It is a team effort, after all.

We get the last cow safely into the hole and I pour ten litres of petrol over our dearly departed bovine friends. Robbie Burns' famous poem, *The Selkirk Grace,* leaps suddenly to mind. To the utter astonishment of the young guys in my rodeo team, I begin to sing out loud with great gusto...

"Some hae meat and cannae eat,
And some wad eat that hae nane,
But we hae meat and we can eat,
So praise the Lord be thanked!"

With the formalities completed, I step back and throw a burning branch into the hole. Whoosh! The petrol ignites, and a great flame rises, and so, the poor creatures are sent on their way to cow Nirvana.

When we return to The Beachcomber, I insist that Tony buy all the vijana sodas, and we take time to reflect on a job well done. I have a shower and pack, and am waiting with my bags ready when Faithfully arrives back with my car and the guests. As she jumps out, I give her a huge hug and whisper,

"All sorted," in her ear. She's delighted, and much relieved.

"How was breakfast?" I ask the VIPs, and they're immediately gushing with reports of the unexpected setting, the fabulous food, the amazing views, the chilled champagne. They loved it.

"That will be a memory I treasure for the rest of my life," the mother raves. They'd never dreamed of having breakfast in such a setting, and were astounded at the effort that must have gone into the preparations.

At this moment, the unmistakable smell of slowly roasting beef wafts tantalizingly past, carried on the gentle sea breeze. The woman's son, who is celebrating his graduation from college with this trip, pipes up cheerily, "Is that a BBQ I smell? If that is lunch for us today, that would be just awesome!"

Josie, the waiter ushers them through to the bar. Faithfully and I turn away before we convulse in laughter, I hug her and jump into my car.

"All in a day's work, eh, Faithfully?" I joke.

"I know I'm a swan, too," she laughs and imitates her legs paddling like mad. "Oh, my God! Now I need to prepare a BBQ!" she shrieks. "I need a Robert!"

She laughs again, and stays to wave me down the drive as I depart for Tanga. I reach the ferry without incident, and as it's on the town side, I have to wait for about twenty minutes for its return to the Bweni side. I spend the time chatting with some of the *wazee* (old men) who seem to spend every day doing nothing much but that: drinking *chai,* watching the ferry come and go, gossiping. I buy my ticket at the kiosk, and then enjoy an ice-cold orange soda as solace against the unrelenting heat. There are a large number of *bodaboda*s waiting for the passengers crossing from town, ready to speed them to Mwera town or the huge number of tiny villages that dot the countryside all down the coast towards Dar Es Salaam. As I drive onto the ferry, I'm greeted by Labda Kesho, the old deck hand who ties the rope around the bollards to secure the ferry each time it crosses, ten times every day. His name means "Maybe Tomorrow," and I tease him when, every time we meet, he asks me for five dollars, and I always reply, "*Labda Kesho, Mzee!*" He always just smiles and shrugs, and the milling crowd of passengers always laugh at my little joke.

Once we spin across on the ferry's one engine, as I drive off, I pause beside Labda Kesho and palm him a five dollar note.

"Siku ya bhati." I laugh. "Lucky day!"

I drive away with the memory of his huge, surprised, but delighted, toothless grin etched on my brain.

The drive to Tanga is blissfully uneventful, save for that moment when I nearly drive over the top of a green mamba snake. A small movement on the road makes me think that something has fallen from the roof of the old bus in front of me, but, as my eyes change focus, I observe this extremely long and very fast bright green snake darting between the bus and my car and straight into the thick bush on the far side of the road. I'm glad not to be on foot.

I turn off the Pangani-Tanga road at Pongwe and cut through the bush. The road here is rutted, and weaves through paddy fields growing rice, palm trees, mango stands, and fields of maize until I reach the tarmac Arusha-Tanga highway. The road transitions here to blissful, immaculate smoothness, and my car climbs past eighty kilometres per hour for the first time in a long time as I enjoy the unusual but pleasurable sensation of speed. The airport lies on this road just south of the city of

Tanga. This is a city of learning, and I know I am getting close as I speed past multiple boarding schools for boys and girls and madrasas for the Islamic community. I also whiz by the huge and ugly cement factories that line this section of road: the price of modernization.

I arrive at the airport in good time, and am waiting in arrivals, savouring the air conditioning, when the small Coastal Aviation plane lands and taxis to a halt in front of the window. Benji gives me a huge wave and thumbs up sign from the pilot's seat, and I smile as I read the call sign emblazoned on the plane's tail: MAD—123. If ever a pilot was made for one plane, then destiny has chosen well. Candy exits down the plane's few steps, and Benji disappears down the runway at great speed bound for Pemba, Zanzibar, and Dar Es Salaam.

Candy brings me up to speed on her time in Arusha as we walk together to the car. Apparently, Rashid was waiting as promised, with the car engine running, as they came down the steps of the plane, but Astrid was virtually unconscious by the time they arrived at the hospital. The doctor was waiting at the door with a wheeled stretcher, and sped her directly into surgery. It was a very long hour and a half before he remerged and found Candy in the waiting room, pleased to announce that all was well, and that Astrid was already in a ward in recovery. Her friends from Denmark had also arrived by this time, and they all agreed to return in the evening during visiting hour. The friends promised to visit each day until Astrid was well enough to be released, and once again offered their lovely home on the outskirts of Arusha for her convalescence.

We're both thrilled and relieved that she's going to make a full recovery. As we begin our drive to the Mkonge Hotel, I start to relate the story of the cow heads, but Candy, laughing, says she doesn't need the details. Faithfully had already called her mobile and recounted the entire episode in graphic detail. Tony is still, she tells me, in the dog house.

We reach the Mkonge Hotel, park under a magnificent flowering flame tree, and check in for the night. Elias, our favourite waiter, is ready to escort us to a table in the garden for pre-dinner drinks, but before heading out, I ask the duty manager if he could lend me some digital scales from the kitchen and have them sent to our room along with our luggage. The Duty Manager is naturally perplexed at such an odd request but before he can voice his concerns Elias leans in to whisper advice.

"Please just send them to the room. It will be most unseemly if the *mzee* starts throwing his shoes at our esteemed management."

This seems to settle the issue, and we retire to the gardens where Elias, miraculously, already has some snacks waiting for us, together with a perfectly chilled bottle of rosé wine in a glistening ice bucket. We thank him profusely, and, with his typical discretion, he leaves us to enjoy our wine and the stunning view over towards the Tanga Yacht Club. Through the trees swaying in the gentle sea breeze, we can make out the masts of the huge variety of different yachts and various other sea cruisers and speed boats, fishing vessels and dhows that are docked in the safe and calm waters in front of the clubhouse that dominates that part of the shoreline.

The club has a rather cunning and rigorously enforced policy for non-members. When I had tried to order two ice cold Kilimanjaro beers on our first visit, the elderly barman had informed me that, as I was not a member, he couldn't accept cash. Rather, I must first purchase a book of vouchers from the

Cash Office, which he indicated was just a short walk away past the lounge. I duly arrived at the grilled counter and was more than a little surprised to find the very same barman waiting to greet me. I asked to purchase the minimum allowance of twenty dollars' worth of vouchers. He took his time noting the serial numbers in an old ledger book, then proceeded to stamp each of the twenty individual one-dollar vouchers with the official club stamp. Then he signed each with a flourish and handed them over to me. By the time I had wandered back to the bar there he was waiting with an immaculate starched white linen towel, with which he was polishing our glasses in anticipation of preparing our order. I ordered the beers, which he poured with perfect control of the level of foam.

"That will be four vouchers, please, sir," he said, with an assumed diffidence.

When I asked what I was to do with the remaining sixteen vouchers, he smiled and informed me that I must keep them for my next visit.

"No refunds, sir. Strict club policy, you know." He smiles.

Luckily, we do now more often visit the Mkonge, where cash is never an issue.

When we return to our room, I'm delighted to find the digital scale from the hotel kitchen sitting proudly on our bed, incongruously wrapped in a red bow.

"If I do the weighing, will you write in the details on the certificates?" I ask Candy as I drag my shoe box and the scales onto the hotel room desk.

We get started. Mostly the stones are singularly unimpressive by sight, and they vary greatly in size, shape and weight. We phone for room service, and sandwiches and coffee are delivered promptly. We work steadily through the shoebox. It's long past dark when we finally finish. Candy does a tally of the weights, and we find that we have 5.45 kilograms of assorted stones, all now neatly boxed and certified. We pack them up into a tidy cardboard box, and add the address in Belgium that Brigitte gave us during her last visit. We'll post it tomorrow.

I grab the kitchen scales, telling Candy I'd better return them before the head chef has palpitations, and I head downstairs to reception. The Duty Manager, while still a bit wary of me, is delighted to accept the scales. I order a bottle of champagne in an ice bucket and some snacks to be sent to our room. We'll skip dinner tonight, and enjoy the very unusual treat of air conditioning and television instead. We have never had a TV in all our years in Africa, and simply don't miss it. We watch movies and series on our computer, and have a stack of hard drives, but we choose when and what we wish to watch.

The manager has the reception TV tuned to CNN, and he asks me what I think of this latest news from China.

"What news?" I ask.

"Covid-19. That coronavirus thing," he replies.

The receptionist adds, *"Shida kubwa kwa macho ndogo lakini hamna shida kwa sisi."* (It's a big problem for the Chinese, but no problem for any of us, I think.)

I'm somewhat concerned, however, as our son and his wife live and work in Shanghai, so when I return to our room, I switch on CNN and tell Candy what I've heard. We wait for the usual news loop of war in Syria, Yemen, Al Shabab, and Boko Haram to pass, and then the China story arrives. It seems the entire city of Wuhan is in complete lock down, with thousands of people being hospitalized, infected with a new virus which apparently has no treatment or cure. We skype Kris and Kirsty, and they confirm that China is starting to lock down. Schools have closed and everyone is having to restrict their movements. They share a video clip one of their friends filmed while cycling on his bicycle through downtown Shanghai, and there is absolutely no one on the streets, no cars, no bicycles. Nothing. In a city we have visited many times, this is incomprehensible, as it has always presented such a huge and sharp contradiction to our own lives. It often takes us a few days to get used to so many people being around.

Kris assures us that they're safe and are just following all the protocols the government has been putting in place. Reassured, we sign off after making them promise to keep in constant contact with us. We next open a chat with our other son, Sean, on Skype in South Korea where he lives. He, too, reassures us that he's safe and well and following all the protocols the Korean government has introduced. Travel restrictions, however, are in place there, he informs us.

It seems inconceivable to us that a virus can be causing so much death and disruption in two such extremely modern and efficient countries. We turn the television off and take our champagne out on to the terrace where we sit hand-in-hand. The moon is still full and it's reflecting brightly over the Indian Ocean. The old disused mosque on Toten Island is a perfect silhouette. The reflection of the moon on the water forms what seems a bright path heading eastwards out to sea, towards where our sons and daughters-in-law are waiting out this Covid storm. Candy sips her champagne, and looks at me.

"I knew there was a good reason we should never watch the television," she says wryly.

I smile and, in silence, we enjoy our wine and the feeling of peace and tranquillity that surrounds us. At least for the moment.

In the morning, while Candy packs up and enjoys a coffee by the pool, I drive into Tanga and post our box to Belgium. It's a beautiful, cool morning. The streets are quiet, merchants only just beginning to set up their market stalls. Children are heading in neat, single-file lines to the many schools around the town.

I return to the hotel, and we make our farewells to Elias and the team, who refuse to allow us to even contemplate carrying even the smallest bag to our car. Everything seems so very normal, but we have this new, nagging feeling that all is not right with our world.

This seems a lull before the storm.

We drive from the Mkonge Hotel past Bombo Hospital, whose gates are thronged as usual. Patients, family, sellers, hawkers, buyers, children. God help us if Covid-19 reaches here. We weave through the streets which are by now clogged with cyclists and buses. Everywhere the cheerful, noisy chatter. Smiles and laughter. Colour and confusion. We're heading to our sanctuary in the bush. To our family—the community who rely on us so heavily for support. For jobs and health. For leadership and pragmatism. For an answer when all else fails.

As we drive deeper into the unrelenting bush, passing elephants and giraffes, gazelles and buffaloes, impalas and baboons, I silently pray that I won't fail our fragile community.

CHAPTER 18
PERCHED ON THE PRECIPICE

Back in our safe haven at Mashetani Ridge Lodge, there's very little talk about Covid-19 amongst the staff. They're all of the opinion that it's a Chinese problem, and as we rarely receive many Chinese guests, they all carry on as usual. The few guests from China we do receive are invariably very polite and respectful, and are always masked against the dust and other perceived dangers. The Maasai staff believe that even if this new virus should become a problem, one particular bush provides them with a solution: they can boil its roots to make an herbal tea that cures anything. When you have malaria, typhus, tuberculosis, AIDS, and tetanus as your close neighbours, you don't need to seek out new and exotic dangers.

Saidi Saidi reinforces this line of thought when he sagely informs us that, "nothing made in China ever lasts more than two weeks, anyway," in a passing reference to the influx of Chinese building materials of highly dubious quality that have in recent years flooded the markets of Tanga.

Guests are still arriving, and we can see no drop in bookings. Indeed, the upcoming year looks set to be our busiest on record. Today we have a full lodge that includes a fashion shoot for a prestigious international magazine, complete with world famous model, Mirandina!, personal assistant—husky-voiced PA with an aura of such command that all quail in her presence—hairdresser, cameramen, make up-artists, and a fashion designer, very topically, all the way from Shanghai, whom the staff immediately christen "Macho Ndogo," or "Little Eyes." I laugh when I recall my son explaining to me that the Chinese have a hundred uncomplimentary nicknames for us for every one we could possibly dream up for them.

Meeting the extremely demanding needs of the photo shoot crew, along with the no less demanding needs of our five-star guests, is a tricky balancing act, and I smile as I recall Faithfully and her VIPs. While, thankfully, there is no sign of any cows' heads lining the beach, we do have someone accompanying the group whom we refer to as a Kenyan Cowboy. Findlay is a fifty-something, white, native third-generation Kenyan guide with a terribly pukka English accent, who needs only a coiled whip on his belt to complete his Indiana Jones-style safari look. He's the quintessential image of a safari guide and a master at getting everything for nothing, as I have already discovered, ruefully, to my frequent cost. Last night in the bar, as I was circulating with our guests, I noticed Findlay's glass was nearly empty, and in passing, I enquired if he'd like a refill. His instant reply was, "That's jolly kind of you to offer, old chap. Make it a double," leaving me with no other socially acceptable option but to pay for the drink myself. Not quite what I'd intended. Well played, Findlay.

Earlier in the day I had accompanied him and the photography team on a reconnoitre safari to let them get a feel for the surrounding bush, and had been left grudgingly in awe of his techniques. With his two Maasai trackers in full regalia, complete with spears, perched precariously front and rear on the roof of his Land Rover, and Findlay at the wheel, they did present a very exotic scene. Completing the team and held in by a seat belt in the rear seat was "Livingston," a full-sized human skeleton, adorned with a bow tie and jaunty red Fez hat. He sported, as well, an arrow protruding through his ribs with a fob watch on a chain attached around the arrow head. I listened intently as Findlay explained that Livingston was only along for use in extreme emergencies and to date had only been called into action once—but the less said about that incident, he assured us, the better. It remained entirely unclear what Livingston's role might be in an "extreme emergency," but he did add considerably to the strangeness of the scene.

As we ambled aimlessly through the bush, Findlay held Mirandina! and the photo crew spellbound with his tales of bush life. After about thirty minutes of seemingly futile wanderings in a distinctly circular fashion, one of the Maasai on the roof quietly whispered to him in Swahili, "Two lions under a tree fifty yards to the left, *Bwana Mkubwa*." Findlay feigned innocence, giving no indication that he had heard, and carried on chatting for a moment or two before slowing to a stop.

Turning in his seat he whispered to his audience, "I think I smell lion."

He then proceeded to arc out of-road to the right and sniffed the wind like a blood hound. Peering into the bush, he veered around and drove directly to the tree under which his spotter had quietly informed him two male lions were reclining in the long grass.

"There they are," he declared loudly, rolling to a stop less than five yards from the two ominous predators. "The old nose never lets me down. You can run and hide, but you won't get away from Old Findlay," he solemnly informed his astonished guests, winking knowingly in my direction. It is a masterclass in bullshit, but I could not but admire his showmanship.

By the time we returned to the lodge, the photoshoot crew were convinced they were in the company of one of the true safari-guiding gods. Shaking my head, I wandered off, as he regaled them with yet more bush tales, pausing only to order another double gin and tonic on the company account. Then, spotting one of the Rose twins, he addressed Saidi Saidi in a loud voice. "I say! Have that gorgeous creature washed and sent to my tent."

Only the outraged and dangerous glare from Rose's eyes made him turn his request into merely a jolly jape.

I can see Candy trying to politely, and with extreme patience, cope with myriad questions and requests from the model's crew.

"Can you get me some false eyelashes, please? We need them urgently."

"Please send a steam cleaner to our dressing tent."

"Why don't you stock Beluga Goldline Vodka? That's all Mirandina! drinks! Well, okay. Give me another, but make sure it's gluten free."

And from the ever-confident PA: "We need a grand piano for tomorrow. See what you can do, will you?"

I seek refuge in engaging some of our other guests, and join a party of four from the home counties in England who are enjoying their first ever taste of Africa. "Tell me, can that chap over by the bar really find lions by smell alone?" one sceptical guy demands.

My reply of, "I'm not sure if that chap could find his ass with both hands, much less walk and chew gum at the same time, but his guests do seem to love him," leaves them a little nonplussed, and I distract them with what we have planned for them for tomorrow's activities. I explain that we're taking them at dawn for a cruise down the river, and plan a bush breakfast on a small sand bar at the mouth of the river where it reaches the Indian Ocean. They'll enjoy fresh cooked eggs benedict and ice-cold champagne. I also promise that we no longer spin the speed boat in a succession of ever decreasing circles to scare away the crocodiles before offering swimming as an added option. If they wish to try the swimming, of course, they can certainly ask the captain to arrange it.

I leave them eagerly discussing the next day's plans and move on to another larger group from Michigan, USA, who are concerned that the risk of malaria is so high in this area. I reassure them that since we're not directly on the coast that the risks are minimal. I do stress, however, that they should all keep taking their anti-malarial drugs. This leads to questions about how Candy and I deal with malaria and what local medical facilities are available. I explain that we always sleep under nets and spray our rooms nightly, and that if we're concerned, we can go to the clinic in the nearby village and take a blood test. In fifteen minutes, we get the result, and any required medication is available to all the staff and the local community. The clinic is very far from being either modern, or even clean, and the "doctor" generally treats everyone who visits for malaria whether they have it or not, but it's our only option. I explain that we regard the first sure sign of having malaria as denial. We always claim that we're just tired, or a bit run down, and then it hits you. Like a train. So, when either of us begins to suffer the onset of malaria, the non-affected one always has to push the other to be tested. The rule-of-thumb is: catch and treat malaria quickly or risk dire consequences.

The reference to thumbs leads me, fuelled by another beer, to regale our guests with the story of when one of our carpenters had recently nearly cut off the top of his thumb with a circular saw. Candy had cleaned the wound, and carefully bandaged him so that the top of his finger was still in place, ready to be stitched back in to position. I had driven him to the clinic where we were somewhat dismayed on arrival to discover that the doctor wasn't there. Another "doctor"—the one who performs the circumcisions for the local Maasai boys—was in residence, however, and he took one look at the thumb and instantly cut off the offending tip, almost severing the entire finger with a bold flourish of his knife, while simultaneously catching the poor carpenter as he fainted, lowering him onto a bed.

"This often happens," he reassured me, administering a tetanus shot to the prostrate fundi. The staff had all found his experience at the hands of the "circumcision doctor" hilarious, and often now joked that he was the only person they knew of who, if he rubbed his thumb, it got bigger!

Assuming I've reassured them, I move onwards and attempt to rescue Candy from the photography crew whom I overhear demanding a Maasai warrior to pose with Mirandina! on tomorrow's photo shoot. I assure the personal assistant that it will be no problem, and grab Ben, the walking guide, who just happens to be passing, and introduce him to her as one of the local Maasai tribe's leading warriors. Ben promises to be available at dawn, and assures her he'll even bring his ostrich feather headdress to mark the occasion. Delighted, the PA heads off to break the news to Mirandina! with a gluten free bottle of vodka under each arm.

Next morning, I'm in the lounge bar area before daybreak. No guests have arrived as yet, but the guides are preparing for their early morning drives, and I can see Ben over by the coffee machine in full Maasai regalia, complete with a huge ringed headdress made from ostrich feathers perched very regally atop his head. I wander over and compliment him on his outfit. I watch with familiar fascination as he pours three double espressos into one large mug and gulps them down.

"I'm useless in the morning until I have my espressos," he remarks. Odd, I think to myself. Having been in Ben's house—which is a very traditional cow dung structure—I don't recall having seen any evidence of electricity, let alone a coffee machine. I'm saved the need for any further comment, as guide Simon arrives and begins to prepare himself a "café limone", which is his own bizarre gift to the world's coffee culture. It comprises a black coffee with half of a fresh cut lemon jammed in the mug.

"Care to join me?" he asks, smiling hopefully in what has now become something of a morning ritual, maintaining his huge, surprised grin when I politely decline, as I do, in fact, every morning. Findlay shambles in a short while later, grabs a large black coffee and demands Saidi Saidi add a tot of Johnny Walker whisky to it.

"Remember and make it a gentleman's measure, my good man," he adds, to ensure he's served his customary double tot. "Fucking cameraman," he muses. "The bastard kept me up at the bar until well-nigh two a.m. Drinks like a bloody fish!" he adds before wandering over to the terrace to light his first cigarette of the day.

I wander through to reception as, along with the first threads of sunrise, the guests start to arrive and make their way,

317

led by their guides, to the safari vehicles or with the captain down to the jetty where the boat is preparing to cast off. I can see Saidi Saidi loading cool boxes onto the boat for the English group's champagne breakfast. Candy emerges from the kitchen in time to witness Mirandina! crash through reception like a tsunami, surrounded by dressers and makeup girls and hairdressers all valiantly still trying to complete her look of the day, and the ubiquitous PA waving her arms like a symphony conductor.

Findlay sprints past me heading outside, cigarette abandoned as he joins his Maasai trackers in the car, and they all depart in a cloud of dust. The trackers are already on the roof scanning for signs of game. Cameras and props protrude from every window. Ben gives me a majestic wave as he, too, departs in the backup vehicle. For one terrible moment, it looks like Livingston, the skeleton, is driving, but thankfully my eyes have deceived me.

The large contingent from Michigan arrive for an early breakfast, and as we show them through to their table, one lady remarks, "Don't you guys ever sleep?"

Candy replies with a disarming grin, "Not until April, when the rains come."

Chattering and laughing, they head through to the restaurant.

"Have you checked your emails?" Candy asks, and when I reply in the negative, she explains that Brigette has sent her a WhatsApp saying she has processed the tanzanites and has sent an email outlining the results. I promise to check, and then stroll down to the jetty to wave off the guests as they depart slowly downstream. I'm delighted to spot a pod of fifteen or so hippo heads appear like synchronized swimmers only a yard from the boat before disappearing once more below the murky surface of the river. A great start to what promises to be a memorable river safari.

Candy finds me some time later in the office. I'm staring at my laptop with a glazed and far off look in my eyes. "Well, what has Brigette said?" she demands. I look up, startled from my reverie, and explain. It seems that Brigette has had all the stones examined and graded. Some are just stones, some industrial quality and some AAA standard. She says she'll transfer the total amount she has calculated from the sale into our French bank account and will send over a statement and breakdown of the details. If I have another shoebox full under my bed, she adds, I should send them to her as soon as possible!

"So how much?" demands Candy, intrigued.

I have to confess that, as yet, I just don't know. My answer of "to be advised" is met with an exasperated shake of her head. I change the subject and inform her that Boss has sent us an email saying that the Covid situation worldwide is getting out of hand, and there's talk of cancelling flights and stopping travel. He says he'll keep us updated. All very disconcerting, especially inasmuch as, if we chose to not access the world news by television or internet here at Mashetani, life would just be carrying on as always. But we agree that we should start to prepare for possible cancellations.

As if to underline the growing crisis, my phone rings shrilly. It's Stanley, our friendly neighbourhood immigration officer, and he's on his way to the lodge with the local Health Officer from Tanga. He tells me there's been a government directive straight from the Minister for Health in Dar Es Salaam that all lodges, hotels, and places of business must introduce new strict hygiene procedures, and that all staff should get a Covid test to make sure our guests remain safe while in Tanzania. No surprise that he expects to arrive just before lunch.

I radio Saidi Saidi and tell him to make sure the fridge is full of cold Kilimanjaro beers.

***

Candy has been doing research, and has already made a bunch of notices which we set about displaying prominently around the lodge:

> Wash your hands.
> Sanitize station.
> Keep a safe distance.
> Our routines change quickly.

We've already started taking all the staff temperatures every morning, and all staff have now been issued PPE face masks. We have begun spacing out the dining tables and using the terraces more for serving of food and drinks. We issue new, more detailed notices to the staff Welfare Committee, and ask for their assistance in ensuring all staff comply.

***

It's reassuring to see the photoshoot party return to the lodge in time for lunch and observe that even Livingston now has a mask on. As Candy deals with all the guests, Stanley and the health officers arrive. Stanley takes up residence in the bar and immediately orders some beer, while I patiently explain to the health officer that, while I'm happy to cooperate and he can begin testing all staff immediately, I will not be giving him fifty dollars for each test completed. After an hour or so of tense negotiation, I agree to paying five dollars per test, having first turned down his offer of ten dollars per staff member and a promise that all the tests would be negative. "Much less disruptive for you!" was his last despairing sales pitch.

With the doctor now suitably motivated, and the testing underway, I wander through to the lounge and join Stanley.

"How much did you settle for?" he immediately asks, and roars with laughter when I explain.

"What exactly happens if someone tests positive?" I ask him.

He explains that it's all very simple. Any positive cases are sent to the "cage" at Bombo Hospital in Tanga. He assures me that he and Rasta Ali visited to inspect the "cage" and found it all perfectly normal. Anyone testing positive is put in the "cage" for seven days and the staff throw some fruit through the bars each day. At the end of this period, they are tested again, and, if negative, they can return to work.

"Throw fruit at them?" I ask incredulously.

Stanley confirms that this is the procedure, and that he and Rasta helped out one day by throwing the fruit themselves, in both the morning and evening.

"All the patients looked completely normal," he says, concluding with a shrug. "It seems like a waste of time to me."

There are no cases in the Tanga region, it seems, apart from a few staff from other lodges and hotels. He does concede that it's more than a little strange that the health officer has found four staff members positive at each establishment they

321

have so far visited.

"Business is business, and life must go on," he concludes, philosophically.

I don't know whether to laugh or cry. Especially again, two hours later, when the Health Officer informs me that four staff have tested positive and must accompany him to Tanga for further assessment and treatment. Following a week of "treatment" and the payment of purportedly related costs incurred, we will be able to collect them—once they test negative, he explains before departing.

I wave him, Stanley, and four of our Maasai gardeners off, and return to the office to find Findlay waiting for me. He tells me that his group have to cut short their stay, what with all the uncertainty over international travel, and that they would all like to leave in the morning. I promise to have a plan in place for Findlay before dinner, and set about attempting to reorganize flights, as he departs in an unusually sombre mood.

Candy arrives and asks if I've seen James, our ancient gardener. She has just passed him in the grounds and was delighted to see him sporting a face mask. On closer inspection, however, the face mask had turned out to be a pink G-String with love-heart bows on each cheek. We are worryingly perplexed as to who its owner might be.

"It's definitely NOT mine!" Candy laughs.

Tomorrow promises to be an eventful day, as subsequent emails have arrived confirming that all of our guests will now be departing then. We have a full-scale evacuation on our hands, with multiple charter flights arriving throughout the morning to ferry all of our guests from the airstrip to either Dar Es Salaam or Kilimanjaro International Airport for flights back to Europe and the USA.

With the guests all frantically packing, I'm in the bar explaining the logistics of the flights for tomorrow to Findlay over a gin and tonic, when Candy arrives and informs us that Kenya has closed the border to Tanzania with immediate effect. This effectively leaves Findlay, his two trackers and Livingston stranded in Tanzania. Findlay orders a round of margaritas, one—an uncharacteristically generous gesture— for me, stating that he thinks better on margaritas. I save him the trouble and offer a solution. Why don't we concentrate tomorrow on getting all of our guests and Findlay's group flown out, and then Findlay can stay overnight with us—free of charge? We can even offer him the deluxe private suite, as we have no other guests, and he can join us for dinner. The next day I can send him and his team overland through the bush with Ali and Ben to guide them across the border, well away from any border checkpoints. They can drop them on the main surfaced road somewhere between Oloitokitok and Kimana Town. From there, it's an easy drive on a highway of five hours to Nairobi. Ben and Ali know exactly which route to take, and Findlay's trackers are both Maasai, albeit from the Mara region, so any Maasai they encounter will gladly assist.

"Let's face it—Livingston does not even have a passport, so it almost makes sense!"

Findlay leaps to his feet and lets out a roar which I take to be of approval. Then he orders another round of margaritas to celebrate, generously insisting they be put on the photoshoot account. Problem solved.

Dinner this evening is a riotous occasion. Led by the head chef, the kitchen staff insist on dancing out into the dining room with each course, along with the wait staff, circling each table in turn before delivering the meals to each guest, all the while blasting out a succession of Swahili and Maasai songs. After dinner, twelve Maasai from the local community perform Maasai dancing, which turns out to be a very interactive affair. The guests take considerable delight in snapping photos of Mirandina! literally letting her hair down as she dances in the middle of the group. Her timing and technique may be slightly off, but she's even taller than most of the Maasai, and her enthusiasm is infectious.

It's almost as though we're trying to insulate ourselves from the outside world, praying the party will continue forever. Life here is so simple and seemingly safe. Great company, great food, great drinks, great dancing, great memories that will last a lifetime. Candy suggests a champagne toast to end the proceedings, and we serve a superbly chilled bottle of Moet et Chandon in a frosted ice bucket to each table. The toast of the evening is *"Maisha Marefu!"* (Long Life!) As the guests slowly begin to depart, escorted to their rooms by Sembuli and Mumbi, I whisper to Candy,

"Oh, by the way... I checked our bank account this evening. It seems we're 4.8 million Euros richer than we were this morning."

There's a very long silence before Candy looks up at me and whispers back, "Are you serious?"

I nod, and reply, "Yup. It seems that Bahati Mbaya really is the unluckiest guy in the world, after all." I suggest we finish our champagne back at our house, and, ice bucket in hand, we walk in silence home.

The next morning is a bit of a whirlwind, and we're on the go from five a.m., as all the guests need to have breakfast, their luggage collected, be checked out, and transported to the airstrip for an exceptional multitude of charter flights. Twice, as our paths cross in the restaurant, Candy whispers to me, "Please tell me I didn't dream that last night," and I assure her that it's all true.

We wave off the last guests, wishing them Godspeed and a safe journey, and the lodge suddenly seems so empty and quiet. Not a single guest, no arrivals expected—not only today, but for months ahead. Boss calls on the mobile from the head office in Dar Es Salaam, and I can immediately tell from his voice that it's bad news. The shareholders have convened an emergency meeting, and the outcome is that the lodge is to close in seven days' time. Indefinitely. We are instructed to please close down and pack away all equipment, mothball the cars and boats, and inform the staff that they must now go on unpaid leave. All but a skeleton staff of nine should return home.

I argue the case that the staff cannot possibly survive on no salaries, and that with only nine staff on site, the jungle will very quickly reclaim the camp and we'll lose everything. I remind Boss that some of the staff actually helped build the camp, and have remained here loyally for over twenty years. I know Boss is hurting, too, and I also know he agrees with me, but since he took on extra investors a few years back, the lodge is sadly not run by him alone now. He has a board of directors to answer to. I make an impassioned plea to allow all the staff who wish to stay on in camp be allowed to do so. At least we can feed and house them, and also maintain the property. With his voice thick with emotion, he promises to take it to the board, and further commits to call back within twenty-four hours with an answer. We both love Boss, but, unfortunately, we also both know that he's no longer the ultimate boss any more. Investors want returns, not sob stories. No one gets rich by being nice.

We call a staff meeting in the Canteen for three p.m., as we have to let everyone know the situation and explain what direction the company has chosen to follow. It's a very sombre meeting. Moses, from the committee, relates the old Maasai proverb which says, "If something is not yours, then do not be surprised when the owner takes it away from you." The staff as one all chant "*Maisha*" as he ends. "Life." That very African acceptance of everything that God can throw at you. I personally think that this time, God has lost the dressing room, so to speak. Even He seems out of his depth on this one. Head Guide Ali ends the meeting with a short speech in which he states that *Bwana Mkubwa*, *Nyati Peke Yake* (the Lone Buffalo), and *Kiboko Kubwa* (the Giant Hippo), all honorific names for me, has never let the staff down, and that if they all pray as hard as they can, then God and Kubwa will find a solution.

All the staff stand as one, and under direction from Mumbi, they all strike one hand in unison in a cutting manner with the other hand and yell, "*Umeme!*" (lightning) in time with the huge cracking sound it generates, all the while stamping one foot hard in time to the floor. This is the traditional end to a Maasai ceremony or discussion.

Candy and I leave in the silence that follows this, and I glance at Candy, muttering, "Well, at least the Big Man is on our side, it's not just us against the world," which makes her smile warmly.

We enjoy a very quiet dinner with Findlay on the terrace outside the bar, under the stars. The two Roses and Saidi Saidi are in great form, and between them and the kitchen team, they spoil us with kindness, making what should have been a glum affair one full of laughter and joy. We depart after dinner to our room. Findlay will be leaving at six a.m. tomorrow to cross the border with Ali and Ben, and I have promised to accompany him to ensure there are no problems.

Candy and I sit on our terrace under a crystal-clear sky fairly bursting with stars. Mars, Saturn, and Uranus are all bright, shining dots picked out dramatically from the Milky Way. We sip an ice-cold glass of Sauvignon Blanc that Rose Kubwa has thoughtfully placed on the terrace for us, and one of our favourite songs comes to sudden life from the speakers of our lounge: *Amazed*, by Lonestar.

Every time our eyes meet
This feeling inside me
Is almost more than I can take
Baby, when you touch me
I can feel how much ya love me
And it just blows me away
I've never been this close to anyone or anything
I can hear your thoughts, I can see your dreams

I don't know how you do what you do
I'm so in love with you
It just keeps gettin' better
I wanna spend the rest of my life with you by my side
Forever and ever
Every little thing that you do
Baby, I'm amazed by you

The smell of your skin
The taste of your kiss

The way you whisper in the dark
Your hair all around me
Baby, you surround me
You touch every place in my heart
Oh, it feels like the first time every time
I wanna spend the whole night in your eyes

I don't know how you do what you do
I'm so in love with you
It just keeps gettin' better
I wanna spend the rest of my life with you by my side
Forever and ever
Every little thing that you do
Baby, I'm amazed by you

Every little thing that you do
I'm so in love with you
It just keeps gettin' better
I wanna spend the rest of my life with you by my side
Forever and ever
Every little thing that you do, oh
Every little thing that you do
Baby, I'm amazed by you

We slow-dance, close together, enveloped in the music, and Candy whispers in my ear, "We can't let everyone down. Especially not when we have millions of Euros burning a hole in our bank account." My silence encourages her to continue, "You would get bored lying on a beach in a week, never mind retiring. We can make both of our boys secure for life and still have loads left over."

As the song finishes, I kiss her gently, and grin. "Glad you mentioned this. I have an idea."

I spin her around, and we collapse laughing onto the sofa on the terrace and fall asleep together under the stars.

It's still dark when we depart the lodge early the next morning. Ali and I are in the lead car, with Findlay and his crew alongside Ben in the second car. We quietly depart the still sleeping lodge, then break to a hard stop as Mumbi leaps from a tree and lands directly in the middle of the track. Once he's assured it is only us, he graciously stands aside, ambush averted. We head onwards towards the border, first by the entrance road to the lodge, and then straight through the bush. Ali turns north, and we slowly skirt the foothills of Mt. Kilimanjaro. By ten a.m., we arrive at the tarmac road, having passed the border without incident.

Following bear hugs all around, we part company with Findlay and his team. He promises to let us know when he reaches Nairobi and home. We watch as they drive off into the distance, and then climb aboard and head back towards Mashetani. Having assured Findlay's safe border crossing, I also wanted the opportunity to speak privately to Ali and Ben. I value their common sense and opinions highly. I also want them to come with me to meet the village chairman, Lelian, on our way back. I explain to them that Candy and I have been awake from three a.m. and have worked out a proposal that we want to put to the staff and the chairman. Without telling them how, I explain that we have access to money that would allow us to keep all the staff on at the lodge and continue to eat from the canteen. I tell them that everyone will continue to receive their full salary, and that if the chairman would gift us some land, we'll propose to build a new clinic and treatment centre, complete with a ward. The staff, I said, will help to build it. This will keep us all safe while the pandemic ravages the outside world, and will bring, as well, some much-needed modern medical facilities to the community. Once completed, we'll even find a way to get some fully trained doctors and nurses to staff it.

Ben leans forward from the back seat and grips my shoulder tightly and whispers, "*Mungu akubariki.*" (God bless you.) Ali's wide smile lights up the car. He quietly chuckles, and says, "I knew you would find a way, Kubwa."

When we reach the village, the chairman, Lelian, joins us. We walk a short distance towards a towering mango tree, laden with ripe fruit. Standing a glorious one hundred feet high, with its wide canopy of leathery, deeply green glossy leaves, its huge, thick trunk supports this iconic symbol of Africa. A small group of children are throwing sticks, trying to dislodge the ripe fruit to take home to their mothers. I ask them to please stop doing that, and they nod and silently depart. The four of us then pause to sit under the cool shade it provides. African-style, we squat in a circle. I lay out my plan in as much detail as I can provide, given that we only hatched it early this morning. Lelian informs me he would be honoured to gift the land required, and promises that all the men of the community will help with the building. He tells me that he thinks this will be a project that will bind the community, the lodge staff, and Candy and I together as one. Our grandchildren will tell stories around the campfire of this day's deeds. I nod and request that I would appreciate if the land he lays aside would include this magnificent mango tree? He smiles at me, nods and simply says "of course, it would be my pleasure, I understand." Somehow, I sense that he really does.

When we arrive back at the lodge, Ali and Ben accompany me to the office, where we find Candy, who has written out our proposal in detail. She has also called the committee to the office, and we again go through in considerable detail what we propose, so that everyone will understand their responsibilities. We are in this together. *Pamoja*. We agree to join all the staff in the canteen this evening at seven thirty to hear their thoughts.

They leave together and we're left alone in the office. We find we can't settle down, our emotions are so engaged, so we decide to go for a short drive. In low gear, we climb to the top of a nearby small hill we often use for sundowner drinks, and park. Looking out over the landscape, it dawns on us that— apart from the staff and village community—we're the only people for miles and miles around. As far as the eye can see, from our lofty position, there are no other people to share this marvellous vista, packed with the most wonderful selection of animals—flora and fauna and unique to Africa, a moment unique to us. As we sit on the bonnet and stare out towards Mount Kilimanjaro, the clouds suddenly clear. Kibo and Mawenzi and Shira, all its peaks, come into view in startling clarity. We can make out the ravines and gullies, and recent heavy rains have left the entire top third of the mountain covered in a thick layer of snow that glows with a rosy tinge as the setting sun is reflected from it. Candy holds my hand and asks, "I wonder, when you climbed Kilimanjaro all those years ago with Gordon, could you ever have imagined you would be sitting here now about to embark on yet another adventure?"

I reflect silently on the path that has led me to this place and this moment, and on the leading role that my late, long-time friend Gordon had played in how my life has so far evolved. Climbing Mount Kilimanjaro and Mount Meru together. Driving to the Serengeti on our own, and getting hopelessly lost. The pure joy from the crazy nights drinking and partying with Stanley and Rasta and a host of other great friends in Pangani and Ushongo. The love we both shared for Africa and the African people that deepened with each turn of the path in us both. I hope against hope, tonight, that he's looking down on me from above, and that he'll remain by my side in spirit as we begin this new adventure. His heart may have failed, but mine is now bursting with pride to be in a position where Candy and I can give something back for the nourishment of our lives that Africa has lavished on us, and help these wonderful, kind, clever, funny and truly amazing people.

I quietly reply to Candy's question, "Never in a million years. No." And I laugh, recalling our first entry to Tanzania so many years before. "But given that I'd never have bought those tanzanites without Gordon's introduction to Bahati, I think we should name the clinic, *The Gordon King Clinic.* Or maybe *The Golden King Clinic* would be even more appropriate!"

Candy hugs me tightly, and we drive silently back to the lodge, tears stinging our eyes. This is one of life's turning points: a moment from which we will always be able to trace, in the future, our past.

We walk the short distance in the growing darkness to the staff canteen and enter to a sea of faces. There's a top table, set complete with starched linen table cloth and candles for Candy and me, plus the committee, the chairman and Ali. All the other tables are laid out facing us. The entire staff is present, as well as many Maasai and the village elders. The unmistakable smell of roasted goat wafts from the kitchen, confirming that the committee have marked the occasion by buying some goats from the village. We begin, as usual, with a prayer, after which Moses rises to his feet, and explains why we are here. He details what we've proposed to do, clarifying that we will all have to work hard to make this happen, and that we must all agree that it is what we want. His duty accomplished, he turns to Candy and me, and informs us that the Rose twins have been nominated to announce the staff's decision and that they'd like to do so before we eat.

Hand-in-hand, Rose Kubwa and Rose Ndogo make their way to the front of the canteen. Shyly, cheeks blushing, they shout in unison their clearly memorized response: "The staff and committee of Mashetani Ridge lodge have received your proposal, and the unanimous verdict is: Let us all join together, in the words of *Baba* Graeme and *Mama* Candy—LET'S JFDI!"